The Complete Slow Cooker Kitchen

500 Easy and Healthy Recipes for Modern Home Cooks

Transform Your Kitchen with Flavorful and Time-Saving Slow Cooker Dishes

Elliot Hart

Table of Contents

Introduction	13
Slow Cooker Breakfast Recipes	14
Apple Crumble	14
Banana and Coconut Oatmeal	14
Breakfast Zucchini Oatmeal	14
Chocolate French Toast	15
Cranberry Quinoa	15
Creamy Yogurt	15
Breakfast Banana Bread	16
Greek Breakfast Casserole	16
Veggie Casserole	16
Mexican Eggs	17
Apple Oatmeal	17
Quinoa and Oats Mix	17
Spiced Pumpkin Oatmeal	18
Quinoa Breakfast Bars	18
Raspberry Oatmeal	18
Artichoke Frittata	19
Spinach Frittata	19
Veggie Omelet	19
Hash Browns and Sausage Casserole	20
Vanilla Oats	20
Ham Quiche	20
Egg Bake	21
Butternut Squash Oatmeal	21
Breakfast Stuffed Peppers	21
Coconut Granola	22
Tropical Granola	22
Creamy Strawberries Oatmeal	22
Breakfast Potatoes	23
Hash Brown Mix	23
Bacon and Egg Casserole	23
Breakfast Rice Pudding	24
Apple Breakfast Rice	24
Quinoa and Banana Mix	24
Dates Quinoa	25
Cinnamon Quinoa	25
Quinoa and Apricots	25

Blueberry Quinoa Oatmeal 26
Lentils and Quinoa Mix 26
Butternut Squash Quinoa 26
Chia Seeds Mix 27
Chia Seeds and Chicken Breakfast 27
Chocolate Quinoa 27
Chai Breakfast Quinoa 28
Quinoa Breakfast Bake 28
Mocha Latte Quinoa Mix 28
Breakfast Butterscotch Pudding 29
French Breakfast Pudding 29
Eggs and Sausage Casserole 29
Cauliflower Rice Pudding 30
Veggies Casserole 30
Arugula Frittata 30
Mixed Egg and Sausage Scramble 31
Worcestershire Asparagus Casserole 31
Peppers, Kale and Cheese Omelet 31
Salmon Frittata 32
Creamy Breakfast 32
Brussels Sprouts Omelet 32
Chicken Frittata 33
Mushrooms Casserole 33
Carrot Pudding 33

Slow Cooker Lunch Recipes 34
Turkey Lunch 34
Lunch Roast 34
Fajitas 35
Teriyaki Pork 35
Beef Stew 36
Apple and Onion Lunch Roast 36
Stuffed Peppers 37
Beans and Pumpkin Chili 37
Chicken and Peppers Mix 38
Chicken Tacos 38
Orange Beef Dish 39
Chicken with Couscous 39
Pork Stew 40
Seafood Stew 40
Pork Sandwiches 41
Peas and Ham Mix 41
Beef and Veggie Stew 41
Hearty Chicken 42
Beef Chili 42
Moist Pork Loin 42

Lunch Meatloaf	43
Mexican Lunch Mix	43
Flavored Turkey	44
Beef Strips	44
BBQ Chicken Thighs	45
Slow Cooker Roast	45
Creamy Chicken	46
Chicken Stew	46
Lemon Chicken	46
Chicken Noodle Soup	47
Lentils Soup	47
Thai Chicken Soup	48
Spinach and Mushroom Soup	48
Creamy Chicken Soup	49
Black Bean Soup	49
Taco Soup	49
Winter Veggie Stew	50
Chickpeas Stew	50
Lentils Curry	51
Quinoa Chili	51
French Veggie Stew	52
Beans and Rice	52
Black Beans Stew	52
Sweet Potato Stew	53
Minestrone Soup	53
Chili Cream	53
Salmon and Cilantro Sauce	54
Chili Salmon	54
Pulled Chicken	54
Chicken Chili	55
Salsa Chicken	55
Thai Chicken	55
Turkey Chili	56
Turkey and Potatoes	56
Chicken Thighs Mix	57
Chicken and Stew	57
Chicken and Cabbage Mix	57
Pork and Chorizo Lunch Mix	58
Lamb Stew	58
Lamb Curry	58
Lamb and Bacon Stew	59
Sweet Potato Soup	59
White Beans Stew	59
Quinoa Chili	60
Pumpkin Chili	60

3 Bean Chili 61
Cod and Asparagus 61
Bulgur Chili 61
Seafood Stew 62
Shrimp Stew 62
Slow Cooker Side Dish Recipes 63
Creamy Hash Brown Mix 63
Broccoli Mix 63
Bean Medley 64
Green Beans Mix 64
Corn and Bacon 64
Peas and Carrots 65
Beans, Carrots and Spinach Salad 65
Scalloped Potatoes 65
Sweet Potatoes with Bacon 66
Cauliflower and Broccoli Mix 66
Wild Rice Mix 66
Mashed Potatoes 67
Orange Glazed Carrots 67
Creamy Risotto 67
Veggie and Garbanzo Mix 68
Cauliflower Pilaf 68
Squash Side Salad 68
Mushrooms and Sausage Mix 69
Glazed Baby Carrots 69
Spinach and Squash Side Salad 69
Buttery Mushrooms 70
Cauliflower Rice and Spinach 70
Maple Sweet Potatoes 70
Creamy Chipotle Sweet Potatoes 71
Kale and Ham Mix 71
Sweet Potato Mash 71
Dill Cauliflower Mash 72
Eggplant and Kale Mix 72
Thai Side Salad 72
Rosemary Potatoes 73
Maple Brussels Sprouts 73
Beets and Carrots 73
Italian Veggie Mix 74
Wild Rice and Barley Pilaf 74
Apples and Potatoes 74
Asparagus and Mushroom Mix 75
Asparagus Mix 75
Chorizo and Cauliflower Mix 75
Easy and Veggies Mix 76

Okra Side Dish 76
Okra Side Dish 76
Okra Mix 77
Stewed Okra 77
Okra and Corn 77
Roasted Beets 78
Thyme Beets 78
Beets Side Salad 78
Lemony Beets 79
Carrot and Beet Side Salad 79
Cauliflower and Carrot Gratin 79
Herbed Beets 80
Summer Squash Mix 80
Easy Veggie Side Salad 80
Italian Squash and Peppers Mix 81
Green Beans and Red Peppers 81
Garlic Butter Green Beans 81
Zucchini Casserole 82
Nut and Berry Side Salad 82
Blueberry and Spinach Salad 82
Rice and Farro Pilaf 83
Pink Rice 83
Pumpkin Rice 83
Rice and Veggies 84
Easy Farro 84
Mexican Rice 84
Goat Cheese Rice 85
Rice and Artichokes 85
Green Beans and Mushrooms 85
Black Beans Mix 86
Rice and Beans 86

Slow cooker Snack Recipes 87
Tamale Dip 87
BBQ Chicken Dip 87
Mexican Dip 87
Tex Mex Dip 88
Artichoke Dip 88
Taco Dip 88
Lasagna Dip 89
Beer and Cheese Dip 89
Queso Dip 89
Crab Dip 90
Slow Cooked Dip 90
Candied Pecans 90
Chicken Bites 91

Peanut Snack	91
Apple Dip	91
Beef and Chipotle Dip	92
Chicken Wings	92
Bean Dip	92
Buffalo Meatballs	93
Glazed Sausages	93
Cheesy Mix	93
Cheeseburger Meatballs	94
Caramel Corn	94
Bourbon Sausage Bites	94
Curried Meatballs	95
Pizza Dip	95
Sauerkraut Dip	95
Spicy Dip	96
Salsa Corn Dip	96
Cheesy Corn Dip	96
White Bean Spread	97
Lentils Rolls	97
Eggplant Salsa	97
Veggie Spread	98
Peas Dip	98
Hummus	98
Cashew Dip	99
Potato Salsa	99
Black Bean Salsa Salad	99
Mushroom Dip	100
Beef Meatballs	100
Jalapeno Poppers	100
Pecans Snack	101
Apple Jelly Sausage Snack	101
Eggplant Dip	101
Lemon Peel Snack	102
Fava Bean Dip	102
Tamales	102
Tostadas	103
Mussels Salad	103
Italian Mussels Salad	103
Spicy Mussels	104
Cheeseburger Dip	104
Onion Dip	104
Caramel Dip	105
Chicken Cordon Bleu Dip	105
Fajita Dip	105
Tomato Salsa	106

- Salsa Snack 106
- Jalapeno Dip 106

Slow Cooker Poultry Recipes 107
- Rotisserie Chicken 107
- Chicken and Dumplings 107
- Balsamic Chicken 108
- Buffalo Chicken 108
- Alfredo Chicken 108
- Slow Cooked Chicken 109
- Slow Cooker Turkey Breast 109
- Chicken Breasts 109
- Turkey Breast and Cranberries 110
- Thyme Chicken 110
- Mediterranean Chicken 110
- Chicken Chowder 111
- Chicken Thighs Delight 111
- Chicken with Peach and Orange Sauce 111
- Flavored Chicken Thighs 112
- Classic Turkey Gumbo 112
- Chinese Duck 112
- Turkey Wings and Veggies 113
- Turkey Wings and Sauce 113
- Chicken and Sauce 113
- Chicken Wings and Mint Sauce 114
- Lemony Chicken 114
- Chicken and Paprika Sauce 114
- Chicken Thighs and Mushrooms 115
- Creamy Duck Breast 115
- Duck Breast and Veggies 115
- Turkey Soup 116
- Slow Cooked Turkey Delight 116
- Turkey Curry 116
- Chicken and Mustard Sauce 117
- Chicken Casserole 117
- Chicken and Broccoli Casserole 117
- Red Chicken Soup 118
- Citrus Chicken 118
- Chicken and Creamy Mushroom Sauce 118
- Slow Cooker Chicken Breasts 119
- Chicken and Sour Cream 119
- Chicken Stroganoff 119
- Pepperoni Chicken 120
- Chicken and Green Onion Sauce 120
- Mushrooms Stuffed With Chicken 120
- Creamy Spinach and Artichoke Chicken 121

Chicken Meatloaf	121
Thai Peanut Chicken	122
Flavored Chicken Drumsticks	122
Chicken Thighs and Romano Cheese Mix	122
Slow Cooker Chicken Thighs	123
Chicken and Tomatillos	123
Duck and Potatoes	123
Chicken Salad	124
Hot Chicken Wings	124
Coca Cola Chicken	124
Duck Chili	125
Cuban Chicken	125
Chicken and Lentils	125
Chicken and Chickpeas	126
Chicken and Sauce	126
Goose Mix	126
Goose and Sauce	127
Chicken Liver Stew	127
Slow cooker Meat Recipes	**128**
Beef Roast	128
Fennel Short Ribs	128
Apple Pork Ribs	129
Beef Chuck Roast	129
Pork Chops and Pineapple Mix	129
Mexican Pork Roast	130
Pork Tenderloin and Apples	130
Lamb Leg and Sweet Potatoes	130
Lamb Shanks	131
Flavored Pork Roast	131
Beef and Onions	131
Artichoke Lamb Shoulder	132
Chinese Pork Shoulder	132
Roast and Pepperoncinis	132
Balsamic Beef Cheeks	133
Seasoned Beef	133
Beef Soup	133
Thai Cocoa Pork	134
Herbed and Cinnamon Beef	134
Beef Brisket and Turnips Mix	134
Veggie Lamb Shanks	135
Lamb Leg and Mushrooms Mix	135
Smoky Lamb	135
Sausage and Onion Jam	136
French Lamb	136
Jamaican Pork	136

- Pork Sirloin Salsa Mix ... 137
- Beef Meatloaf ... 137
- Pork Loin and Cauliflower Rice ... 137
- Lamb and Spinach Salad ... 138
- Lamb Stew ... 138
- Sausages and Celeriac Mash ... 138
- Pork Belly and Applesauce ... 139
- Stuffed Pork ... 139
- Pork Rolls ... 140
- Pork Chops ... 140
- Worcestershire Pork Chops ... 140
- Rosemary Pork ... 141
- Oregano Pork Chops ... 141
- Spicy Pork ... 141
- Beef Meatballs Casserole ... 142
- Beef Stuffed Squash ... 142
- Beef and Tzatziki ... 142
- German Beef Soup ... 143
- Paprika Lamb ... 143
- Lamb Casserole ... 144
- Lavender and Orange Lamb ... 144
- Lamb and Orange Sauce ... 144
- Lamb and Mint Pesto ... 145
- Lamb and Fennel Mix ... 145
- Beef and Pancetta ... 145
- Veal Stew ... 146
- Veal and Tomatoes ... 146
- Wine Piccata ... 146
- Onion Sausage Mix ... 147
- Cheesy Sausage Casserole ... 147
- Sausage Soup ... 147
- Italian Sausage Soup ... 148
- Beef Curry ... 148
- Spicy Beef Mix ... 148

Slow Cooker Fish Recipes ... 149
- Salmon and Green Onions Mix ... 149
- Seafood Chowder ... 149
- Asian Salmon Mix ... 149
- Shrimp Mix ... 150
- Asian Steamed Fish ... 150
- Poached Cod and Pineapple Mix ... 150
- Chili Catfish ... 151
- Tuna Loin Mix ... 151
- Creamy Sea Bass ... 151
- Flavored Cod Fillets ... 152

Shrimp and Baby Carrots Mix	152
Dill Trout	152
Fish Pie	153
Slow Cooked Haddock	153
Buttery Trout	153
Salmon and Kimchi Sauce	154
Salmon Meatballs and Sauce	154
Salmon and Caper Sauce	154
Tabasco Halibut	155
Creamy Salmon	155
Chinese Cod	155
Mustard Fish Mix	156
Italian Barramundi and Tomato Relish	156
Spicy Creole Shrimp	156
Sriracha Shrimp	157
Shrimp and Peas Soup	157
Calamari and Sauce	157
Calamari and Shrimp	158
Clam Chowder	158
Shrimp Salad	158
Italian Clams	159
Orange Salmon	159
Tuna and Chimichurri	159
Cider Clams	160
Mustard Salmon	160
Salmon and Relish	160
Mussels Soup	161
Fish and Olives Mix	161
Indian Fish	161
Cod and Peas	162
Salmon and Rice	162
Milky Fish	162
Salmon and Raspberry Vinaigrette	163
Fish Pudding	163
Jambalaya	163
Tasty Tuna Mix	164
Delicious Mackerel	164
Chinese Mackerel	164
Mackerel and Lemon	165
Mussels and Sausage Mix	165
Mussels, Clams and Chorizo Mix	165
Crab Legs	166
Shrimp and Sausage Boil	166
Mushroom and Shrimp Curry	166
Dill Shrimp Mix	167

Japanese Shrimp 167
Octopus and Veggies Mix 167
Mediterranean Octopus 168
Stuffed Squid 168
Flavored Squid 168

Slow Cooker Dessert Recipes 169
Pudding Cake 169
Peanut Butter Cake 169
Blueberry Cake 169
Peach Pie 170
Sweet Strawberry Mix 170
Sweet Plums 170
Bananas and Sweet Sauce 171
Orange Cake 171
Apples Stew 171
Pears and Sauce 172
Vanilla Cookies 172
Pumpkin Pie 172
Strawberries Marmalade 173
Rhubarb Marmalade 173
Sweet Potato Pudding 173
Cherry Jam 174
Sweet Cookies 174
Maple Pears 174
Stuffed Apples 175
Chocolate Cake 175
Berry Cobbler 175
Apple Bread 176
Banana Cake 176
Chocolate Pudding 176
Cauliflower Pudding 177
Chia Pudding 177
Stewed Grapefruit 177
Cocoa Cherry Compote 178
Cashew Cake 178
Lemon Pudding 178
Lemon Jam 179
Chocolate Cream 179
Coconut and Macadamia Cream 179
Strawberry Pie 180
Sweet Raspberry Mix 180
Sweet Mascarpone Cream 180
Lemon Cream 181
Coconut Vanilla Cream 181
Avocado Pudding 181

- Coconut Pudding 182
- Simple Cake 182
- Dark Chocolate Cream 182
- Mango Cream 183
- Lime Cheesecake 183
- Caramel Cream 183
- Ricotta Cream 184
- Green Tea Pudding 184
- Sweet Lemon Mix 184
- Banana Bread 185
- Candied Lemon 185
- Chocolate and Liquor Cream 185
- Butternut Squash Sweet Mix 186
- Tapioca Pudding 186
- Orange Cream Mix 186
- Pears and Wine Sauce 187
- Pears and Grape Sauce 187
- Rice Pudding 187
- Orange Marmalade 188
- Berry Marmalade 188
- Pears Jam 188

Conclusion 189

Introduction

Welcome to a world where the joy of cooking is not eclipsed by the dread of adverse time and effort. We understand all too well the common predicament of home chefs worldwide; the grueling bouts of long prep hours, endless cleaning, and the clutter of pots and pans that besieges your kitchen.

But now, you can heave a sigh of relief. The solution to your culinary conundrums is here - the awe-inspiring Slow Cooker! This one-pot wonder is your ticket to simpler, healthier, and more exciting cooking experiences. It opens up a whole new panorama of endless culinary possibilities with minimal input required from your end.

With a Slow Cooker, there's no need for formal culinary training or expert instincts. All you need is the right set of ingredients, a splash of passion, and voilà! You're all set to stir up gastronomical magic. Delicious, flavorful, rich, and teeming with perfect textures — this is what you can anticipate from every meal prepared in your Slow Cooker.

Across the globe, joyous cooks are discovering the delight of making their kitchen routine not only more fun but also incredibly effortless. You too can now join the burgeoning legion of these contented culinary mavericks simply by welcoming a Slow Cooker into your kitchen.

So, you've decided to bring home a Slow Cooker? Let's kick things up a notch with this splendid cookbook that will serve as your trusty companion in your Slow Cooker journey. It is a treasure trove of recipes, designed to guide you into crafting the most exhilarating slow-cooked dishes.

From heart-warming breakfasts, fulfilling lunches, divine side dishes to savory poultry, meat and fish dishes, this cookbook covers it all. And for the sweet finale, it offers simple and delightful desserts. Can you imagine anything better?

The thought itself is mouth-watering, isn't it? Get ready to take the culinary plunge with your Slow Cooker and this special cookbook, marking the genesis of an innovative, enjoyable, and unparalleled journey in your kitchen.

You're all set for an unforgettable gastronomic adventure. Embrace the fun, lavish in the flavours, and relish your spectacular Slow Cooker creations. Bon appétit!

Slow Cooker Breakfast Recipes

Apple Crumble

Preparation time: 10 minutes | Cooking time: 4 hours | Servings: 6

Ingredients:
- 2 green apples, peeled, cored and sliced
- ½ cup granola
- ½ cup bran flakes
- ¼ cup apple juice
- 1/8 cup maple syrup
- 1 teaspoon cinnamon powder
- 2 tablespoons soft butter
- ½ teaspoon nutmeg, ground

Directions:
In your Slow cooker, mix apples with granola, bran flakes, apple juice, maple syrup, cinnamon, butter and nutmeg, toss, cover, cook on Low for 4 hours, divide into bowls and serve for breakfast.

Nutrition: calories 363, fat 5, fiber 6, carbs 20, protein 6

Banana and Coconut Oatmeal

Preparation time: 10 minutes | Cooking time: 7 hours | Servings: 6

Ingredients:
- Cooking spray
- 2 bananas, sliced
- 1 cup steel cut oats
- 28 ounces canned coconut milk
- ½ cup water
- 1 tablespoon butter
- 2 tablespoons brown sugar
- ¼ teaspoon nutmeg, ground
- ½ teaspoon cinnamon powder
- ½ teaspoon vanilla extract
- 1 tablespoon flaxseed, ground

Directions:
Grease your Slow cooker with cooking spray, add banana slices, oats, coconut milk, water, butter, sugar, cinnamon, butter, vanilla and flaxseed, toss a bit, cover and cook on Low for 7 hours. Divide into bowls and serve for breakfast.

Nutrition: calories 251, fat 6, fiber 8, carbs 16, protein 6

Breakfast Zucchini Oatmeal

Preparation time: 10 minutes | Cooking time: 8 hours | Servings: 4

Ingredients:
- ½ cup steel cut oats
- 1 carrot, grated
- 1 and ½ cups coconut milk
- ¼ zucchini, grated
- A pinch of cloves, ground
- A pinch of nutmeg, ground
- ½ teaspoon cinnamon powder
- 2 tablespoons brown sugar
- ¼ cup pecans, chopped

Directions:
In your Slow cooker, mix oats with carrot, milk, zucchini, cloves, nutmeg, cinnamon and sugar, stir, cover and cook on Low for 8 hours. Add pecans, toss, divide into bowls and serve.

Nutrition: calories 251, fat 6, fiber 8, carbs 19, protein 6

Chocolate French Toast

Preparation time: 10 minutes | Cooking time: 4 hours | Servings: 4

Ingredients:
- Cooking spray
- 1 loaf of bread, cubed
- ¾ cup brown sugar
- 3 eggs
- 1 and ½ cups milk
- 1 teaspoon vanilla extract
- ¾ cup chocolate chips
- 1 teaspoon cinnamon powder

Directions:
Grease your Slow cooker with the cooking spray and arrange bread cubes inside. In a bowl, mix the eggs with milk, sugar, vanilla, cinnamon and chocolate chips, whisk well, add to the slow cooker, cover and cook on Low for 4 hours. Divide into bowls and serve for breakfast.

Nutrition: calories 261, fat 6, fiber 5, carbs 19, protein 6

Cranberry Quinoa

Preparation time: 10 minutes | Cooking time: 2 hours | Servings: 4

Ingredients:
- 3 cups coconut water
- 1 teaspoon vanilla extract
- 1 cup quinoa
- 3 teaspoons honey
- 1/8 cup almonds, sliced
- 1/8 cup coconut flakes
- ¼ cup cranberries, dried

Directions:
In your Slow cooker, mix coconut water with vanilla, quinoa, honey, almonds, coconut flakes and cranberries, toss, cover and cook on High for 2 hours. Divide quinoa mix into bowls and serve.

Nutrition: calories 261, fat 7, fiber 8, carbs 18, protein 4

Creamy Yogurt

Preparation time: 10 minutes | Cooking time: 10 hours | Servings: 8

Ingredients:
- 3 teaspoons gelatin
- ½ gallon milk
- 7 ounces plain yogurt
- 1 and ½ tablespoons vanilla extract
- ½ cup maple syrup

Directions:
Put the milk in your Slow cooker, cover and cook on Low for 3 hours. In a bowl, mix 1 cup of hot milk from the slow cooker with the gelatin, whisk well, pour into the slow cooker, cover and leave aside for 2 hours. Combine 1 cup of milk with the yogurt, whisk really well and pour into the pot. Also add vanilla and maple syrup, stir, cover and cook on Low for 7 more hours. Leave yogurt aside to cool down and serve it for breakfast.

Nutrition: calories 200, fat 4, fiber 5, carbs 10, protein 5

Breakfast Banana Bread

Preparation time: 10 minutes | Cooking time: 4 hours | Servings: 4

Ingredients:
- 2 eggs
- 1 cup sugar
- 2 cups flour
- ½ cup butter
- 1 teaspoon baking powder
- 3 bananas, mashed
- ½ teaspoon baking soda

Directions:
In a bowl, mix butter with sugar and eggs and whisk well. Add baking soda, baking powder, flour and bananas, stir really well and pour into a bread pan that fits your Slow cooker. Put the pan into your Slow cooker, cover and cook on Low for 4 hours. Slice and serve for breakfast.

Nutrition: calories 261, fat 9, fiber 6, carbs 20, protein 16

Greek Breakfast Casserole

Preparation time: 10 minutes | Cooking time: 4 hours | Servings: 4

Ingredients:
- 12 eggs, whisked
- Salt and black pepper to the taste
- ½ cup milk
- 1 red onion, chopped
- 1 cup baby bell mushrooms, sliced
- ½ cup sun-dried tomatoes
- 1 teaspoon garlic, minced
- 2 cups spinach
- ½ cup feta cheese, crumbled

Directions:
In a bowl, mix the eggs with salt, pepper and milk and whisk well. Add garlic, onion, mushrooms, spinach and tomatoes, toss well, pour this into your Slow cooker, sprinkle cheese all over, cover and cook on Low for 4 hours. Slice, divide between plates and serve for breakfast.

Nutrition: calories 325, fat 7, fiber 7, carbs 27, protein 18

Veggie Casserole

Preparation time: 10 minutes | Cooking time: 4 hours | Servings: 8

Ingredients:
- 4 egg whites
- 8 eggs
- Salt and black pepper to the taste
- 2 teaspoons ground mustard
- ¾ cup milk
- 30 ounces hash browns
- 4 bacon strips, cooked and chopped
- 1 broccoli head, chopped
- 2 bell peppers, chopped
- Cooking spray
- 6 ounces cheddar cheese, shredded
- 1 small onion, chopped

Directions:
In a bowl, mix the egg white with eggs, salt, pepper, mustard and milk and whisk really well. Grease your Slow cooker with the spray, add hash browns, broccoli, bell peppers and onion. Pour eggs mix, sprinkle bacon and cheddar on top, cover and cook on Low for 4 hours. Divide between plates and serve hot for breakfast.

Nutrition: calories 300, fat 4, fiber 8, carbs 18, protein 8

Mexican Eggs

Preparation time: 10 minutes | Cooking time: 2 hours 15 minutes | Servings: 8

Ingredients:
- Cooking spray
- 10 eggs
- 12 ounces Monterey jack, shredded
- 1 cup half and half
- ½ teaspoon chili powder
- 1 garlic clove, minced
- A pinch of salt and black pepper
- 10 ounces taco sauce
- 4 ounces canned green chilies, chopped
- 8 corn tortillas

Directions:
In a bowl, mix the eggs with half and half, 8 ounces of cheese, salt, pepper, chili powder, green chilies and garlic and whisk everything. Grease your Slow cooker with cooking spray, add eggs mix, cover and cook on Low for 2 hours. Spread taco sauce and the rest of the cheese all over, cover and cook on Low for 15 minutes more. Divide eggs on tortillas, wrap and serve for breakfast.

Nutrition: calories 312, fat 4, fiber 8, carbs 12, protein 5

Apple Oatmeal

Preparation time: 10 minutes | Cooking time: 10 hours | Servings: 4

Ingredients:
- 2 tablespoons butter, soft
- ¾ cup brown sugar
- 4 apples, cored, peeled and chopped
- 2 cups old-fashioned oats
- 1 and ½ tablespoons cinnamon powder
- 4 cups water

Directions:
Spread butter in your Slow cooker. Add sugar, apples, oats, cinnamon and water, cover and cook on Low for 8 hours. Stir oatmeal, divide into bowls and serve for breakfast.

Nutrition: calories 282, fat 4, fiber 9, carbs 20, protein 5

Quinoa and Oats Mix

Preparation time: 10 minutes | Cooking time: 7 hours | Servings: 6

Ingredients:
- ½ cup quinoa
- 1 and ½ cups steel cut oats
- 4 and ½ cups almond milk
- 2 tablespoons maple syrup
- 4 tablespoons brown sugar
- 1 and ½ teaspoons vanilla extract
- Cooking spray

Directions:
Grease your Slow cooker with cooking spray, add quinoa, oats, almond milk, maple syrup, sugar and vanilla extract, cover and cook on Low for 7 hours. Stir, divide into bowls and serve for breakfast.

Nutrition: calories 251, fat 8, fiber 8, carbs 20, protein 5

Spiced Pumpkin Oatmeal

Preparation time: 10 minutes | Cooking time: 9 hours | Servings: 4

Ingredients:
- Cooking spray
- 1 cup steel cut oats
- ½ cup milk
- 4 cups water
- 2 tablespoons brown sugar
- ½ cup pumpkin puree
- ½ teaspoon cinnamon powder
- A pinch of cloves, ground
- A pinch of ginger, grated
- A pinch of allspice, ground
- A pinch of nutmeg, ground

Directions:
Grease your Slow cooker with cooking spray, add oats, milk, water, sugar, pumpkin puree, cinnamon, cloves, ginger, allspice and nutmeg, cover and cook on Low for 9 hours. Stir your oatmeal, divide into bowls and serve for breakfast.

Nutrition: calories 342, fat 5, fiber 8, carbs 20, protein 5

Quinoa Breakfast Bars

Preparation time: 10 minutes | Cooking time: 4 hours | Servings: 8

Ingredients:
- 2 tablespoons maple syrup
- 2 tablespoons almond butter, melted
- Cooking spray
- ½ teaspoon cinnamon powder
- 1 cup almond milk
- 2 eggs
- ½ cup raisins
- 1/3 cup quinoa
- 1/3 cup almonds, roasted and chopped
- 1/3 cup dried apples, chopped
- 2 tablespoons chia seeds

Directions:
In a bowl, mix almond butter with maple syrup, cinnamon, milk, eggs, quinoa, raisins, almonds, apples and chia seeds and stir really well. Grease your Slow cooker with the spray, line it with parchment paper, spread quinoa mix, cover and cook on Low for 4 hours. Leave mix aside to cool down, slice and serve for breakfast.

Nutrition: calories 300, fat 7, fiber 8, carbs 22, protein 5

Raspberry Oatmeal

Preparation time: 10 minutes | Cooking time: 8 hours | Servings: 4

Ingredients:
- 2 cups water
- 1 tablespoon coconut oil
- 1 cup steel cut oats
- 1 tablespoon sugar
- 1 cup milk
- ½ teaspoon vanilla extract
- 1 cup raspberries
- 4 tablespoons walnuts, chopped

Directions:
In your Slow cooker, mix oil with water, oats, sugar, milk, vanilla and raspberries, cover and cook on Low for 8 hours. Stir oatmeal, divide into bowls, sprinkle walnuts on top and serve for breakfast.

Nutrition: calories 200, fat 10, fiber 4, carbs 20, protein 4

Artichoke Frittata

Preparation time: 10 minutes | Cooking time: 3 hours | Servings: 4

Ingredients:
- 14 ounces canned artichokes hearts, drained and chopped
- 12 ounces roasted red peppers, chopped
- 8 eggs, whisked
- ¼ cup green onions, chopped
- 4 ounces feta cheese, crumbled
- Cooking spray

Directions:
Grease your Slow cooker with cooking spray and add artichokes, roasted peppers and green onions. Add eggs, sprinkle cheese all over, cover and cook on Low for 3 hours. Divide frittata between plates and serve.

Nutrition: calories 232, fat 7, fiber 9, carbs 17, protein 6

Spinach Frittata

Preparation time: 10 minutes | Cooking time: 2 hours | Servings: 6

Ingredients:
- 1 tablespoon olive oil
- 1 yellow onion, chopped
- 1 cup mozzarella cheese, shredded
- 3 egg whites
- 3 eggs
- 2 tablespoons milk
- Salt and black pepper to the taste
- 1 cup baby spinach
- 1 tomato, chopped

Directions:
Grease your Slow cooker with the oil and spread onion, spinach and tomatoes on the bottom. In a bowl, mix the eggs with egg whites, milk, salt and pepper, whisk well and pour over the veggies from the pot. Sprinkle mozzarella all over, cover slow cooker, cook on Low for 2 hours, slice, divide between plates and serve for breakfast.

Nutrition: calories 200, fat 8, fiber 2, carbs 5, protein 12

Veggie Omelet

Preparation time: 10 minutes | Cooking time: 2 hours | Servings: 4

Ingredients:
- ½ cup milk
- 6 eggs
- Salt and black pepper to the taste
- A pinch of chili powder
- A pinch of garlic powder
- 1 red bell pepper, chopped
- 1 cup broccoli florets
- 1 yellow onion, chopped
- 1 garlic clove, minced
- 1 tablespoon cheddar cheese, shredded
- Cooking spray

Directions:
In a bowl, mix the eggs with milk, salt, pepper, chili powder, garlic powder, broccoli, garlic, bell pepper and onion and whisk well. Grease your Slow cooker with cooking spray, add eggs mix, spread, cover slow cooker and cook on High for 2 hours. Slice omelet, divide it between plates and serve hot for breakfast.

Nutrition: calories 142, fat 7, fiber 1, carbs 8, protein 10

Hash Browns and Sausage Casserole

Preparation time: 10 minutes | Cooking time: 4 hours | Servings: 12

Ingredients:
- 30 ounces hash browns
- 1 pound sausage, browned and sliced
- 8 ounces mozzarella cheese, shredded
- 8 ounces cheddar cheese, shredded
- 6 green onions, chopped
- ½ cup milk
- 12 eggs
- Cooking spray

Directions:
Grease your Slow cooker with cooking spray and add half of the hash browns, half of the sausage, half of the mozzarella, cheddar and green onions. In a bowl, mix the eggs with salt, pepper and milk and whisk well. Add half of the eggs mix into the slow cooker, then layer the remaining hash browns, sausages, mozzarella, cheddar and green onions. Top with the rest of the eggs, cover the slow cooker and cook on High for 4 hours. Divide between plates and serve hot.

Nutrition: calories 300, fat 3, fiber 7, carbs 10, protein 12

Vanilla Oats

Preparation time: 10 minutes | Cooking time: 8 hours | Servings: 4

Ingredients:
- 1 cup steel cut oats
- 2 teaspoons vanilla extract
- 2 cups vanilla almond milk
- 2 tablespoons maple syrup
- 2 teaspoons cinnamon powder
- 2 cups water
- 2 teaspoons flaxseed
- 2 tablespoons blackberries

Directions:
Grease your Slow cooker with the cooking spray and add oats, vanilla extract, almond milk, maple syrup, cinnamon, water and flaxseed, cover and cook on Low for 8 hours. Stir oats, divide into bowls, sprinkle blackberries on top and serve for breakfast.

Nutrition: calories 200, fat 3, fiber 6, carbs 9, protein 3

Ham Quiche

Preparation time: 10 minutes | Cooking time: 3 hours | Servings: 6

Ingredients:
- 1 pie crust
- 1 cup ham, cooked and chopped
- 2 cups Swiss cheese, shredded
- 6 eggs
- 1 cup whipping cream
- 4 green onions, chopped
- Salt and black pepper to the taste
- A pinch of nutmeg, ground

Directions:
Grease your Slow cooker with cooking spray, add pie crust inside, cover and cook on High for 1 hour and 30 minutes. In a bowl, mix the eggs with salt, pepper, nutmeg and whipping cream and whisk well. Pour this into pie crust, sprinkle cheese, ham and green onions, cover slow cooker and cook on High for 1 hour and 30 minutes. Slice quiche, divide it between plates and serve for breakfast.

Nutrition: calories 300, fat 4, fiber 7, carbs 15, protein 5

Egg Bake

Preparation time: 10 minutes | Cooking time: 8 hours | Servings: 8

Ingredients:
- 20 ounces tater tots
- 2 yellow onions, chopped
- 6 ounces bacon, chopped
- 2 cups cheddar cheese, shredded
- 12 eggs
- ¼ cup parmesan, grated
- 1 cup milk
- Salt and black pepper to the taste
- 4 tablespoons white flour
- Cooking spray

Directions:
Grease your Slow cooker with cooking spray and layer half of the tater tots, onions, bacon, cheddar and parmesan. Continue layering the rest of the tater tots, bacon, onions, parmesan and cheddar. In a bowl, mix the eggs with milk, salt, pepper and flour and whisk well. Pour this into the slow cooker, cover and cook on Low for 8 hours. Slice, divide between plates and serve for breakfast.

Nutrition: calories 290, fat 9, fiber 1, carbs 9, protein 22

Butternut Squash Oatmeal

Preparation time: 10 minutes | Cooking time: 8 hours | Servings: 6

Ingredients:
- ½ cup almonds, soaked for 12 hours in water and drained
- ½ cup walnuts, chopped
- 2 apples, peeled, cored and cubed
- 1 butternut squash, peeled and cubed
- ½ teaspoon nutmeg, ground
- 1 cup milk

Directions:
In your Slow cooker, mix almonds with walnuts, apples, squash, nutmeg, cinnamon, sugar and milk, cover and cook on Low for 8 hours. Stir oatmeal, divide into bowls and serve.

Nutrition: calories 178, fat 7, fiber 7, carbs 9, protein 4

Breakfast Stuffed Peppers

Preparation time: 10 minutes | Cooking time: 4 hours | Servings: 3

Ingredients:
- 3 bell peppers, halved and deseeded
- Salt and black pepper to the taste
- 4 eggs
- ½ cup milk
- 2 tablespoons green onions, chopped
- ½ cup ham, chopped
- ¼ cup spinach, chopped
- ¾ cup cheddar cheese, shredded

Directions:
In a bowl, mix the eggs with salt, pepper, green onion, milk, spinach, ham and half of the cheese and stir well. Line your Slow cooker with tin foil, divide eggs mix in each bell pepper half, arrange them all in the slow cooker, sprinkle the rest of the cheese all over them, cover and cook on Low for 4 hours. Divide peppers between plates and serve for breakfast.

Nutrition: calories 162, fat 4, fiber 1, carbs 6, protein 11

Coconut Granola

Preparation time: 10 minutes | Cooking time: 2 hours | Servings: 8

Ingredients:

- 5 cups old-fashioned rolled oats
- 1/3 cup coconut oil
- 2/3 cup honey
- ½ cup almonds, chopped
- ½ cup peanut butter
- 1 tablespoon vanilla
- 2 teaspoons cinnamon powder
- 1 cup craisins
- Cooking spray

Directions:

Grease your Slow cooker with cooking spray, add oats, oil, honey, almonds, peanut butter, vanilla, craisins and cinnamon, toss just a bit, cover and cook on High for 2 hours, stirring every 30 minutes. Divide into bowls and serve for breakfast.

Nutrition: calories 200, fat 3, fiber 6, carbs 9, protein 4

Tropical Granola

Preparation time: 10 minutes | Cooking time: 1 hour 30 minutes | Servings: 6

Ingredients:

- 1 cup almonds, sliced
- 4 cups old-fashioned oats
- ½ cup pecans, chopped
- ½ teaspoon ginger, ground
- ½ cup coconut oil
- ½ cup dried coconut
- ½ cup raisins
- ½ cup dried cherries
- ½ cup pineapple, dried

Directions:

In your Slow cooker, mix oil with almonds, oats, pecans, ginger, coconut, raisins, cherries and pineapple, toss, cover, cook on High for 1 hour and 30 minutes, stir again, divide into bowls and serve for breakfast.

Nutrition: calories 172, fat 5, fiber 8, carbs 10, protein 4

Creamy Strawberries Oatmeal

Preparation time: 10 minutes | Cooking time: 8 hours | Servings: 8

Ingredients:

- 6 cups water
- 2 cups milk
- 2 cups steel cut oats
- 1 cup Greek yogurt
- 1 teaspoon cinnamon powder
- 2 cups strawberries, halved
- 1 teaspoon vanilla extract

Directions:

In your Slow cooker, mix water with milk, oats, yogurt, cinnamon, strawberries and vanilla, toss, cover and cook on Low for 8 hours. Divide into bowls and serve for breakfast.

Nutrition: calories 200, fat 4, fiber 6, carbs 8, protein 4

Breakfast Potatoes

Preparation time: 10 minutes | Cooking time: 4 hours | Servings: 8

Ingredients:
- 3 potatoes, peeled and cubed
- 1 green bell pepper, chopped
- 1 red bell pepper, chopped
- 1 yellow onion, chopped
- 12 ounces smoked chicken sausage, sliced
- 1 and ½ cups cheddar cheese, shredded
- ¼ teaspoon oregano, dried
- ½ cup sour cream
- ¼ teaspoon basil, dried
- 10 ounces cream of chicken soup
- 2 tablespoons parsley, chopped
- Salt and black pepper to the taste

Directions:

In your Slow cooker, mix potatoes with red bell pepper, green bell pepper, sausage, onion, oregano, basil, cheese, salt, pepper and cream of chicken, cover and cook on Low for 4 hours. Add parsley, divide between plates and serve for breakfast.

Nutrition: calories 320, fat 5, fiber 7, carbs 10, protein 5

Hash Brown Mix

Preparation time: 10 minutes | Cooking time: 3 hours | Servings: 6

Ingredients:
- 3 tablespoons butter
- ½ cup sour cream
- ¼ cup mushrooms, sliced
- ¼ teaspoon garlic powder
- ¼ cup yellow onion, chopped
- 1 cup milk
- 3 tablespoons flour
- 20 ounces hash browns
- Salt and black pepper to the taste
- 1 cup cheddar cheese, shredded
- Cooking spray

Directions:

Heat up a pan with the butter over medium-high heat, add mushrooms, onion and garlic powder, stir and cook for a few minutes. Add flour and whisk well. Add milk, stir really well and transfer everything to your Slow cooker greased with cooking spray. Add hash browns, salt, pepper, sour cream and cheese, toss, cover and cook on High for 3 hours. Divide between plates and serve for breakfast

Nutrition: calories 262, fat 6, fiber 4, carbs 12, protein 6

Bacon and Egg Casserole

Preparation time: 10 minutes | Cooking time: 5 hours | Servings: 8

Ingredients:
- 20 ounces hash browns
- Cooking spray
- 8 ounces cheddar cheese, shredded
- 8 bacon slices, cooked and chopped
- 6 green onions, chopped
- ½ cup milk
- 12 eggs
- Salt and black pepper to the taste
- Salsa for serving

Directions:

Grease your Slow cooker with cooking spray, spread hash browns, cheese, bacon and green onions and toss. In a bowl, mix the eggs with salt, pepper and milk and whisk really well. Pour this over hash browns, cover and cook on Low for 5 hours. Divide between plates and serve with salsa on top.

Nutrition: calories 300, fat 5, fiber 5, carbs 9, protein 5

Breakfast Rice Pudding

Preparation time: 10 minutes | Cooking time: 4 hours | Servings: 4

Ingredients:
- 1 cup coconut milk
- 2 cups water
- 1 cup almond milk
- ½ cup raisins
- 1 cup brown rice
- 2 teaspoons vanilla extract
- 2 tablespoons flaxseed
- 1 teaspoon cinnamon powder
- 2 tablespoons coconut sugar
- Cooking spray

Directions:
Grease your Slow cooker with the cooking spray, add coconut milk, water, almond milk, raisins, rice, vanilla, flaxseed and cinnamon, cover, cook on Low for 4 hours, stir, divide into bowls, sprinkle coconut sugar all over and serve.

Nutrition: calories 213, fat 3, fiber 6, carbs 10, protein 4

Apple Breakfast Rice

Preparation time: 10 minutes | Cooking time: 7 hours | Servings: 4

Ingredients:
- 4 apples, cored, peeled and chopped
- 2 tablespoons butter
- 2 teaspoons cinnamon powder
- 1 and ½ cups brown rice
- ½ teaspoon vanilla extract
- A pinch of nutmeg, ground
- 5 cups milk

Directions:
Put the butter in your Slow cooker, add apples, cinnamon, rice, vanilla, nutmeg and milk, cover, cook on Low for 7 hours, stir, divide into bowls and serve for breakfast.

Nutrition: calories 214, fat 4, fiber 5, carbs 7, protein 4

Quinoa and Banana Mix

Preparation time: 10 minutes | Cooking time: 6 hours | Servings: 8

Ingredients:
- 2 cups quinoa
- 2 bananas, mashed
- 4 cups water
- 2 cups blueberries
- 2 teaspoons vanilla extract
- 2 tablespoons maple syrup
- 1 teaspoon cinnamon powder
- Cooking spray

Directions:
Grease your Slow cooker with cooking spray, add quinoa, bananas, water, blueberries, vanilla, maple syrup and cinnamon, stir, cover and cook on Low for 6 hours. Stir again, divide into bowls and serve for breakfast.

Nutrition: calories 200, fat 4, fiber 6, carbs 12, protein 4

Dates Quinoa

Preparation time: 10 minutes | Cooking time: 3 hours | Servings: 4

Ingredients:
- 1 cup quinoa
- 4 medjol dates, chopped
- 3 cups milk
- 1 apple, cored and chopped
- ¼ cup pepitas
- 2 teaspoons cinnamon powder
- 1 teaspoon vanilla extract
- ¼ teaspoon nutmeg, ground

Directions:

In your Slow cooker, mix quinoa with dates, milk, apple, pepitas, cinnamon, nutmeg and vanilla, stir, cover and cook on High for 3 hours. Stir again, divide into bowls and serve.

Nutrition: calories 241, fat 4, fiber 4, carbs 10, protein 3

Cinnamon Quinoa

Preparation time: 10 minutes | Cooking time: 4 hours | Servings: 4

Ingredients:
- 1 cup quinoa
- 2 cups milk
- 2 cups water
- ¼ cup stevia
- 1 teaspoon cinnamon powder
- 1 teaspoon vanilla extract

Directions:

In your Slow cooker, mix quinoa with milk, water, stevia, cinnamon and vanilla, stir, cover, cook on Low for 3 hours and 30 minutes, stir, cook for 30 minutes more, divide into bowls and serve for breakfast.

Nutrition: calories 172, fat 4, fiber 3, carbs 8, protein 2

Quinoa and Apricots

Preparation time: 10 minutes | Cooking time: 10 hours | Servings: 6

Ingredients:
- ¾ cup quinoa
- ¾ cup steel cut oats
- 2 tablespoons honey
- 1 cup apricots, chopped
- 6 cups water
- 1 teaspoon vanilla extract
- ¾ cup hazelnuts, chopped

Directions:

In your Slow cooker, mix quinoa with oats honey, apricots, water, vanilla and hazelnuts, stir, cover and cook on Low for 10 hours. Stir quinoa mix again, divide into bowls and serve for breakfast.

Nutrition: calories 200, fat 3, fiber 5, carbs 8, protein 6

Blueberry Quinoa Oatmeal

Preparation time: 10 minutes | Cooking time: 8 hours | Servings: 4

Ingredients:
- ½ cup quinoa
- 1 cup steel cut oats
- 1 teaspoon vanilla extract
- 5 cups water
- Zest of 1 lemon, grated
- 1 teaspoon vanilla extract
- 2 tablespoons flaxseed
- 1 tablespoon butter, melted
- 3 tablespoons maple syrup
- 1 cup blueberries

Directions:
In your Slow cooker, mix butter with quinoa, water, oats, vanilla, lemon zest, flaxseed, maple syrup and blueberries, stir, cover and cook on Low for 8 hours. Divide into bowls and serve for breakfast.

Nutrition: calories 189, fat 5, fiber 5, carbs 20, protein 5

Lentils and Quinoa Mix

Preparation time: 10 minutes | Cooking time: 8 hours | Servings: 6

Ingredients:
- 3 garlic cloves, minced
- 1 yellow onion, chopped
- 1 celery stalk, chopped
- 2 red bell peppers, chopped
- 12 ounces canned tomatoes, chopped
- 4 cups veggie stock
- 1 cup lentils
- 14 ounces pinto beans
- 2 tablespoons chili powder
- ½ cup quinoa
- 1 tablespoons oregano, chopped
- 2 teaspoon cumin, ground

Directions:
In your Slow cooker, mix garlic with the onion, celery, bell peppers, tomatoes, stock, lentils, pinto beans, chili powder, quinoa, oregano and cumin, stir, cover, cook on Low for 8 hours, divide between plates and serve for breakfast.

Nutrition: calories 231, fat 4, fiber 5, carbs 16, protein 4

Butternut Squash Quinoa

Preparation time: 10 minutes | Cooking time: 6 hours | Servings: 6

Ingredients:
- 1 yellow onion, chopped
- 1 tablespoon olive oil
- 3 garlic cloves, minced
- 2 teaspoons oregano, dried
- 1 and ½ pound chicken breasts, skinless, boneless and chopped
- 2 teaspoons parsley, dried
- 2 teaspoons curry powder
- ½ teaspoon chili flakes
- Salt and black pepper to the taste
- 1 butternut squash, peeled and cubed
- 2/3 cup quinoa
- 12 ounces canned tomatoes, chopped
- 4 cups veggie stock

Directions:
In your Slow cooker, mix onion with oil, garlic, oregano, chicken, parsley, curry powder, chili, squash, quinoa, salt, pepper, tomatoes and stock, stir, cover and cook on Low for 6 hours. Divide into bowls and serve for breakfast.

Nutrition: calories 231, fat 4, fiber 6, carbs 20, protein 5

Chia Seeds Mix

Preparation time: 10 minutes | Cooking time: 8 hours | Servings: 4

Ingredients:
- 1 cup steel cut oats
- 1 cup water
- 3 cups almond milk
- 2 tablespoons chia seeds
- ¼ cup pomegranate seeds
- ¼ cup dried blueberries
- ¼ cup almonds, sliced

Directions:
In your Slow cooker, mix oats with water, almond milk, chia seeds, pomegranate ones, blueberries and almonds, stir, cover and cook on Low for 8 hours. Stir again, divide into bowls and serve for breakfast.

Nutrition: calories 200, fat 3, fiber 7, carbs 16, protein 3

Chia Seeds and Chicken Breakfast

Preparation time: 10 minutes | Cooking time: 3 hours | Servings: 4

Ingredients:
- 1 pound chicken breasts, skinless, boneless and cubed
- ½ teaspoon basil, dried
- ¾ cup flaxseed, ground
- ¼ cup chia seeds
- ¼ cup parmesan, grated
- ½ teaspoon oregano, chopped
- Salt and black pepper to the taste
- 2 eggs
- 2 garlic cloves, minced

Directions:
In a bowl, mix flaxseed with chia seeds, parmesan, salt, pepper, oregano, garlic and basil and stir. Put the eggs in a second bowl and whisk them well. Dip chicken in eggs mix, then in chia seeds mix, put them in your Slow cooker after you've greased it with cooking spray, cover and cook on High for 3 hours. Serve them right away for a Sunday breakfast.

Nutrition: calories 212, fat 3, fiber 4, carbs 17, protein 4

Chocolate Quinoa

Preparation time: 10 minutes | Cooking time: 6 hours | Servings: 4

Ingredients:
- 1 cup quinoa
- 1 cup coconut milk
- 1 cup milk
- 2 tablespoons cocoa powder
- 3 tablespoons maple syrup
- 4 dark chocolate squares, chopped

Directions:
In your Slow cooker, mix quinoa with coconut milk, milk, cocoa powder, maple syrup and chocolate, stir, cover and cook on Low for 6 hours. Stir quinoa mix again, divide into bowls and serve.

Nutrition: calories 215, fat 5, fiber 8, carbs 17, protein 4

Chai Breakfast Quinoa

Preparation time: 10 minutes | Cooking time: 6 hours | Servings: 2

Ingredients:
- 1 cup quinoa
- 1 egg white
- 2 cups milk
- ¼ teaspoon vanilla extract
- 1 and ½ tablespoons brown sugar
- ¼ teaspoon cardamom, ground
- ¼ teaspoon ginger, grated
- ¼ teaspoon cinnamon powder
- ¼ teaspoon vanilla extract
- ¼ teaspoon nutmeg, ground
- 1 tablespoons coconut flakes

Directions:
In your Slow cooker, mix quinoa with egg white, milk, vanilla, sugar, cardamom, ginger, cinnamon, vanilla and nutmeg, stir a bit, cover and cook on Low for 6 hours. Stir, divide into bowls and serve for breakfast with coconut flakes on top.

Nutrition: calories 211, fat 4, fiber 6, carbs 10, protein 4

Quinoa Breakfast Bake

Preparation time: 10 minutes | Cooking time: 7 hours | Servings: 4

Ingredients:
- 1 cup quinoa
- 4 tablespoons olive oil
- 2 cups water
- ½ cup dates, chopped
- 3 bananas, chopped
- ¼ cup coconut, shredded
- 2 teaspoons cinnamon powder
- 2 tablespoons brown sugar
- 1 cup walnuts, toasted and chopped

Directions:
Put the oil in your Slow cooker, add quinoa, water, dates, bananas, coconut, cinnamon, brown sugar and walnuts, stir, cover and cook on Low for 7 hours. Divide into bowls and serve for breakfast.

Nutrition: calories 241, fat 4, fiber 8, carbs 16, protein 6

Mocha Latte Quinoa Mix

Preparation time: 10 minutes | Cooking time: 6 hours | Servings: 4

Ingredients:
- 1 cup hot coffee
- 1 cup quinoa
- 1 cup coconut water
- ¼ cup chocolate chips
- ½ cup coconut cream

Directions:
In your Slow cooker, mix quinoa with coffee, coconut water and chocolate chips, cover and cook on Low for 6 hours. Stir, divide into bowls, spread coconut cream all over and serve for breakfast.

Nutrition: calories 251, fat 4, fiber 7, carbs 15, protein 4

Breakfast Butterscotch Pudding

Preparation time: 10 minutes | Cooking time: 1 hour 40 minutes | Servings: 6

Ingredients:
- 4 ounces butter, melted
- 2 ounces brown sugar
- 7 ounces flour
- ¼ pint milk
- 1 teaspoon vanilla extract
- Zest of ½ lemon, grated
- 2 tablespoons maple syrup
- Cooking spray
- 1 egg

Directions:
In a bowl, mix butter with sugar, milk, vanilla, lemon zest, maple syrup and eggs and whisk well. Add flour and whisk really well again. Grease your Slow cooker with cooking spray, add pudding mix, spread, cover and cook on High for 1 hour and 30 minutes. Divide between plates and serve for breakfast.

Nutrition: calories 271, fat 5, fiber 5, carbs 17, protein 4

French Breakfast Pudding

Preparation time: 10 minutes | Cooking time: 1 hour 30 minutes | Servings: 4

Ingredients:
- 3 egg yolks
- 6 ounces double cream
- 1 teaspoon vanilla extract
- 2 tablespoons caster sugar

Directions:
In a bowl, mix the egg yolks with sugar and whisk well. Add cream and vanilla extract, whisk well, pour into your 4 ramekins, place them in your Slow cooker, add some water to the slow cooker, cover and cook on High for 1 hour and 30 minutes. Leave aside to cool down and serve.

Nutrition: calories 261, fat 5, fiber 6, carbs 15, protein 2

Eggs and Sausage Casserole

Preparation time: 10 minutes | Cooking time: 8 hours | Servings: 4

Ingredients:
- 8 eggs, whisked
- 1 yellow onion, chopped
- 1 pound pork sausage, chopped
- 2 teaspoons basil, dried
- 1 tablespoon garlic powder
- Salt and black pepper to the taste
- 1 yellow bell pepper, chopped
- 1 teaspoon olive oil

Directions:
Grease your Slow cooker with the olive oil, add eggs, onion, pork sausage, basil, garlic powder, salt, pepper and yellow bell pepper, toss, cover and cook on Low for 8 hours. Slice, divide between plates and serve for breakfast.

Nutrition: calories 301, fat 4, fiber 4, carbs 14, protein 7

Cauliflower Rice Pudding

Preparation time: 10 minutes | Cooking time: 2 hours | Servings: 2

Ingredients:
- ¼ cup maple syrup
- 3 cups almond milk
- 1 cup cauliflower rice
- 2 tablespoons vanilla extract

Directions:
Put cauliflower rice in your Slow cooker, add maple syrup, almond milk and vanilla extract, stir, cover and cook on High for 2 hours. Stir your pudding again, divide into bowls and serve for breakfast.

Nutrition: calories 240, fat 2, fiber 2, carbs 15, protein 5

Veggies Casserole

Preparation time: 10 minutes | Cooking time: 4 hours | Servings: 8

Ingredients:
- 8 eggs
- 4 egg whites
- 2 teaspoons mustard
- ¾ cup almond milk
- A pinch of salt and black pepper
- 2 red bell peppers, chopped
- 1 yellow onion, chopped
- 1 teaspoon sweet paprika
- 4 bacon strips, chopped
- 6 ounces cheddar cheese, shredded
- Cooking spray

Directions:
In a bowl, mix the eggs with egg whites, mustard, milk, salt, pepper and sweet paprika and whisk well. Grease your Slow cooker with cooking spray and spread bell peppers, bacon and onion on the bottom. Add mixed eggs, sprinkle cheddar all over, cover and cook on Low for 4 hours. Divide between plates and serve for breakfast.

Nutrition: calories 262, fat 6, fiber 3, carbs 15, protein 7

Arugula Frittata

Preparation time: 10 minutes | Cooking time: 4 hours | Servings: 4

Ingredients:
- 8 eggs
- Salt and black pepper to the taste
- ½ cup milk
- 1 teaspoon oregano, dried
- 4 cups baby arugula
- 1 and ¼ cup roasted red peppers, chopped
- ½ cup red onion, chopped
- ¾ cup goat cheese, crumbled
- Cooking spray

Directions:
In a bowl, mix the eggs with milk, oregano, salt and pepper and whisk well. Grease your Slow cooker with cooking spray and spread roasted peppers, onion and arugula. Add eggs mix, sprinkle goat cheese all over, cover, cook on Low for 4 hours, divide frittata between plates and serve for breakfast.

Nutrition: calories 269, fat 3, fiber 6, carbs 15, protein 4

Mixed Egg and Sausage Scramble

Preparation time: 10 minutes | Cooking time: 6 hours | Servings: 6

Ingredients:
- 12 eggs
- 14 ounces sausages, sliced
- 1 cup milk
- 16 ounces cheddar cheese, shredded
- A pinch of salt and black pepper
- 1 teaspoon basil, dried
- 1 teaspoon oregano, dried
- Cooking spray

Directions:
Grease your Slow cooker with cooking spray, spread sausages on the bottom, crack eggs, add milk, basil, oregano, salt and pepper, whisk a bit, sprinkle cheddar all over, cover and cook on Low for 6 hours. Divide egg and sausage scramble between plates and serve.

Nutrition: calories 267, fat 4, fiber 5, carbs 12, protein 9

Worcestershire Asparagus Casserole

Preparation time: 10 minutes | Cooking time: 5 hours | Servings: 4

Ingredients:
- 2 pounds asparagus spears, cut into 1-inch pieces
- 1 cup mushrooms, sliced
- 1 teaspoon olive oil
- Salt and black pepper to the taste
- 2 cups coconut milk
- 1 teaspoon Worcestershire sauce
- 5 eggs, whisked

Directions:
Grease your Slow cooker with the oil and spread asparagus and mushrooms on the bottom. In a bowl, mix the eggs with milk, salt, pepper and Worcestershire sauce, whisk, pour into the slow cooker, toss everything, cover and cook on Low for 6 hours. Divide between plates and serve right away for breakfast.

Nutrition: calories 211, fat 4, fiber 4, carbs 8, protein 5

Peppers, Kale and Cheese Omelet

Preparation time: 10 minutes | Cooking time: 3 hours | Servings: 4

Ingredients:
- 1 teaspoon olive oil
- 7 ounces roasted red peppers, chopped
- 6 ounces baby kale
- Salt and black pepper to the taste
- 6 ounces feta cheese, crumbled
- ¼ cup green onions, sliced
- 7 eggs, whisked

Directions:
In a bowl, mix the eggs with cheese, kale, red peppers, green onions, salt and pepper, whisk well, pour into the Slow cooker after you've greased it with the oil, cover, cook on Low for 3 hours, divide between plates and serve right away.

Nutrition: calories 231, fat 7, fiber 4, carbs 7, protein 14

Salmon Frittata

Preparation time: 10 minutes | Cooking time: 3 hours 40 minutes | Servings: 3

Ingredients:
- 4 eggs, whisked
- ½ teaspoon olive oil
- 2 tablespoons green onions, chopped
- Salt and black pepper to the taste
- 4 ounces smoked salmon, chopped

Directions:

Drizzle the oil in your Slow cooker, add eggs, salt and pepper, whisk, cover and cook on Low for 3 hours. Add salmon and green onions, toss a bit, cover, cook on Low for 40 minutes more and divide between plates. Serve right away for breakfast.

Nutrition: calories 220, fat 10, fiber 2, carbs 15, protein 7

Creamy Breakfast

Preparation time: 5 minutes | Cooking time: 3 hours | Servings: 1

Ingredients:
- 1 teaspoon cinnamon powder
- ½ teaspoon nutmeg, ground
- ½ cup almonds, chopped
- 1 teaspoon sugar
- 1 and ½ cup heavy cream
- ¼ teaspoon cardamom, ground
- ¼ teaspoon cloves, ground

Directions:

In your Slow cooker, mix cream with cinnamon, nutmeg, almonds, sugar, cardamom and cloves, stir, cover, cook on Low for 3 hours, divide into bowls and serve for breakfast

Nutrition: calories 250, fat 12, fiber 4, carbs 8, protein 16

Brussels Sprouts Omelet

Preparation time: 10 minutes | Cooking time: 4 hours | Servings: 4

Ingredients:
- 4 eggs, whisked
- Salt and black pepper to the taste
- 1 tablespoon olive oil
- 2 green onions, minced
- 2 garlic cloves, minced
- 12 ounces Brussels sprouts, sliced
- 2 ounces bacon, chopped

Directions:

Drizzle the oil on the bottom of your Slow cooker and spread Brussels sprouts, garlic, bacon, green onions, eggs, salt and pepper, toss, cover and cook on Low for 4 hours. Divide between plates and serve right away for breakfast.

Nutrition: calories 240, fat 7, fiber 4, carbs 7, protein 13

Chicken Frittata

Preparation time: 10 minutes | Cooking time: 3 hours | Servings: 2

Ingredients:
- ½ cup chicken, cooked and shredded
- 1 teaspoon mustard
- 1 tablespoon mayonnaise
- 1 tomato, chopped
- 2 bacon slices, cooked and crumbled
- 4 eggs
- 1 small avocado, pitted, peeled and chopped
- Salt and black pepper to the taste

Directions:
In a bowl, mix the eggs with salt, pepper, chicken, avocado, tomato, bacon, mayo and mustard, toss, transfer to your Slow cooker, cover and cook on Low for 3 hours. Divide between plates and serve for breakfast

Nutrition: calories 300, fat 32, fiber 6, carbs 15, protein 25

Mushrooms Casserole

Preparation time: 10 minutes | Cooking time: 4 hours | Servings: 4

Ingredients:
- 1 teaspoon lemon zest, grated
- 10 ounces goat cheese, cubed
- 1 tablespoon lemon juice
- 1 tablespoon apple cider vinegar
- 1 tablespoon olive oil
- 2 garlic cloves, minced
- 10 ounces spinach, torn
- ½ cup yellow onion, chopped
- ½ teaspoon basil, dried
- 8 ounces mushrooms, sliced
- Salt and black pepper to the taste
- Cooking spray

Directions:
Spray your Slow cooker with cooking spray, arrange cheese cubes on the bottom and add lemon zest, lemon juice, vinegar, olive oil, garlic, spinach, onion, basil, mushrooms, salt and pepper. Toss well, cover, cook on Low for 4 hours, divide between plates and serve for breakfast right away.

Nutrition: calories 276, fat 6, fiber 5, carbs 7, protein 4

Carrot Pudding

Preparation time: 10 minutes | Cooking time: 8 hours | Servings: 4

Ingredients:
- 4 carrots, grated
- 1 and ½ cups milk
- A pinch of nutmeg, ground
- A pinch of cloves, ground
- ½ teaspoon cinnamon powder
- 2 tablespoons maple syrup
- ¼ cup walnuts, chopped
- 1 teaspoon vanilla extract

Directions:
In your Slow cooker, mix carrots with milk, cloves, nutmeg, cinnamon, maple syrup, walnuts and vanilla extract, stir, cover and cook on Low for 8 hours. Divide into bowls and serve for breakfast.

Nutrition: calories 215, fat 4, fiber 4, carbs 7, protein 7

Slow Cooker Lunch Recipes

Turkey Lunch

Preparation time: 10 minutes | Cooking time: 4 hours 20 minutes | Servings: 12

Ingredients:
- ½ teaspoon thyme, dried
- ½ teaspoon garlic powder
- Salt and black pepper to the taste
- 2 turkey breast halves, boneless
- 1/3 cup water
- 1 cup grape juice
- 2 cups raspberries
- 2 apples, peeled and chopped
- 2 cups blueberries
- A pinch of red pepper flakes, crushed
- ¼ teaspoon ginger powder

Directions:
In your Slow cooker, mix water with salt, pepper, thyme and garlic powder and stir. Add turkey breast halves, toss, cover and cook on Low for 4 hours. Meanwhile, heat up a pan over medium-high heat, add grape juice, apples, raspberries, blueberries, pepper flakes and ginger, stir, bring to a simmer, cook for 20 minutes and take off heat. Divide turkey between plates, drizzle berry sauce all over and serve for lunch.

Nutrition: calories 215, fat 2, fiber 3, carbs 12, protein 26

Lunch Roast

Preparation time: 10 minutes | Cooking time: 8 hours | Servings: 8

Ingredients:
- 2 pounds beef chuck roast
- Salt and black pepper to the taste
- 1 yellow onion, chopped
- 2 teaspoons olive oil
- 8 ounces tomato sauce
- ¼ cup lemon juice
- ¼ cup water
- ¼ cup ketchup
- ¼ cup apple cider vinegar
- 1 tablespoons Worcestershire sauce
- 2 tablespoons brown sugar
- ½ teaspoon mustard powder
- ½ teaspoons paprika

Directions:
In your Slow cooker, mix beef with salt, pepper, onion oil, tomato sauce, lemon juice, water, ketchup, vinegar, Worcestershire sauce, sugar, mustard and paprika, toss well, cover and cook on Low for 8 hours. Slice roast, divide between plates, drizzle cooking sauce all over and serve for lunch.

Nutrition: calories 243, fat 12, fiber 2, carbs 10, protein 23

Fajitas

Preparation time: 10 minutes | Cooking time: 3 hours | Servings: 8

Ingredients:
- 1 and ½ pounds beef sirloin, cut into thin strips
- 2 tablespoons lemon juice
- 2 tablespoons olive oil
- 1 garlic clove, minced
- 1 and ½ teaspoon cumin, ground
- Salt and black pepper to the taste
- ½ teaspoon chili powder
- A pinch of red pepper flakes, crushed
- 1 red bell pepper, cut into thin strips
- 1 yellow onion, cut into thin strips
- 8 mini tortillas

Directions:
Heat up a pan with the oil over medium-high heat, add beef strips, brown them for a few minutes and transfer to your Slow cooker. Add lemon juice, garlic, cumin, salt, pepper, chili powder and pepper flakes to the slow cooker as well, cover and cook on High for 2 hours. Add bell pepper and onion, stir and cook on High for 1 more hour. Divide beef mix between your mini tortillas and serve for lunch.

Nutrition: calories 220, fat 9, fiber 2, carbs 14, protein 20

Teriyaki Pork

Preparation time: 10 minutes | Cooking time: 7 hours | Servings: 8

Ingredients:
- 2 tablespoons sugar
- 2 tablespoons soy sauce
- ¾ cup apple juice
- 1 teaspoon ginger powder
- 1 tablespoon white vinegar
- Salt and black pepper to the taste
- ¼ teaspoon garlic powder
- 3 pounds pork loin roast, halved
- 7 teaspoons cornstarch
- 3 tablespoons water

Directions:
In your Slow cooker, mix apple juice with sugar, soy sauce, vinegar, ginger, garlic powder, salt, pepper and pork loin, toss well, cover and cook on Low for 7 hours. Transfer cooking juices to a small pan, heat up over medium-high heat, add cornstarch mixed with water, stir well, cook for 2 minutes until it thickens and take off heat. Slice roast, divide between plates, drizzle sauce all over and serve for lunch.

Nutrition: calories 247, fat 8, fiber 1, carbs 9, protein 33

Beef Stew

Preparation time: 10 minutes | Cooking time: 7 hours 30 minutes | Servings: 5

Ingredients:
- 2 potatoes, peeled and cubed
- 1 pound beef stew meat, cubed
- 11 ounces tomato juice
- 14 ounces beef stock
- 2 celery ribs, chopped
- 2 carrots, chopped
- 3 bay leaves
- 1 yellow onion, chopped
- Salt and black pepper to the taste
- ½ teaspoon chili powder
- ½ teaspoon thyme, dried
- 1 tablespoon water
- 2 tablespoons cornstarch
- ½ cup peas
- ½ cup corn

Directions:
In your Slow cooker, mix potatoes with beef, tomato juice, stock, ribs, carrots, bay leaves, onion, salt, pepper, chili powder and thyme, stir, cover and cook on Low for 7 hours. Add cornstarch mixed with water, peas and corn, stir, cover and cook on Low for 30 minutes more. Divide into bowls and serve for lunch.

Nutrition: calories 273, fat 7, fiber 6, carbs 30, protein 22

Apple and Onion Lunch Roast

Preparation time: 10 minutes | Cooking time: 5 hours | Servings: 8

Ingredients:
- 1 beef sirloin roast, halved
- Salt and black pepper to the taste
- 1 cup water
- ½ teaspoon soy sauce
- 1 apple, cored and quartered
- ¼ teaspoon garlic powder
- ½ teaspoon Worcestershire sauce
- 1 yellow onion, cut into medium wedges
- 2 tablespoons water
- 2 tablespoons cornstarch
- 1/8 teaspoon browning sauce
- Cooking spray

Directions:
Grease a pan with the cooking spray, heat it up over medium-high heat, add roast, brown it for a few minutes on each side and transfer to your Slow cooker. Add salt, pepper, soy sauce, garlic powder, Worcestershire sauce, onion and apple, cover and cook on Low for 6 hours. Transfer cooking juices from the slow cooker to a pan, heat it up over medium heat, add cornstarch, water and browning sauce, stir well, cook for a few minutes and take off heat. Slice roast, divide between plates, drizzle sauce all over and serve for lunch.

Nutrition: calories 242, fat 8, fiber 1, carbs 8, protein 34

Stuffed Peppers

Preparation time: 10 minutes | Cooking time: 4 hours | Servings: 4

Ingredients:
- 15 ounces canned black beans, drained
- 4 sweet red peppers, tops and seeds discarded
- 1 cup pepper jack cheese, shredded
- 1 yellow onion, chopped
- ¾ cup salsa
- ½ cup corn
- 1/3 cup white rice
- ½ teaspoon cumin, ground
- 1 and ½ teaspoons chili powder

Directions:
In a bowl, mix black beans with cheese, salsa, onion, corn, rice, cumin and chili powder and stir well. Stuff peppers with this mix, place them in your Slow cooker, cover and cook on Low for 4 hours. Divide between plates and serve them for lunch.

Nutrition: calories 317, fat 10, fiber 8, carbs 43, protein 12

Beans and Pumpkin Chili

Preparation time: 10 minutes | Cooking time: 4 hours | Servings: 10

Ingredients:
- 1 yellow bell pepper, chopped
- 1 yellow onion, chopped
- 3 garlic cloves, minced
- 2 tablespoons olive oil
- 3 cups chicken stock
- 30 ounces canned black beans, drained
- 14 ounces pumpkin, cubed
- 2 and ½ cups turkey meat, cooked and cubed
- 2 teaspoons parsley, dried
- 1 and ½ teaspoon oregano, dried
- 2 teaspoons chili powder
- 1 and ½ teaspoon cumin, ground
- Salt and black pepper to the taste

Directions:
Heat up a pan with the oil over medium-high heat, add bell pepper, onion and garlic, stir, cook for a few minutes and transfer to your Slow cooker. Add stock, beans, pumpkin, turkey, parsley, oregano, chili powder, cumin, salt and pepper, stir, cover and cook on Low for 4 hours. Divide into bowls and serve right away for lunch.

Nutrition: calories 200, fat 5, fiber 7, carbs 20, protein 15

Chicken and Peppers Mix

Preparation time: 10 minutes | Cooking time: 4 hours | Servings: 6

Ingredients:

- 24 ounces tomato sauce
- ¼ cup parmesan, grated
- 1 yellow onion, chopped
- 2 garlic cloves, minced
- 1 teaspoon basil, dried
- 1 teaspoon oregano, dried
- Salt and black pepper to the taste
- 6 chicken breast halves, skinless and boneless
- ½ green bell pepper, chopped
- ½ yellow bell pepper, chopped
- ½ red bell pepper, chopped

Directions:

In your Slow cooker, mix tomato sauce with parmesan, onion, garlic, basil, oregano, salt, pepper, chicken, green bell pepper, yellow bell pepper and red bell pepper, toss, cover and cook on Low for 4 hours. Divide between plates and serve for lunch.

Nutrition: calories 221, fat 6, fiber 3, carbs 16, protein 26

Chicken Tacos

Preparation time: 10 minutes | Cooking time: 5 hours | Servings: 16

Ingredients:

- 2 mangos, peeled and chopped
- 2 tomatoes, chopped
- 1 and ½ cups pineapple chunks
- 1 red onion, chopped
- 2 small green bell peppers, chopped
- 1 tablespoon lime juice
- 2 green onions, chopped
- 1 teaspoon sugar
- 4 pounds chicken breast halves, skinless
- Salt and black pepper to the taste
- 32 taco shells, warm
- ¼ cup cilantro, chopped
- ¼ cup brown sugar

Directions:

In a bowl, mix mango with pineapple, red onion, tomatoes, and bell peppers, green onions, lime juice, and toss. Put chicken in your Slow cooker, add salt, pepper and sugar and toss. Add mango mix, cover and cook on Low for 5 hours. Transfer chicken to a cutting board, cool it down, discard bones and shred meat. Divide meat and mango mix between taco shells and serve them for lunch.

Nutrition: calories 246, fat 7, fiber 2, carbs 25, protein 21

Orange Beef Dish

Preparation time: 10 minutes | Cooking time: 5 hours | Servings: 5

Ingredients:
- 1 pound beef sirloin steak, cut into medium strips
- 2 and ½ cups shiitake mushrooms, sliced
- 1 yellow onion, cut into medium wedges
- 3 red hot chilies, dried
- ¼ cup brown sugar
- ¼ cup orange juice
- ¼ cup soy sauce
- 2 tablespoons cider vinegar
- 1 tablespoon cornstarch
- 1 tablespoon ginger, grated
- 1 tablespoon sesame oil
- 1 cup snow peas
- 2 garlic cloves, minced
- 1 tablespoon orange zest, grated

Directions:
In your Slow cooker, mix steak strips with mushrooms, onion, chilies, sugar, orange juice, soy sauce, vinegar, cornstarch, ginger, oil, garlic and orange zest, toss, cover and cook on Low for 4 hours and 30 minutes. Add snow peas, cover, cook on Low for 30 minutes more, divide between plates and serve.

Nutrition: calories 310, fat 7, fiber 4, carbs 26, protein 33

Chicken with Couscous

Preparation time: 10 minutes | Cooking time: 3 hours | Servings: 6

Ingredients:
- 2 sweet potatoes, peeled and cubed
- 1 sweet red peppers, chopped
- 1 and ½ pounds chicken breasts, skinless and boneless
- 13 ounces canned stewed tomatoes
- Salt and black pepper to the taste
- ¼ cup raisins
- ¼ teaspoon cinnamon powder
- ¼ teaspoon cumin, ground

For the couscous:
- 1 cup whole wheat couscous
- 1 cup water
- Salt to the taste

Directions:
In your Slow cooker, mix potatoes with red peppers, chicken, tomatoes, salt, pepper, raisins, cinnamon and cumin, toss, cover, cook on Low for 3 hours and shred meat using 2 forks. Meanwhile, heat up a pan with the water over medium-high heat, add salt, bring water to a boil, add couscous, stir, leave aside covered for 10 minutes and fluff with a fork. Divide chicken mix between plates, add couscous on the side and serve.

Nutrition: calories 351, fat 4, fiber 7, carbs 45, protein 30

Pork Stew

Preparation time: 10 minutes | Cooking time: 5 hours | Servings: 8

Ingredients:

- 2 pork tenderloins, cubed
- Salt and black pepper to the taste
- 2 carrots, sliced
- 1 yellow onion, chopped
- 2 celery ribs, chopped
- 2 tablespoons tomato paste
- 3 cups beef stock
- 1/3 cup plums, dried, pitted and chopped
- 1 rosemary spring
- 1 thyme spring
- 2 bay leaves
- 4 garlic cloves, minced
- 1/3 cup green olives, pitted and sliced
- 1 tablespoon parsley, chopped

Directions:

In your Slow cooker, mix pork with salt, pepper, carrots, onion, celery, tomato paste, stock, plums, rosemary, thyme, bay leaves, garlic, olives and parsley, cover and cook on Low for 5 hours. Discard thyme, rosemary and bay leaves, divide stew into bowls and serve for lunch.

Nutrition: calories 200, fat 4, fiber 2, carbs 8, protein 23

Seafood Stew

Preparation time: 10 minutes | Cooking time: 4 hours 30 minutes | Servings: 8

Ingredients:

- 8 ounces clam juice
- 2 yellow onions, chopped
- 28 ounces canned tomatoes, chopped
- 6 ounces tomato paste
- 3 celery ribs, chopped
- ½ cup white wine
- 1 tablespoon red vinegar
- 5 garlic cloves, minced
- 1 tablespoon olive oil
- 1 teaspoon Italian seasoning
- 1 bay leaf
- 1 pound haddock fillets, boneless and cut into medium pieces
- ½ teaspoon sugar
- 1 pound shrimp, peeled and deveined
- 6 ounces crabmeat
- 6 ounces canned clams
- 2 tablespoons parsley, chopped

Directions:

In your Slow cooker, mix tomatoes with onions, clam juice, tomato paste, celery, wine, vinegar, garlic, oil, seasoning, sugar and bay leaf, stir, cover and cook on Low for 4 hours. Add shrimp, haddock, crabmeat and clams, cover, cook on Low for 30 minutes more, divide into bowls and serve with parsley sprinkled on top.

Nutrition: calories 205, fat 4, fiber 4, carbs 14, protein 27

Pork Sandwiches

Preparation time: 10 minutes | Cooking time: 8 hours | Servings: 12

Ingredients:
- 1 tablespoon steak seasoning
- 1 tablespoon fennel seeds
- A pinch of cayenne pepper
- Salt and black pepper to the taste
- 3 pounds pork shoulder butt, boneless
- 2 green bell peppers, chopped
- 1 tablespoon olive oil
- 2 yellow onions, chopped
- 14 ounces canned tomatoes, chopped
- 12 hamburger buns, split

Directions:
In your Slow cooker, mix pork butt with steak seasoning, fennel, cayenne, salt, pepper, bell peppers, oil, onions and tomatoes, toss, cover and cook on Low for 8 hours. Shred meat using 2 forks, divide the whole mix between your hamburger buns and serve for lunch.

Nutrition: calories 288, fat 8, fiber 5, carbs 28, protein 25

Peas and Ham Mix

Preparation time: 10 minutes | Cooking time: 5 hours | Servings: 12

Ingredients:
- ½ cup ham, cooked and chopped
- 16 ounces black-eyed peas
- 1 yellow onion, chopped
- 1 red bell pepper, chopped
- 5 bacon strips, cooked and crumbled
- 1 jalapeno pepper, chopped
- 2 garlic cloves, minced
- 1 teaspoon cumin, ground
- Salt and black pepper to the taste
- A pinch of cayenne pepper
- 6 cups water
- 1 tablespoon cilantro, chopped

Directions:
In your Slow cooker, mix ham with peas, onion, bell pepper, bacon, jalapeno, garlic, cumin, salt, pepper, cayenne and water, toss, cover and cook on Low for 5 hours. Add cilantro, stir, divide into bowls and serve for lunch.

Nutrition: calories 170, fat 3, fiber 6, carbs 26, protein 13

Beef and Veggie Stew

Preparation time: 10 minutes | Cooking time: 6 hours 30 minutes | Servings: 8

Ingredients:
- 3 potatoes, cubed
- 1 and ½ pound beef chuck roast, boneless and cubed
- 10 ounces canned tomato soup
- 1 and ½ cup baby carrots
- 3 and ¾ cups water
- 1 celery rib, chopped
- 1 yellow onion, chopped
- 2 tablespoons Worcestershire sauce
- 1 garlic clove, minced
- Salt and black pepper to the taste
- 1 teaspoon sugar
- 2 cups peas
- ¼ cup cornstarch

Directions:
In your Slow cooker, mix potatoes with beef cubes, tomato soup, baby carrots, 3 cups water, celery, onion, Worcestershire sauce, garlic, salt, pepper and sugar, stir, cover and cook on Low for 6 hours. Add cornstarch mixed with the rest of the water and the peas, stir, cover and cook on Low for 30 minutes more. Divide into bowls and serve for lunch.

Nutrition: calories 287, fat 4, fiber 5, carbs 31, protein 20

Hearty Chicken

Preparation time: 10 minutes | Cooking time: 6 hours | Servings: 2

Ingredients:
- 1 small yellow onion, chopped
- 2 carrots, sliced
- 1 cup green beans
- ½ celery rib, chopped
- 2 chicken breast halves, boneless and skinless
- 2 small red potatoes, halved
- 2 bacon strips, cooked and crumbled
- Salt and black pepper to the taste
- ¾ cup water
- ¼ teaspoon basil, dried
- ¼ teaspoon thyme, dried

Directions:

In your Slow cooker, mix onion with carrots, green beans, celery, chicken, red potatoes, bacon, salt, pepper, water, basil and thyme, cover and cook on Low for 6 hours. Divide between plates and serve for lunch.

Nutrition: calories 304, fat 7, fiber 5, carbs 20, protein 37

Beef Chili

Preparation time: 10 minutes | Cooking time: 10 hours | Servings: 8

Ingredients:
- 3 chipotle chili peppers in adobo sauce, chopped
- 2 pounds beef steak, cubed
- 1 yellow onion, chopped
- 2 garlic cloves, minced
- 1 tablespoon chili powder
- Salt and black pepper to the taste
- 45 canned tomato puree
- ½ teaspoon cumin, ground
- 14 ounces beef stock
- 2 tablespoons cilantro, chopped

Directions:

In your Slow cooker, chipotle chilies with beef, onion, garlic, chili powder, salt, pepper, tomato puree, cumin and stock, stir, cover and cook on Low for 6 hours. Add cilantro, stir, divide into bowls and serve for lunch.

Nutrition: calories 230, fat 8, fiber 2, carbs 12, protein 25

Moist Pork Loin

Preparation time: 10 minutes | Cooking time: 5 hours | Servings: 8

Ingredients:
- 3 pound pork loin roast
- 1 teaspoon onion powder
- 1 teaspoon mustard powder
- 2 cups chicken stock
- 2 tablespoons olive oil
- ¼ cup cornstarch
- ¼ cup water

Directions:

In your Slow cooker, mix pork with onion powder, mustard powder, stock and oil, cover and cook on Low for 5 hours. Transfer roast to a cutting board, slice and divide between plates. Transfer cooking juices to a pan and heat it up over medium heat. Add water and cornstarch, stir, cook until it thickens, drizzle over roast and serve for lunch.

Nutrition: calories 300, fat 11, fiber 1, carbs 10, protein 34

Lunch Meatloaf

Preparation time: 10 minutes | Cooking time: 4 hours | Servings: 8

Ingredients:
- ½ cup breadcrumbs
- 1 yellow onion, chopped
- 1 green bell pepper, chopped
- 2 eggs, whisked
- 2 tablespoons brown mustard
- ½ cup chili sauce
- Salt and black pepper to the taste
- 4 garlic cloves, minced
- ¼ teaspoon oregano, dried
- 2 pounds beef meat, ground
- ¼ teaspoon basil, dried
- Cooking spray

Directions:
In a bowl, mix beef with onion, breadcrumbs, bell pepper, mustard, chili sauce, eggs, salt, pepper, garlic, oregano and basil and stir well. Line your Slow cooker with tin foil, grease with cooking spray, add beef meat, shape your meatloaf with your hands, cover and cook on Low for 4 hours. Divide between plates and serve for lunch.

Nutrition: calories 253, fat 11, fiber 1, carbs 12, protein 25

Mexican Lunch Mix

Preparation time: 10 minutes | Cooking time: 7 hours | Servings: 12

Ingredients:
- 12 ounces beer
- ¼ cup flour
- 2 tablespoons tomato paste
- 1 jalapeno pepper, chopped
- 1 bay leaf
- 4 teaspoons Worcestershire sauce
- 2 teaspoons red pepper flakes, crushed
- 1 and ½ teaspoons cumin, ground
- 2 teaspoons chili powder
- Salt and black pepper to the taste
- 2 garlic cloves, minced
- ½ teaspoon sweet paprika
- ½ teaspoon red vinegar
- 3 pounds pork shoulder butter, cubed
- 2 potatoes, chopped
- 1 yellow onion, chopped

Directions:
In your Slow cooker, mix pork with potatoes, onion, beef, flour, tomato paste, jalapeno, bay leaf, Worcestershire sauce, pepper flakes, cumin, chili powder, garlic, paprika and vinegar, toss, cover and cook on Low for 7 hours. Divide between plates and serve for lunch.

Nutrition: calories 261, fat 12, fiber 2, carbs 16, protein 21

Flavored Turkey

Preparation time: 8 minutes | Cooking time: 3 hours 30 minutes | Servings: 12

Ingredients:

- 14 ounces chicken stock
- ¼ cup brown sugar
- ½ cup lemon juice
- ¼ cup lime juice
- ¼ cup sage, chopped
- ¼ cup cider vinegar
- 2 tablespoons mustard
- ¼ cup olive oil
- 1 tablespoon marjoram, chopped
- 1 teaspoon sweet paprika
- Salt and black pepper to the taste
- 1 teaspoon garlic powder
- 2 turkey breast halves, boneless and skinless

Directions:

In your blender, mix stock with brown sugar, lemon juice, lime juice, sage, vinegar, mustard, oil, marjoram, paprika, salt, pepper and garlic powder and pulse well. Put turkey breast halves in a bowl, add blender mix, cover and leave aside in the fridge for 8 hours. Transfer everything to your Slow cooker, cover and cook on High for 3 hours and 30 minutes. Divide between plates and serve for lunch.

Nutrition: calories 219, fat 4, fiber 1, carbs 5, protein 36

Beef Strips

Preparation time: 10 minutes | Cooking time: 6 hours | Servings: 4

Ingredients:

- ½ pound baby mushrooms, sliced
- 1 yellow onion, chopped
- 1 pound beef sirloin steak, cubed
- Salt and black pepper to the taste
- 1/3 cup red wine
- 2 teaspoons olive oil
- 2 cups beef stock
- 1 tablespoon Worcestershire sauce

Directions:

In your Slow cooker, mix beef strips with onion, mushrooms, salt, pepper, wine, olive oil, beef stock and Worcestershire sauce, toss, cover and cook on Low for 6 hours. Divide between plates and serve for lunch.

Nutrition: calories 212, fat 7, fiber 1, carbs 8, protein 26

BBQ Chicken Thighs

Preparation time: 10 minutes | Cooking time: 5 hours | Servings: 6

Ingredients:
- 6 chicken thighs, skinless and boneless
- 1 yellow onion, chopped
- ½ teaspoon poultry seasoning
- 14 ounces canned tomatoes, chopped
- 8 ounces tomato sauce
- ½ cup bbq sauce
- 1 teaspoon garlic powder
- ¼ cup orange juice
- ½ teaspoon hot pepper sauce
- ¾ teaspoon oregano, dried
- Salt and black pepper to the taste

Directions:
In your Slow cooker, mix chicken with onion, poultry seasoning, tomatoes, tomato sauce, bbq sauce, garlic powder, orange juice, pepper sauce, oregano, salt and pepper, toss, cover and cook on Low for 5 hours. Divide between plates and serve with the sauce drizzled on top.

Nutrition: calories 211, fat 9, fiber 2, carbs 12, protein 23

Slow Cooker Roast

Preparation time: 10 minutes | Cooking time: 6 hours | Servings: 6

Ingredients:
- 2 sweet potatoes, cubed
- 2 carrots, chopped
- 2 pounds beef chuck roast, cubed
- ¼ cup celery, chopped
- 1 tablespoon canola oil
- 2 garlic cloves, minced
- 1 yellow onion, chopped
- 1 tablespoon flour
- 1 tablespoon brown sugar
- 1 tablespoon sugar
- 1 teaspoon cumin, ground
- Salt and black pepper to the taste
- ¾ teaspoon coriander, ground
- ½ teaspoon oregano, dried
- 1 teaspoon chili powder
- 1/8 teaspoon cinnamon powder
- ¾ teaspoon orange peel grated
- 15 ounces tomato sauce

Directions:
In your Slow cooker, mix potatoes with carrots, beef cubes, celery, oil, garlic, onion, flour, brown sugar, sugar, cumin, salt pepper, coriander, oregano, chili powder, cinnamon, orange peel and tomato sauce, stir, cover and cook on Low for 6 hours. Divide into bowls and serve for lunch.

Nutrition: calories 278, fat 12, fiber 2, carbs 16, protein 25

Creamy Chicken

Preparation time: 10 minutes | Cooking time: 8 hours 30 minutes | Servings: 6

Ingredients:
- 10 ounces canned cream of chicken soup
- Salt and black pepper to the taste
- A pinch of cayenne pepper
- 3 tablespoons flour
- 1 pound chicken breasts, skinless, boneless and cubed
- 1 celery rib, chopped
- ½ cup green bell pepper, chopped
- ¼ cup yellow onion, chopped
- 10 ounces peas
- 2 tablespoons pimientos, chopped

Directions:

In your Slow cooker, mix cream of chicken with salt, pepper, cayenne and flour and whisk well. Add chicken, celery, bell pepper and onion, toss, cover and cook on Low for 8 hours. Add peas and pimientos, stir, cover and cook on Low for 30 minutes more. Divide into bowls and serve for lunch.

Nutrition: calories 200, fat 3, fiber 4, carbs 16, protein 17

Chicken Stew

Preparation time: 10 minutes | Cooking time: 8 hours | Servings: 6

Ingredients:
- 32 ounces chicken stock
- 3 spicy chicken sausage links, cooked and sliced
- 28 ounces canned tomatoes, chopped
- 1 yellow onion, chopped
- 1 cup lentils
- 1 carrot, chopped
- 2 garlic cloves, minced
- 1 celery rib, chopped
- ½ teaspoon thyme, dried
- Salt and black pepper to the taste

Directions:

In your Slow cooker, mix stock with sausage, tomatoes, onion, lentils, carrot, garlic, celery, thyme, salt and pepper, stir, cover and cook on Low for 8 hours. Divide into bowls and serve for lunch.

Nutrition: calories 231, fat 4, fiber 12, carbs 31, protein 15

Lemon Chicken

Preparation time: 10 minutes | Cooking time: 5 hours | Servings: 6

Ingredients:
- 6 chicken breast halves, skinless and bone in
- Salt and black pepper to the taste
- 1 teaspoon oregano, dried
- ¼ cup water
- 2 tablespoons butter
- 3 tablespoons lemon juice
- 2 garlic cloves, minced
- 1 teaspoon chicken bouillon granules
- 2 teaspoons parsley, chopped

Directions:

In your Slow cooker, mix chicken with salt, pepper, water, butter, lemon juice, garlic and chicken granules, stir, cover and cook on Low for 5 hours. Add parsley, stir, divide between plates and serve for lunch.

Nutrition: calories 336, fat 10, fiber 1, carbs 1, protein 46

Chicken Noodle Soup

Preparation time: 10 minutes | Cooking time: 6 hours 15 minutes | Servings: 4

Ingredients:

- 1 and ½ pound chicken breast, boneless, skinless and cubed
- 1 yellow onion, chopped
- 3 carrots, chopped
- 2 celery stalks, chopped
- 3 garlic cloves minced
- 2 bay leaves
- 1 cup water
- 6 cups chicken stock
- 1 teaspoon Italian seasoning
- 2 cup cheese tortellini
- 1 tablespoon parsley, chopped

Directions:

In your Slow cooker, mix chicken with onion, carrots, celery, garlic, bay leaves, water, stock and seasoning, stir, cover and cook on Low for 6 hours. Add tortellini, stir, cover, cook on Low for 15 minutes more, ladle into bowls and serve for lunch.

Nutrition: calories 231, fat 3, fiber 4, carbs 17, protein 22

Lentils Soup

Preparation time: 10 minutes | Cooking time: 6 hours | Servings: 6

Ingredients:

- 1 yellow onion, chopped
- 6 carrots, sliced
- 1 yellow bell pepper, chopped
- 4 garlic cloves, minced
- A pinch of cayenne pepper
- 3 cups red lentils
- 4 cups chicken stock
- Salt and black pepper to the taste
- 2 cups water
- 1 teaspoon lemon zest, grated
- 1 teaspoon lemon juice
- 1 tablespoon rosemary, chopped

Directions:

In your Slow cooker, mix onion with carrots, bell pepper, garlic, cayenne, lentils, stock, salt, pepper and water, stir, cover and cook on Low for 6 hours. Add lemon zest, lemon juice and rosemary, stir, ladle into bowls and serve for lunch.

Nutrition: calories 281, fat 4, fiber 3, carbs 38, protein 17

Thai Chicken Soup

Preparation time: 10 minutes | Cooking time: 7 hours | Servings: 4

Ingredients:
- 1 pound chicken breasts, skinless and boneless
- 1 cup wild rice
- 1 tablespoon olive oil
- 1 sweet potato, peeled and cubed
- 1 cup butternut squash, peeled and cubed
- 1 zucchini, chopped
- 1 green apple, cored and chopped
- 1 yellow onion, chopped
- 1 tablespoon ginger, grated
- ¼ cup red curry paste
- 4 garlic cloves, minced
- 2 tablespoons brown sugar
- 2 tablespoons fish sauce
- 2 tablespoons soy sauce
- 1 tablespoon basil, dried
- 1 teaspoon cumin, ground
- Salt and black pepper to the taste
- 28 ounces coconut milk
- 5 cups chicken stock

Directions:
In your Slow cooker, mix chicken with rice, oil, sweet potato, squash, zucchini, apple, onion, ginger, curry paste, garlic, sugar, fish, soy sauce, basil, cumin, salt, pepper, coconut milk and stock, stir, cover and cook on Low for 7 hours. Transfer meat to a cutting board, shred using 2 forks, return to slow cooker, stir, ladle soup into bowls and serve for lunch.

Nutrition: calories 300, fat 4, fiber 6, carbs 28, protein 17

Spinach and Mushroom Soup

Preparation time: 10 minutes | Cooking time: 3 hours | Servings: 6

Ingredients:
- 2/3 cup yellow onion, chopped
- 16 ounces baby spinach
- 3 tablespoons butter
- Salt and black pepper to the taste
- 5 cups veggie stock
- 3 garlic cloves, minced
- ½ teaspoon Italian seasoning
- 1 and ½ cups half and half
- ¼ teaspoon thyme, dried
- 16 ounces cheese tortellini
- 2 teaspoons garlic powder
- 3 cups mushrooms, sliced
- ½ cup parmesan, grated

Directions:
Heat up a pan with the butter over medium-high heat, add onion, garlic, mushrooms and spinach, stir and cook for a few minutes. Transfer to your Slow cooker, add salt, pepper, stock, Italian seasoning, half and half, thyme, garlic powder and parmesan, cover and cook on High for 2 hours and 30 minutes. Add tortellini, stir, cover, cook on High for 30 minutes more, ladle into bowls and serve for lunch.

Nutrition: calories 231, fat 5, fiber 6, carbs 14, protein 5

Creamy Chicken Soup

Preparation time: 10 minutes | Cooking time: 6 hours | Servings: 6

Ingredients:
- 2 chicken breasts, skinless and boneless
- 1 cup yellow corn
- 1 cup peas
- 1 celery stalk, chopped
- 1 cup carrots, chopped
- 2 gold potatoes, cubed
- 4 ounces cream cheese, soft
- 1 yellow onion, chopped
- 4 cups chicken stock
- 2 teaspoons garlic powder
- 3 cups heavy cream
- Salt and black pepper to the taste

Directions:
In your Slow cooker, mix chicken with corn, peas, carrots, potatoes, celery, cream cheese, onion, garlic powder, stock, heavy cream, salt and pepper, stir, cover and cook on Low for 6 hours. Transfer chicken to a cutting board, shred meat using 2 forks, return to the slow cooker, stir, ladle soup into bowls and serve for lunch.

Nutrition: calories 300, fat 6, fiber 5, carbs 20, protein 22

Black Bean Soup

Preparation time: 10 minutes | Cooking time: 6 hours | Servings: 6

Ingredients:
- 1 pound black beans
- 2 celery stalks, chopped
- 2 garlic cloves, minced
- 1 yellow onion, chopped
- 2 carrots, chopped
- 1 tablespoon chili powder
- 1 cup salsa
- 1 teaspoon oregano, dried
- ½ tablespoon cumin, ground
- 2 cups water
- 4 cups veggie stock

Directions:
In your Slow cooker, mix beans with celery, garlic, onion, carrots, chili powder, salsa, oregano, cumin, water and stock, stir, cover and cook on Low for 6 hours. Blend soup using an immersion blender, ladle into bowls and serve for lunch.

Nutrition: calories 300, fat 4, fiber 7, carbs 20, protein 16

Taco Soup

Preparation time: 10 minutes | Cooking time: 6 hours | Servings: 4

Ingredients:
- 1 tablespoon olive oil
- 4 red bell peppers, chopped
- 1 yellow onion, chopped
- 2 pounds beef, ground
- 2 tablespoons chili powder
- 2 tablespoons cumin, ground
- Salt and black pepper to the taste
- 1 teaspoon cinnamon powder
- 1 teaspoon sweet paprika
- ½ teaspoon onion powder
- ½ teaspoon garlic powder
- A pinch of cayenne pepper
- 24 ounces beef stock
- 28 ounces canned tomatoes, chopped
- 8 ounces canned green chilies, chopped
- 6 ounces coconut milk

Directions:
In your Slow cooker, mix oil with bell peppers, onion, beef, chili powder, cumin, salt, pepper, cinnamon, paprika, onion powder, garlic powder, cayenne, stock, tomatoes chilies and coconut milk, stir well, cover and cook on Low for 6 hours. Ladle into bowls and serve for lunch.

Nutrition: calories 403, fat 12, fiber 4, carbs 14, protein 45

Winter Veggie Stew

Preparation time: 10 minutes | Cooking time: 4 hours | Servings: 8

Ingredients:
- 1 yellow onion, chopped
- 1 teaspoon olive oil
- 2 red potatoes, chopped
- Salt and black pepper to the taste
- 1 tablespoon sugar
- 1 tablespoon curry powder
- 1 tablespoon ginger, grated
- 3 garlic cloves, minced
- 30 ounces canned chickpeas, drained
- 1 green bell pepper, chopped
- 2 cups chicken stock
- 1 red bell pepper, chopped
- 1 cauliflower head, florets separated
- 28 ounces canned tomatoes, chopped
- 1 cup coconut milk
- 10 ounces baby spinach

Directions:
In your slow cooker, mix oil with onion, potatoes, salt, pepper, sugar, curry powder, ginger, garlic, chickpeas, red and green bell pepper, stock, cauliflower, tomatoes, spinach and milk, stir, cover and cook on High for 4 minutes. Stir your stew again, divide into bowls and serve for lunch.

Nutrition: calories 319, fat 10, fiber 13, carbs 45, protein 14

Chickpeas Stew

Preparation time: 10 minutes | Cooking time: 4 hours 10 minutes | Servings: 6

Ingredients:
- 1 yellow onion, chopped
- 1 tablespoon ginger, grated
- 1 tablespoon olive oil
- 6 ounces canned chickpeas, drained
- 4 garlic cloves, minced
- Salt and black pepper to the taste
- 2 red Thai chilies, chopped
- ½ teaspoon turmeric powder
- 2 tablespoons garam masala
- 4 ounces tomato paste
- 2 cups chicken stock
- 2 tablespoons cilantro, chopped

Directions:
Heat up a pan with the oil over medium-high heat, add ginger and onions, stir and cook for 4-5 minutes. Add garlic, salt, pepper, Thai chilies, garam masala and turmeric, stir, cook for 2 minutes more and transfer everything to your slow cooker. Add stock, chickpeas and tomato paste, stir, cover and cook on Low for 4 hours. Add cilantro, stir, divide into bowls and serve for lunch.

Nutrition: calories 225, fat 7, fiber 4, carbs 14, protein 7

Lentils Curry

Preparation time: 10 minutes | Cooking time: 8 hours | Servings: 16

Ingredients:
- 4 garlic cloves, minced
- 4 cups brown lentils
- 2 yellow onions, chopped
- 1 tablespoon ginger, grated
- 4 tablespoons olive oil
- 1 tablespoon garam masala
- 4 tablespoons red curry paste
- 2 teaspoons sugar
- 1 and ½ teaspoons turmeric powder
- A pinch of salt and black pepper
- 45 ounces canned tomato puree
- ½ cup coconut milk
- 1 tablespoon cilantro, chopped

Directions:
In your slow cooker, mix lentils with onions, garlic, ginger, oil, curry paste, garam masala, turmeric, salt, pepper, sugar and tomato puree, stir, cover and cook on Low for 7 hours and 20 minutes. Add coconut milk and cilantro, stir, cover, cook on Low for 40 minutes, divide into bowls and serve for lunch.

Nutrition: calories 268, fat 5, fiber 4, carbs 18, protein 6

Quinoa Chili

Preparation time: 10 minutes | Cooking time: 3 hours | Servings: 4

Ingredients:
- 15 ounces canned black beans, drained
- 2 and ¼ cups veggie stock
- ½ cup quinoa
- 14 ounces canned tomatoes, chopped
- ¼ cup red bell pepper, chopped
- 1 carrot, sliced
- ¼ cup green bell pepper, chopped
- 2 garlic cloves, minced
- ½ chili pepper, chopped
- ½ cup corn
- 2 teaspoons chili powder
- 1 small yellow onion, chopped
- Salt and black pepper to the taste
- 1 teaspoon oregano, dried
- 1 teaspoon cumin, ground

Directions:
In your slow cooker, mix black beans with stock, quinoa, tomatoes, red and green bell pepper, carrot, garlic, chili, chili powder, onion, salt, pepper, oregano, cumin and corn, stir, cover and cook on High for 3 hours. Divide chili into bowls and serve for lunch.

Nutrition: calories 291, fat 7, fiber 4, carbs 28, protein 8

French Veggie Stew

Preparation time: 10 minutes | Cooking time: 9 hours | Servings: 6

Ingredients:
- 2 yellow onions, chopped
- 1 eggplant, sliced
- 4 zucchinis, sliced
- 2 garlic cloves, minced
- 2 green bell peppers, cut into medium strips
- 6 ounces canned tomato paste
- 2 tomatoes, cut into medium wedges
- 1 teaspoon oregano, dried
- 1 teaspoon sugar
- 1 teaspoon basil, dried
- Salt and black pepper to the taste
- 2 tablespoons parsley, chopped
- ¼ cup olive oil
- A pinch of red pepper flakes, crushed

Directions:
In your Slow cooker, mix oil with onions, eggplant, zucchinis, garlic, bell peppers, tomato paste, basil, sugar, oregano, salt and pepper, cover and cook on Low for 9 hours. Add pepper flakes and parsley, stir gently, divide into bowls and serve for lunch.

Nutrition: calories 269, fat 7, fiber 6, carbs 17, protein 4

Beans and Rice

Preparation time: 10 minutes | Cooking time: 3 hours | Servings: 6

Ingredients:
- 1 pound pinto beans, dried
- 1/3 cup hot sauce
- Salt and black pepper to the taste
- 1 tablespoon garlic, minced
- 1 teaspoon garlic powder
- ½ teaspoon cumin, ground
- 1 tablespoon chili powder
- 3 bay leaves
- ½ teaspoon oregano, dried
- 1 cup white rice, cooked

Directions:
In your slow cooker, mix pinto beans with hot sauce, salt, pepper, garlic, garlic powder, cumin, chili powder, bay leaves and oregano, stir, cover and cook on High for 3 hours. Divide rice between plates, add pinto beans on top and serve for lunch

Nutrition: calories 381, fat 7, fiber 12, carbs 35, protein 10

Black Beans Stew

Preparation time: 10 minutes | Cooking time: 6 hours 20 minutes | Servings: 6

Ingredients:
- 1 yellow onion, chopped
- 1 tablespoon olive oil
- 1 red bell pepper, chopped
- 1 jalapeno, chopped
- 2 garlic cloves, minced
- 1 teaspoon ginger, grated
- ½ teaspoon cumin
- ½ teaspoon allspice, ground
- ½ teaspoon oregano, dried
- 30 ounces canned black beans, drained
- ½ teaspoon sugar
- 1 cup chicken stock
- Salt and black pepper
- 3 cups brown rice, cooked
- 2 mangoes, peeled and chopped

Directions:
Heat up a pan with the oil over medium-high heat, add onion, stir and cook for 3-4 minutes, Add garlic, ginger and jalapeno, stir, cook for 3 minutes more and transfer to your slow cooker. Add red bell pepper, cumin, allspice, oregano, black beans, sugar, stock, salt and pepper, stir, cover and cook on Low for 6 hours. Add rice and mangoes, stir, cover, cook on Low for 10 minutes more, divide between plates and serve.

Nutrition: calories 490, fat 6, fiber 20, carbs 80, protein 17

Sweet Potato Stew

Preparation time: 10 minutes | Cooking time: 8 hours | Servings: 8

Ingredients:
- 1 yellow onion, chopped
- ½ cup red beans, dried
- 2 red bell peppers, chopped
- 2 tablespoons ginger, grated
- 4 garlic cloves, minced
- 2 pounds sweet, peeled and cubed
- 3 cups chicken stock
- 14 ounces canned tomatoes, chopped
- 2 jalapeno peppers, chopped
- Salt and black pepper to the taste
- ½ teaspoon cumin, ground
- ½ teaspoon coriander, ground
- ¼ teaspoon cinnamon powder
- ¼ cup peanuts, roasted and chopped
- Juice of ½ lime

Directions:
In your slow cooker, mix onion with red beans, red bell peppers, ginger, garlic, potatoes, stock, tomatoes, jalapenos, salt, pepper, cumin, coriander and cinnamon, stir, cover and cook on Low for 8 hours. Divide into bowls, divide peanuts on top, drizzle limejuice and serve for lunch.

Nutrition: calories 259, fat 8, fiber 7, carbs 42, protein 8

Minestrone Soup

Preparation time: 10 minutes | Cooking time: 4 hours | Servings: 8

Ingredients:
- 2 zucchinis, chopped
- 3 carrots, chopped
- 1 yellow onion, chopped
- 1 cup green beans, halved
- 3 celery stalks, chopped
- 4 garlic cloves, minced
- 10 ounces canned garbanzo beans
- 1 pound lentils, cooked
- 4 cups veggie stock
- 28 ounces canned tomatoes, chopped
- 1 teaspoon curry powder
- ½ teaspoon garam masala
- ½ teaspoon cumin, ground
- Salt and black pepper to the taste

Directions:
In your slow cooker, mix zucchinis with carrots, onion, green beans, celery, garlic, garbanzo beans, lentils, stock, tomatoes, salt, pepper, cumin, curry powder and garam masala, stir, cover, cook on High for 4 hours, ladle into bowls and serve for lunch.

Nutrition: calories 273, fat 12, fiber 7, carbs 34, protein 10

Chili Cream

Preparation time: 10 minutes | Cooking time: 6 hours | Servings: 6

Ingredients:
- 2 jalapeno chilies, chopped
- 1 cup yellow onion, chopped
- 1 tablespoon olive oil
- 4 poblano chilies, chopped
- 4 Anaheim chilies, chopped
- 3 cups corn
- 6 cups veggie stock
- ½ bunch cilantro, chopped
- Salt and black pepper to the taste

Directions:
In your slow cooker, mix jalapenos with onion, oil, poblano chilies, Anaheim chilies, corn and stock, stir, cover and cook on Low for 6 hours. Add cilantro, salt and pepper, stir, transfer to your blender, pulse well, divide into bowls and serve for lunch.

Nutrition: calories 209, fat 5, fiber 5, carbs 33, protein 5

Salmon and Cilantro Sauce

Preparation time: 10 minutes | Cooking time: 2 hours 30 minutes | Servings: 4

Ingredients:
- 2 garlic cloves, minced
- 4 salmon fillets, boneless
- ¾ cup cilantro, chopped
- 3 tablespoons lime juice
- 1 tablespoon olive oil
- Salt and black pepper to the taste

Directions:
Grease your Slow cooker with the oil, add salmon fillets inside skin side down, also add garlic, cilantro, lime juice, salt and pepper, cover and cook on Low for 2 hours and 30 minutes. Divide salmon fillets on plates, drizzle the cilantro sauce all over and serve for lunch.

Nutrition: calories 200, fat 3, fiber 2, carbs 14, protein 8

Chili Salmon

Preparation time: 10 minutes | Cooking time: 2 hours | Servings: 2

Ingredients:
- 2 medium salmon fillets, boneless
- A pinch of nutmeg, ground
- A pinch of cloves, ground
- A pinch of ginger powder
- Salt and black pepper to the taste
- 2 teaspoons sugar
- 1 teaspoon onion powder
- ¼ teaspoon chipotle chili powder
- ½ teaspoon cayenne pepper
- ½ teaspoon cinnamon, ground
- 1/8 teaspoon thyme, dried

Directions:
In a bowl, mix salmon fillets with nutmeg, cloves, ginger, salt, coconut sugar, onion powder, chili powder, cayenne black pepper, cinnamon and thyme, toss, transfer fish to 2 tin foil pieces, wrap, add to your Slow cooker, cover and cook on Low for 2 hours. Unwrap fish, divide between plates and serve with a side salad for lunch.

Nutrition: calories 220, fat 4, fiber 2, carbs 7, protein 4

Pulled Chicken

Preparation time: 10 minutes | Cooking time: 6 hours | Servings: 2

Ingredients:
- 2 tomatoes, chopped
- 2 red onions, chopped
- 2 chicken breasts, skinless and boneless
- 2 garlic cloves, minced
- 1 tablespoon maple syrup
- 1 teaspoon chili powder
- 1 teaspoon basil, dried
- 3 tablespoons water
- 1 teaspoon cloves, ground

Directions:
In your Slow cooker, mix onion with tomatoes, chicken, garlic, maple syrup, chili powder, basil, water and cloves, toss well, cover and cook on Low for 6 hours. Shred chicken, divide it along with the veggies between plates and serve for lunch.

Nutrition: calories 220, fat 3, fiber 3, carbs 14, protein 6

Chicken Chili

Preparation time: 10 minutes | Cooking time: 7 hours | Servings: 4

Ingredients:
- 16 ounces salsa
- 8 chicken thighs
- 1 yellow onion, chopped
- 16 ounces canned tomatoes, chopped
- 1 red bell pepper, chopped
- 2 tablespoons chili powder

Directions:
Put the salsa in your slow cooker, add chicken, onion, tomatoes, bell pepper and chili powder, stir, cover, cook on Low for 7 hours, divide into bowls and serve for lunch.

Nutrition: calories 250, fat 3, fiber 3, carbs 14, protein 8

Salsa Chicken

Preparation time: 10 minutes | Cooking time: 7 hours | Servings: 4

Ingredients:
- 4 chicken breasts, skinless and boneless
- ½ cup veggie stock
- Salt and black pepper to the taste
- 16 ounces salsa
- 1 and ½ tablespoons parsley, dried
- 1 teaspoon garlic powder
- ½ tablespoon cilantro, chopped
- 1 teaspoon onion powder
- ½ tablespoons oregano, dried
- ½ teaspoon paprika, smoked
- 1 teaspoon chili powder
- ½ teaspoon cumin, ground

Directions:
Put the stock in your slow cooker, add chicken breasts, add salsa, parsley, garlic powder, cilantro, onion powder, oregano, paprika, chili powder, cumin, salt and black pepper to the taste, stir, cover and cook on Low for 7 hours. Divide chicken between plates, drizzle the sauces on top and serve for lunch.

Nutrition: calories 270, fat 4, fiber 2, carbs 14, protein 9

Thai Chicken

Preparation time: 10 minutes | Cooking time: 4 hours | Servings: 6

Ingredients:
- 1 and ½ pound chicken breast, boneless, skinless and cubed
- 1 tablespoon olive oil
- 3 tablespoons soy sauce
- 2 tablespoons flour
- Salt and black pepper to the taste
- 1 tablespoon ketchup
- 2 tablespoons white vinegar
- 1 teaspoon ginger, grated
- 2 tablespoons sugar
- ½ cup cashews, chopped
- 2 garlic cloves, minced
- 1 green onion, chopped

Directions:
Put chicken pieces in a bowl, season with salt, black pepper, add flour and toss well. Heat up a pan with the oil over medium-high heat, add chicken, cook for 5 minutes and transfer to your slow cooker. Add soy sauce, ketchup, vinegar, ginger, sugar and garlic, stir well, cover, cook on Low for 4 hours, add cashews and green onion, stir, divide into bowls and serve for lunch.

Nutrition: calories 200, fat 3, fiber 2, carbs 13, protein 12

Turkey Chili

Preparation time: 10 minutes | Cooking time: 4 hours | Servings: 8

Ingredients:
- 1 red bell pepper, chopped
- 2 pounds turkey meat, ground
- 28 ounces canned tomatoes, chopped
- 1 red onion, chopped
- 1 green bell pepper, chopped
- 4 tablespoons tomato paste
- 1 tablespoon oregano, dried
- 3 tablespoon chili powder
- 3 tablespoons cumin, ground
- Salt and black pepper to the taste

Directions:
Heat up a pan over medium-high heat, add turkey, brown it for a few minutes, transfer to your slow cooker, add red and green bell pepper, onion, tomatoes, tomato paste, chili powder, oregano, cumin, salt and black pepper to the taste, stir, cover and cook on High for 4 hours. Divide into bowls and serve for lunch.

Nutrition: calories 225, fat 6, fiber 4, carbs 15, protein 18

Turkey and Potatoes

Preparation time: 10 minutes | Cooking time: 8 hours | Servings: 4

Ingredients:
- 3 pounds turkey breast, skinless and boneless
- 1 cup cranberries, chopped
- 2 sweet potatoes, chopped
- ½ cup raisins
- ½ cup walnuts, chopped
- 1 sweet onion, chopped
- 2 tablespoons lemon juice
- 1 cup sugar
- 1 teaspoon ginger, grated
- ½ teaspoon nutmeg, ground
- 1 teaspoon cinnamon powder
- ½ cup veggie stock
- 1 teaspoon poultry seasoning
- Salt and black pepper to the taste
- 3 tablespoons olive oil

Directions:
Heat up a pan with the oil over medium-high heat, add cranberries, walnuts, raisins, onion, lemon juice, sugar, ginger, nutmeg, cinnamon, stock and black pepper, stir well and bring to a simmer. Place turkey breast in your slow cooker, add sweet potatoes, cranberries mix and poultry seasoning, cover and cook on Low for 8 hours. Slice turkey breast and divide between plates, add sweet potatoes, drizzle sauce from the slow cooker and serve for lunch.

Nutrition: calories 264, fat 4, fiber 6, carbs 8, protein 15

Chicken Thighs Mix

Preparation time: 10 minutes | Cooking time: 6 hours | Servings: 6

Ingredients:
- 2 and ½ pounds chicken thighs, skinless and boneless
- 1 and ½ tablespoon olive oil
- 2 yellow onions, chopped
- 1 teaspoon cinnamon powder
- ¼ teaspoon cloves, ground
- ¼ teaspoon allspice, ground
- Salt and black pepper to the taste
- A pinch of saffron
- A handful pine nuts
- A handful mint, chopped

Directions:
In a bowl, mix oil with onions, cinnamon, allspice, cloves, salt, pepper and saffron, whisk and transfer to your slow cooker. Add the chicken, toss well, cover and cook on Low for 6 hours. Sprinkle pine nuts and mint on top before serving,

Nutrition: calories 223, fat 3, fiber 2, carbs 6, protein 13

Chicken and Stew

Preparation time: 10 minutes | Cooking time: 5 hours | Servings: 4

Ingredients:
- 4 chicken breasts, skinless and boneless
- 6 Italian sausages, sliced
- 5 garlic cloves, minced
- 1 white onion, chopped
- 1 teaspoon Italian seasoning
- A drizzle of olive oil
- 1 teaspoon garlic powder
- 29 ounces canned tomatoes, chopped
- 15 ounces tomato sauce
- 1 cup water
- ½ cup balsamic vinegar

Directions:
Put chicken and sausage slices in your slow cooker, add garlic, onion, Italian seasoning, oil, tomatoes, tomato sauce, garlic powder, water and the vinegar, cover and cook on High for 5 hours. Stir the stew, divide between plates and serve for lunch

Nutrition: calories 267, fat 4, fiber 3, carbs 15, protein 13

Chicken and Cabbage Mix

Preparation time: 10 minutes | Cooking time: 5 hours 20 minutes | Servings: 6

Ingredients:
- 6 garlic cloves, minced
- 4 scallions, sliced
- 1 cup veggie stock
- 1 tablespoon olive oil
- 2 teaspoons sugar
- 1 tablespoon soy sauce
- 1 teaspoon ginger, minced
- 2 pounds chicken thighs, skinless and boneless
- 2 cups cabbage, shredded

Directions:
In your Slow cooker, mix stock with oil, scallions, garlic, sugar, soy sauce, ginger and chicken, stir, cover and cook on Low for 5 hours. Transfer chicken to plates, add cabbage to the slow cooker, cover, cook on High for 20 minutes more, add next to the chicken and serve for lunch.

Nutrition: calories 240, fat 3, fiber 4, carbs 14, protein 10

Pork and Chorizo Lunch Mix

Preparation time: 10 minutes | Cooking time: 4 hours | Servings: 8

Ingredients:
- 1 pound chorizo, ground
- 1 pound pork, ground
- 3 tablespoons olive oil
- 1 tomato, chopped
- 1 avocado, pitted, peeled and chopped
- Salt and black pepper to the taste
- 1 small red onion, chopped
- 2 tablespoons enchilada sauce

Directions:

Heat up a pan with the oil over medium-high heat, add pork, stir, brown for a couple of minutes, transfer to your slow cooker, add salt, pepper, chorizo, onion and enchilada sauce, stir, cover and cook on Low for 4 hours. Divide between plates and serve with chopped tomato and avocado on top

Nutrition: calories 300, fat 12, fiber 3, carbs 15, protein 17

Lamb Stew

Preparation time: 10 minutes | Cooking time: 8 hours | Servings: 4

Ingredients:
- 1 and ½ pounds lamb meat, cubed
- ¼ cup flour
- Salt and black pepper to the taste
- 2 tablespoons olive oil
- 1 teaspoon rosemary, dried
- 1 onion, sliced
- ½ teaspoon thyme, dried
- 2 cups water
- 1 cup baby carrots
- 2 cups sweet potatoes, chopped

Directions:

In a bowl, mix lamb with flour and toss. Heat up a pan with the oil over medium-high heat, add meat, brown it on all sides and transfer to your slow cooker. Add onion, salt, pepper, rosemary, thyme, water, carrots and sweet potatoes, cover and cook on Low for 8 hours. Divide lamb stew between plates and serve for lunch

Nutrition: calories 350, fat 8, fiber 3, carbs 20, protein 16

Lamb Curry

Preparation time: 10 minutes | Cooking time: 4 hours | Servings: 4

Ingredients:
- 1 and ½ tablespoons sweet paprika
- 3 tablespoons curry powder
- Salt and black pepper to the taste
- 2 pounds lamb meat, cubed
- 2 tablespoons olive oil
- 3 carrots, chopped
- 4 celery stalks, chopped
- 1 onion, chopped
- 4 celery stalks, chopped
- 1 cup chicken stock
- 4 garlic cloves minced
- 1 cup coconut milk

Directions:

Heat up a pan with the oil over medium-high heat, add lamb meat, brown it on all sides and transfer to your slow cooker. Add stock, onions, celery and carrots to the slow cooker and stir everything gently. In a bowl, mix paprika with a pinch of salt, black pepper and curry powder and stir. Add spice mix to the cooker, also add coconut milk, cover, cook on High for 4 hours, divide into bowls and serve for lunch.

Nutrition: calories 300, fat 4, fiber 4, carbs 16, protein 13

Lamb and Bacon Stew

Preparation time: 10 minutes | Cooking time: 7 hours 10 minutes | Servings: 6

Ingredients:

- 2 tablespoons flour
- 2 ounces bacon, cooked and crumbled
- 1 and ½ pounds lamb loin, chopped
- Salt and black pepper to the taste
- 1 garlic clove, minced
- 1 cup yellow onion, chopped
- 3 and ½ cups veggie stock
- 1 cup carrots, chopped
- 1 cup celery, chopped
- 2 cups sweet potatoes, chopped
- 1 tablespoon thyme, chopped
- 1 bay leaf
- 2 tablespoons olive oil

Directions:

Put lamb meat in a bowl, add flour, salt and pepper and toss to coat. Heat up a pan with the oil over medium-high heat, add lamb, brown for 5 minutes on each side and transfer to your slow cooker. Add onion, garlic, bacon, carrots, potatoes, bay leaf, stock, thyme and celery to the slow cooker as well, stir gently, cover and cook on Low for 7 hours. Discard bay leaf, stir your stew, divide into bowls and serve for lunch

Nutrition: calories 360, fat 5, fiber 3, carbs 16, protein 17

Sweet Potato Soup

Preparation time: 10 minutes | Cooking time: 5 hours 20 minutes | Servings: 6

Ingredients:

- 5 cups veggie stock
- 3 sweet potatoes, peeled and chopped
- 2 celery stalks, chopped
- 1 cup yellow onion, chopped
- 1 cup milk
- 1 teaspoon tarragon, dried
- 2 garlic cloves, minced
- 2 cups baby spinach
- 8 tablespoons almonds, sliced
- Salt and black pepper to the taste

Directions:

In your slow cooker, mix stock with potatoes, celery, onion, milk, tarragon, garlic, salt and pepper, stir, cover and cook on High for 5 hours. Blend soup using an immersion blender, add spinach and almonds, toss, cover and leave aside for 20 minutes. Divide soup into bowls and serve for lunch.

Nutrition: calories 301, fat 5, fiber 4, carbs 12, protein 5

White Beans Stew

Preparation time: 10 minutes | Cooking time: 4 hours | Servings: 10

Ingredients:

- 2 pounds white beans
- 3 celery stalks, chopped
- 2 carrots, chopped
- 1 bay leaf
- 1 yellow onion, chopped
- 3 garlic cloves, minced
- 1 teaspoon rosemary, dried
- 1 teaspoon oregano, dried
- 1 teaspoon thyme, dried
- 10 cups water
- Salt and black pepper to the taste
- 28 ounces canned tomatoes, chopped
- 6 cups chard, chopped

Directions:

In your slow cooker, mix white beans with celery, carrots, bay leaf, onion, garlic, rosemary, oregano, thyme, water, salt, pepper, tomatoes and chard, cover and cook on High for 4 hours. Stir, divide into bowls and serve for lunch,

Nutrition: calories 341, fat 8, fiber 12, carbs 20, protein 6

Quinoa Chili

Preparation time: 10 minutes | Cooking time: 6 hours | Servings: 6

Ingredients:
- 2 cups veggie stock
- ½ cup quinoa
- 30 ounces canned black beans, drained
- 28 ounces canned tomatoes, chopped
- 1 green bell pepper, chopped
- 1 yellow onion, chopped
- 2 sweet potatoes, cubed
- 1 tablespoon chili powder
- 2 tablespoons cocoa powder
- 2 teaspoons cumin, ground
- Salt and black pepper to the taste
- ¼ teaspoon smoked paprika

Directions:
In your slow cooker, mix stock with quinoa, black beans, tomatoes, bell pepper, onion, sweet potatoes, chili powder, cocoa, cumin, paprika, salt and pepper, stir, cover and cook on High for 6 hours. Divide into bowls and serve for lunch.

Nutrition: calories 342, fat 6, fiber 7, carbs 18, protein 4

Pumpkin Chili

Preparation time: 10 minutes | Cooking time: 5 hours | Servings: 6

Ingredients:
- 1 cup pumpkin puree
- 30 ounces canned kidney beans, drained
- 30 ounces canned roasted tomatoes, chopped
- 2 cups water
- 1 cup red lentils, dried
- 1 cup yellow onion, chopped
- 1 jalapeno pepper, chopped
- 1 tablespoon chili powder
- 1 tablespoon cocoa powder
- ½ teaspoon cinnamon powder
- 2 teaspoons cumin, ground
- A pinch of cloves, ground
- Salt and black pepper to the taste
- 2 tomatoes, chopped

Directions:
In your Slow cooker, mix pumpkin puree with kidney beans, roasted tomatoes, water, lentils, onion, jalapeno, chili powder, cocoa, cinnamon, cumin, cloves, salt and pepper, stir, cover and cook on High for 5 hours. Divide into bowls, top with chopped tomatoes and serve for lunch.

Nutrition: calories 266, fat 6, fiber 4, carbs 12, protein 4

3 Bean Chili

Preparation time: 10 minutes | Cooking time: 8 hours | Servings: 6

Ingredients:
- 15 ounces canned kidney beans, drained
- 30 ounces canned chili beans in sauce
- 15 ounces canned black beans, drained
- 2 green bell peppers, chopped
- 30 ounces canned tomatoes, crushed
- 2 tablespoons chili powder
- 2 yellow onions, chopped
- 2 garlic cloves, minced
- 1 teaspoon oregano, dried
- 1 tablespoon cumin, ground
- Salt and black pepper to the taste

Directions:
In your Slow cooker, mix kidney beans with chili beans, black beans, bell peppers, tomatoes, chili powder, onion, garlic, oregano, cumin, salt and pepper, stir, cover and cook on Low for 8 hours. Divide into bowls and serve for lunch.

Nutrition: calories 314, fat 6, fiber 5, carbs 14, protein 4

Cod and Asparagus

Preparation time: 10 minutes | Cooking time: 2 hours | Servings: 4

Ingredients:
- 4 cod fillets, boneless
- 1 bunch asparagus
- 12 tablespoons lemon juice
- 2 tablespoons olive oil

Directions:
Divide cod fillets between tin foil pieces, top each with asparagus spears, lemon juice, lemon pepper and oil and wrap them. Arrange wrapped fish in your Slow cooker, cover and cook on High for 2 hours. Unwrap fish, divide it and asparagus between plates and serve for lunch.

Nutrition: calories 202, fat 3, fiber 6, carbs 7, protein 3

Bulgur Chili

Preparation time: 10 minutes | Cooking time: 8 hours | Servings: 4

Ingredients:
- 2 cups white mushrooms, sliced
- ¾ cup bulgur, soaked in 1 cup hot water for 15 minutes and drained
- 2 cups yellow onion, chopped
- ½ cup red bell pepper, chopped
- 1 cup veggie stock
- 2 garlic cloves, minced
- 1 cup strong brewed coffee
- 14 ounces canned kidney beans, drained
- 14 ounces canned pinto beans, drained
- 2 tablespoons sugar
- 2 tablespoons chili powder
- 1 tablespoon cocoa powder
- 1 teaspoon oregano, dried
- 2 teaspoons cumin, ground
- 1 bay leaf
- Salt and black pepper to the taste

Directions:
In your Slow cooker, mix mushrooms with bulgur, onion, bell pepper, stock, garlic, coffee, kidney and pinto beans, sugar, chili powder, cocoa, oregano, cumin, bay leaf, salt and pepper, stir gently, cover and cook on Low for 12 hours. Discard bay leaf, divide chili into bowls and serve for lunch.

Nutrition: calories 351, fat 4, fiber 6, carbs 20, protein 4

Seafood Stew

Preparation time: 10 minutes | *Cooking time:* 7 hours | *Servings:* 4

Ingredients:
- 28 ounces canned tomatoes, crushed
- 4 cups veggie stock
- 3 garlic cloves, minced
- 1 pound sweet potatoes, cubed
- ½ cup yellow onion, chopped
- 2 pounds mixed seafood
- 1 teaspoon thyme, dried
- 1 teaspoon cilantro, dried
- 1 teaspoon basil, dried
- Salt and black pepper to the taste
- A pinch of red pepper flakes, crushed

Directions:
In your Slow cooker, mix tomatoes with stock, garlic, sweet potatoes, onion, thyme, cilantro, basil, salt, pepper and pepper flakes, stir, cover and cook on Low for 6 hours. Add seafood, stir, cover, and cook on High for 1 more hour, divide stew into bowls and serve for lunch.

Nutrition: calories 270, fat 4, fiber 4, carbs 12, protein 3

Shrimp Stew

Preparation time: 10 minutes | *Cooking time:* 4 hours 30 minutes | *Servings:* 8

Ingredients:
- 29 ounces canned tomatoes, chopped
- 2 yellow onions, chopped
- 2 celery ribs, chopped
- ½ cup fish stock
- 4 garlic cloves, minced
- 1 tablespoon red vinegar
- 2 tablespoons olive oil
- 3 pounds shrimp, peeled and deveined
- 6 ounces canned clams
- 2 tablespoons cilantro, chopped

Directions:
In your Slow cooker, mix tomatoes with onion, celery, stock, vinegar and oil, stir, cover and cook on Low for 4 hours. Add shrimp, clams and cilantro, stir, cover, cook on Low for 30 minutes more, divide into bowls and serve for lunch.

Nutrition: calories 255, fat 4, fiber 3, carbs 14, protein 26

Slow Cooker Side Dish Recipes

Creamy Hash Brown Mix

Preparation time: 10 minutes | Cooking time: 3 hours | Servings: 12

Ingredients:
- 2 pounds hash browns
- 1 and ½ cups milk
- 10 ounces cream of chicken soup
- 1 cup cheddar cheese, shredded
- ½ cup butter, melted
- Salt and black pepper to the taste
- ¾ cup cornflakes, crushed

Directions:

In a bowl, mix hash browns with milk, cream of chicken, cheese, butter, salt and pepper, stir, transfer to your Slow cooker, cover and cook on Low for 3 hours. Add cornflakes, divide between plates and serve as a side dish.

Nutrition: calories 234, fat 12, fiber 2, carbs 22, protein 6

Broccoli Mix

Preparation time: 10 minutes | Cooking time: 2 hours | Servings: 10

Ingredients:
- 6 cups broccoli florets
- 1 and ½ cups cheddar cheese, shredded
- 10 ounces canned cream of celery soup
- ½ teaspoon Worcestershire sauce
- ¼ cup yellow onion, chopped
- Salt and black pepper to the taste
- 1 cup crackers, crushed
- 2 tablespoons soft butter

Directions:

In a bowl, mix broccoli with cream of celery soup, cheese, salt, pepper, onion and Worcestershire sauce, toss and transfer to your Slow cooker. Add butter, toss again, sprinkle crackers, cover and cook on High for 2 hours. Serve as a side dish.

Nutrition: calories 159, fat 11, fiber 1, carbs 11, protein 6

Bean Medley

Preparation time: 10 minutes | Cooking time: 5 hours | Servings: 12

Ingredients:
- 2 celery ribs, chopped
- 1 and ½ cups ketchup
- 1 green bell pepper, chopped
- 1 yellow onion, chopped
- 1 sweet red pepper, chopped
- ½ cup brown sugar
- ½ cup Italian dressing
- ½ cup water
- 1 tablespoon cider vinegar
- 2 bay leaves
- 16 ounces kidney beans, drained
- 15 ounces canned black-eyed peas, drained
- 15 ounces canned northern beans, drained
- 15 ounces canned corn, drained
- 15 ounces canned lima beans, drained
- 15 ounces canned black beans, drained

Directions:
In your Slow cooker, mix celery with ketchup, red and green bell pepper, onion, sugar, Italian dressing, water, vinegar, bay leaves, kidney beans, black-eyed peas, northern beans, corn, lima beans and black beans, stir, cover and cook on Low for 5 hours. Divide between plates and serve as a side dish.

Nutrition: calories 255, fat 4, fiber 9, carbs 45, protein 6

Green Beans Mix

Preparation time: 10 minutes | Cooking time: 2 hours | Servings: 12

Ingredients:
- 16 ounces green beans
- ½ cup brown sugar
- ½ cup butter, melted
- ¾ teaspoon soy sauce
- Salt and black pepper to the taste

Directions:
In your Slow cooker, mix green beans with sugar, butter, soy sauce, salt and pepper, stir, cover and cook on Low for 2 hours. Divide between plates and serve as a side dish.

Nutrition: calories 176, fat 4, fiber 7, carbs 14, protein 4

Corn and Bacon

Preparation time: 10 minutes | Cooking time: 4 hours | Servings: 20

Ingredients:
- 10 cups corn
- 24 ounces cream cheese, cubed
- ½ cup milk
- ½ cup melted butter
- ½ cup heavy cream
- ¼ cup sugar
- A pinch of salt and black pepper
- 4 bacon strips, cooked and crumbled
- 2 tablespoons green onions, chopped

Directions:
In your Slow cooker, mix corn with cream cheese, milk, butter, cream, sugar, salt, pepper, bacon and green onions, cover and cook on Low for 4 hours. Stir the corn, divide between plates and serve as a side dish.

Nutrition: calories 259, fat 20, fiber 2, carbs 18, protein 5

Peas and Carrots

Preparation time: 10 minutes | Cooking time: 5 hours | Servings: 12

Ingredients:
- 1 yellow onion, chopped
- 1 pound carrots, sliced
- 16 ounces peas
- ¼ cup melted butter
- ¼ cup water
- ¼ cup honey
- 4 garlic cloves, minced
- A pinch of salt and black pepper
- 1 teaspoon marjoram, dried

Directions:

In your Slow cooker, mix onion with carrots, peas, butter, water, honey, garlic, salt, pepper and marjoram, cover and cook on Low for 5 hours. Stir peas and carrots mix, divide between plates and serve as a side dish.

Nutrition: calories 105, fat 4, fiber 3, carbs 16, protein 4

Beans, Carrots and Spinach Salad

Preparation time: 10 minutes | Cooking time: 7 hours | Servings: 6

Ingredients:
- 1 and ½ cups northern beans
- 1 yellow onion, chopped
- 5 carrots, chopped
- 2 garlic cloves, minced
- ½ teaspoon oregano, dried
- Salt and black pepper to the taste
- 4 and ½ cups chicken stock
- 5 ounces baby spinach
- 2 teaspoons lemon peel, grated
- 1 avocado, peeled, pitted and chopped
- 3 tablespoons lemon juice
- ¾ cup feta cheese, crumbled
- 1/3 cup pistachios, chopped

Directions:

In your Slow cooker, mix beans with onion, carrots, garlic, oregano, salt, pepper and stock, stir, cover and cook on Low for 7 hours. Drain beans and veggies, transfer them to a salad bowl, add baby spinach, lemon peel, avocado, lemon juice, pistachios and cheese, toss, divide between plates and serve as a side dish.

Nutrition: calories 300, fat 8, fiber 14, carbs 43, protein 16

Scalloped Potatoes

Preparation time: 10 minutes | Cooking time: 6 hours | Servings: 6

Ingredients:
- Cooking spray
- 2 and ½ pounds gold potatoes, sliced
- 10 ounces canned cream of potato soup
- 1 yellow onion, roughly chopped
- 8 ounces sour cream
- 1 cup gouda cheese, shredded
- ½ cup blue cheese, crumbled
- ½ cup parmesan, grated
- ½ cup chicken stock
- Salt and black pepper to the taste
- 1 tablespoon chives, chopped

Directions:

Grease your Slow cooker with cooking spray and arrange potato slices on the bottom. Add cream of potato soup, onion, sour cream, Gouda cheese, blue cheese, parmesan, stock, salt and pepper, cover and cook on Low for 6 hours. Add chives, divide between plates and serve as a side dish.

Nutrition: calories 306, fat 14, fiber 4, carbs 33, protein 12

Sweet Potatoes with Bacon

Preparation time: 10 minutes | Cooking time: 5 hours | Servings: 6

Ingredients:
- 4 pounds sweet potatoes, peeled and sliced
- 3 tablespoons brown sugar
- ½ cup orange juice
- ½ teaspoon sage, dried
- ½ teaspoon thyme, dried
- 4 bacon slices, cooked and crumbled
- 2 tablespoons soft butter

Directions:
Arrange sweet potato slices in your Slow cooker, add sugar, orange juice, sage, thyme, butter and bacon, cover and cook on Low for 5 hours. Divide between plates and serve them as a side dish.

Nutrition: calories 200, fat 4, fiber 4, carbs 30, protein 4

Cauliflower and Broccoli Mix

Preparation time: 10 minutes | Cooking time: 7 hours | Servings: 10

Ingredients:
- 4 cups broccoli florets
- 4 cups cauliflower florets
- 7 ounces Swiss cheese, torn
- 14 ounces Alfredo sauce
- 1 yellow onion, chopped
- Salt and black pepper to the taste
- 1 teaspoon thyme, dried
- ½ cup almonds, sliced

Directions:
In your Slow cooker, mix broccoli with cauliflower, cheese, sauce, onion, salt, pepper and thyme, stir, cover and cook on Low for 7 hours. Add almonds, divide between plates and serve as a side dish.

Nutrition: calories 177, fat 7, fiber 2, carbs 10, protein 7

Wild Rice Mix

Preparation time: 10 minutes | Cooking time: 6 hours | Servings: 16

Ingredients:
- 45 ounces chicken stock
- 1 cup carrots, sliced
- 2 and ½ cups wild rice
- 4 ounces mushrooms, sliced
- 2 tablespoons butter, soft
- Salt and black pepper to the taste
- 2 teaspoons marjoram, dried
- 2/3 cup dried cherries
- 2/3 cup green onions, chopped
- ½ cup pecans, chopped

Directions:
In your Slow cooker, mix stock with carrots, rice, mushrooms, butter, salt, pepper and marjoram, cover and cook on Low for 6 hours. Add cherries, green onions and pecans, toss, divide between plates and serve as a side dish.

Nutrition: calories 169, fat 6, fiber 4, carbs 27, protein 5

Mashed Potatoes

Preparation time: 10 minutes | Cooking time: 4 hours | Servings: 12

Ingredients:
- 3 pounds gold potatoes, peeled and cubed
- 1 bay leaf
- 6 garlic cloves, minced
- 28 ounces chicken stock
- 1 cup milk
- ¼ cup butter
- Salt and black pepper to the taste

Directions:
In your Slow cooker, mix potatoes with bay leaf, garlic, salt, pepper and stock, cover and cook on Low for 4 hours. Drain potatoes, mash them, mix with butter and milk, blend really, divide between plates and serve as a side dish.

Nutrition: calories 135, fat 4, fiber 2, carbs 22, protein 4

Orange Glazed Carrots

Preparation time: 10 minutes | Cooking time: 8 hours | Servings: 10

Ingredients:
- 3 pounds carrots, cut into medium chunks
- 1 cup orange juice
- 2 tablespoons orange peel, grated
- ½ cup orange marmalade
- ½ cup veggie stock
- ¼ cup white wine
- 1 tablespoon tapioca, crushed
- ¼ cup parsley, chopped
- 3 tablespoons butter
- Salt and black pepper to the taste

Directions:
In your Slow cooker, mix carrots with orange juice, orange peel, marmalade, stock, wine, tapioca, parsley, butter, salt and pepper, cover and cook on Low for 8 hours. Toss carrots, divide between plates and serve as a side dish.

Nutrition: calories 160, fat 4, fiber 4, carbs 31, protein 3

Creamy Risotto

Preparation time: 10 minutes | Cooking time: 1 hours | Servings: 4

Ingredients:
- 4 ounces mushrooms, sliced
- ½ quart veggie stock
- 1 teaspoon olive oil
- 2 tablespoons porcini mushrooms
- 2 cups white rice
- A small bunch of parsley, chopped

Directions:
In your Slow cooker, mix mushrooms with stock, oil, porcini mushrooms and rice, stir, cover and cook on High for 1 hour. Add parsley, stir, divide between plates and serve as a side dish.

Nutrition: calories 346, fat 3, fiber 4, carbs 35, protein 10

Veggie and Garbanzo Mix

Preparation time: 10 minutes | Cooking time: 6 hours | Servings: 4

Ingredients:

- 15 ounces canned garbanzo beans, drained
- 3 cups cauliflower florets
- 1 cup green beans
- 1 cup carrot, sliced
- 14 ounces veggie stock
- ½ cup onion, chopped
- 2 teaspoons curry powder
- ¼ cup basil, chopped
- 14 ounces coconut milk

Directions:

In your Slow cooker, mix beans with cauliflower, green beans, carrot, onion, stock, curry powder, basil and milk, stir, cover and cook on Low for 6 hours. Stir veggie mix again, divide between plates and serve as a side dish.

Nutrition: calories 219, fat 5, fiber 8, carbs 32, protein 7

Cauliflower Pilaf

Preparation time: 10 minutes | Cooking time: 3 hours | Servings: 6

Ingredients:

- 1 cup cauliflower rice
- 6 green onions, chopped
- 3 tablespoons ghee, melted
- 2 garlic cloves, minced
- ½ pound Portobello mushrooms, sliced
- 2 cups warm water
- Salt and black pepper to the taste

Directions:

In your Slow cooker, mix cauliflower rice with green onions, melted ghee, garlic, mushrooms, water, salt and pepper, stir well, cover and cook on Low for 3 hours. Divide between plates and serve as a side dish.

Nutrition: calories 200, fat 5, fiber 3, carbs 14, protein 4

Squash Side Salad

Preparation time: 10 minutes | Cooking time: 4 hours | Servings: 8

Ingredients:

- 1 tablespoon olive oil
- 1 cup carrots, chopped
- 1 yellow onion, chopped
- 1 teaspoon sugar
- 1 and ½ teaspoons curry powder
- 1 garlic clove, minced
- 1 big butternut squash, peeled and cubed
- A pinch of sea salt and black pepper
- ¼ teaspoon ginger, grated
- ½ teaspoon cinnamon powder
- 3 cups coconut milk

Directions:

In your Slow cooker, mix oil with carrots, onion, sugar, curry powder, garlic, squash, salt, pepper, ginger, cinnamon and coconut milk, stir well, cover and cook on Low for 4 hours. Stir, divide between plates and serve as a side dish.

Nutrition: calories 200, fat 4, fiber 4, carbs 17, protein 4

Mushrooms and Sausage Mix

Preparation time: 10 minutes | Cooking time: 2 hours 30 minutes | Servings: 12

Ingredients:
- ½ cup butter, melted
- 1 pound pork sausage, ground
- ½ pound mushrooms, sliced
- 6 celery ribs, chopped
- 2 yellow onions, chopped
- 2 garlic cloves, minced
- 1 tablespoon sage, chopped
- 1 cup cranberries, dried
- ½ cup cauliflower florets, chopped
- ½ cup veggie stock

Directions:
Heat up a pan with the butter over medium-high heat, add sausage, stir, and cook for a couple of minutes and transfer to your Slow cooker. Add mushrooms, celery, onion, garlic, sage, cranberries, cauliflower and stock, stir, cover and cook on High for 2 hours and 30 minutes. Divide between plates and serve as a side dish.

Nutrition: calories 200, fat 3, fiber 6, carbs 9, protein 4

Glazed Baby Carrots

Preparation time: 10 minutes | Cooking time: 6 hours | Servings: 6

Ingredients:
- ½ cup peach preserves
- ½ cup butter, melted
- 2 pounds baby carrots
- 2 tablespoon sugar
- 1 teaspoon vanilla extract
- A pinch of salt and black pepper
- A pinch of nutmeg, ground
- ½ teaspoon cinnamon powder
- 2 tablespoons water

Directions:
Put baby carrots in your Slow cooker, add butter, peach preserves, sugar, vanilla, salt, pepper, nutmeg, cinnamon and water, toss well, cover and cook on Low for 6 hours. Divide between plates and serve as a side dish.

Nutrition: calories 283, fat 14, fiber 4, carbs 28, protein 3

Spinach and Squash Side Salad

Preparation time: 10 minutes | Cooking time: 4 hours | Servings: 12

Ingredients:
- 3 pounds butternut squash, peeled and cubed
- 1 yellow onion, chopped
- 2 teaspoons thyme, chopped
- 3 garlic cloves, minced
- A pinch of salt and black pepper
- 10 ounces veggie stock
- 6 ounces baby spinach

Directions:
In your Slow cooker, mix squash cubes with onion, thyme, salt, pepper and stock, stir, cover and cook on Low for 4 hours. Transfer squash mix to a bowl, add spinach, toss, divide between plates and serve as a side dish.

Nutrition: calories 100, fat 1, fiber 4, carbs 18, protein 4

Buttery Mushrooms

Preparation time: 10 minutes | Cooking time: 4 hours | Servings: 6

Ingredients:
- 1 yellow onion, chopped
- 1 pounds mushrooms, halved
- ½ cup butter, melted
- 1 teaspoon Italian seasoning
- Salt and black pepper to the taste
- 1 teaspoon sweet paprika

Directions:

In your Slow cooker, mix mushrooms with onion, butter, Italian seasoning, salt, pepper and paprika, toss, cover and cook on Low for 4 hours. Divide between plates and serve as a side dish.

Nutrition: calories 120, fat 6, fiber 1, carbs 8, protein 4

Cauliflower Rice and Spinach

Preparation time: 10 minutes | Cooking time: 3 hours | Servings: 8

Ingredients:
- 2 garlic cloves, minced
- 2 tablespoons butter, melted
- 1 yellow onion, chopped
- ¼ teaspoon thyme, dried
- 3 cups veggie stock
- 20 ounces spinach, chopped
- 6 ounces coconut cream
- Salt and black pepper to the taste
- 2 cups cauliflower rice

Directions:

Heat up a pan with the butter over medium heat, add onion, stir and cook for 4 minutes. Add garlic, thyme and stock, stir, cook for 1 minute more and transfer to your Slow cooker. Add spinach, coconut cream, cauliflower rice, salt and pepper, stir a bit, cover and cook on High for 3 hours. Divide between plates and serve as a side dish.

Nutrition: calories 200, fat 4, fiber 4, carbs 8, protein 2

Maple Sweet Potatoes

Preparation time: 10 minutes | Cooking time: 5 hours | Servings: 10

Ingredients:
- 8 sweet potatoes, halved and sliced
- 1 cup walnuts, chopped
- ½ cup cherries, dried and chopped
- ½ cup maple syrup
- ¼ cup apple juice
- A pinch of salt

Directions:

Arrange sweet potatoes in your slow cooker, add walnuts, dried cherries, maple syrup, apple juice and a pinch of salt, toss a bit, cover and cook on Low for 5 hours. Divide between plates and serve as a side dish.

Nutrition: calories 271, fat 6, fiber 4, carbs 26, protein 6

Creamy Chipotle Sweet Potatoes
Preparation time: 10 minutes | Cooking time: 4 hours | Servings: 10

Ingredients:
- 1 sweet onion, chopped
- 2 tablespoons olive oil
- ¼ cup parsley, chopped
- 2 shallots, chopped
- 2 teaspoons chipotle pepper, crushed
- Salt and black pepper
- 4 big sweet potatoes, shredded
- 8 ounces coconut cream
- 16 ounces bacon, cooked and chopped
- ½ teaspoon sweet paprika

Directions:
Heat up a pan with the oil over medium-high heat, add shallots and onion stir, cook for 6 minutes and transfer to a bowl. Add parsley, chipotle pepper, salt, pepper, sweet potatoes, coconut cream, paprika and bacon, stir, pour everything in your Slow cooker after you've greased it with some cooking spray, cover, cook on Low for 4 hours, leave aside to cool down a bit, divide between plates and serve as a side dish.

Nutrition: calories 260, fat 14, fiber 6, carbs 20, protein 15

Kale and Ham Mix
Preparation time: 10 minutes | Cooking time: 6 hours | Servings: 6

Ingredients:
- 8 ounces ham hock slices
- 1 and ½ cups water
- 1 cup chicken stock
- 12 cups kale leaves, torn
- A pinch of salt and cayenne pepper
- 2 tablespoons olive oil
- 1 yellow onion, chopped
- 2 tablespoons apple cider vinegar

Directions:
Put ham in a heatproof bowl, add the water and the stock, cover and microwave for 3 minutes. Heat up a pan with the oil over medium-high heat, add onion, stir and cook for 5 minutes. Drain ham and add it to your slow cooker, add onions, kale, salt, cayenne and vinegar, toss, cover and cook on Low for 6 hours. Divide between plates and serve as a side dish.

Nutrition: calories 200, fat 4, fiber 7, carbs 10, protein 3

Sweet Potato Mash
Preparation time: 10 minutes | Cooking time: 5 hours | Servings: 6

Ingredients:
- 2 pounds sweet potatoes, peeled and sliced
- 1 tablespoon cinnamon powder
- 1 cup apple juice
- 1 teaspoon nutmeg, ground
- ¼ teaspoon cloves, ground
- ½ teaspoon allspice
- 1 tablespoon butter, melted

Directions:
In your Slow cooker, mix sweet potatoes with cinnamon, apple juice, nutmeg, cloves and allspice, stir, cover and cook on Low for 5 hours. Mash using a potato masher, add butter, whisk well, divide between plates and serve as a side dish.

Nutrition: calories 111, fat 2, fiber 2, carbs 16, protein 3

Dill Cauliflower Mash

Preparation time: 10 minutes | Cooking time: 5 hours | Servings: 6

Ingredients:
- 1 cauliflower head, florets separated
- 1/3 cup dill, chopped
- 6 garlic cloves
- 2 tablespoons butter, melted
- A pinch of salt and black pepper

Directions:
Put cauliflower in your Slow cooker, add dill, garlic and water to cover cauliflower, cover and cook on High for 5 hours. Drain cauliflower and dill, add salt, pepper and butter, mash using a potato masher, whisk well and serve as a side dish.

Nutrition: calories 187, fat 4, fiber 5, carbs 12, protein 3

Eggplant and Kale Mix

Preparation time: 10 minutes | Cooking time: 2 hours | Servings: 6

Ingredients:
- 14 ounces canned roasted tomatoes and garlic
- 4 cups eggplant, cubed
- 1 yellow bell pepper, chopped
- 1 red onion, cut into medium wedges
- 4 cups kale leaves
- 2 tablespoons olive oil
- 1 teaspoon mustard
- 3 tablespoons red vinegar
- 1 garlic clove, minced
- Salt and black pepper to the taste
- ½ cup basil, chopped

Directions:
In your Slow cooker, mix the eggplant with tomatoes, bell pepper and onion, toss, cover and cook on High for 2 hours. Add kale, toss, cover slow cooker and leave aside for now. In a bowl, mix oil with vinegar, mustard, garlic, salt, pepper, and whisk well. Add this over eggplant mix, also add basil, toss, divide between plates and serve as a side dish.

Nutrition: calories 251, fat 9, fiber 6, carbs 34, protein 8

Thai Side Salad

Preparation time: 10 minutes | Cooking time: 3 hours | Servings: 8

Ingredients:
- 8 ounces yellow summer squash, peeled and roughly chopped
- 12 ounces zucchini, halved and sliced
- 2 cups button mushrooms, quartered
- 1 red sweet potatoes, chopped
- 2 leeks, sliced
- 2 tablespoons veggie stock
- 2 garlic cloves, minced
- 2 tablespoon Thai red curry paste
- 1 tablespoon ginger, grated
- 1/3 cup coconut milk
- ¼ cup basil, chopped

Directions:
In your Slow cooker, mix zucchini with summer squash, mushrooms, red pepper, leeks, garlic, stock, curry paste, ginger, coconut milk and basil, toss, cover and cook on Low for 3 hours. Stir your Thai mix one more time, divide between plates and serve as a side dish.

Nutrition: calories 69, fat 2, fiber 2, carbs 8, protein 2

Rosemary Potatoes

Preparation time: 10 minutes | Cooking time: 3 hours | Servings: 12

Ingredients:
- 2 tablespoons olive oil
- 3 pounds new potatoes, halved
- 7 garlic cloves, minced
- 1 tablespoon rosemary, chopped
- A pinch of salt and black pepper

Directions:

In your Slow cooker, mix oil with potatoes, garlic, rosemary, salt and pepper, toss, cover and cook on High for 3 hours. Divide between plates and serve as a side dish.

Nutrition: calories 102, fat 2, fiber 2, carbs 18, protein 2

Maple Brussels Sprouts

Preparation time: 10 minutes | Cooking time: 3 hours | Servings: 12

Ingredients:
- 1 cup red onion, chopped
- 2 pounds Brussels sprouts, trimmed and halved
- Salt and black pepper to the taste
- ¼ cup apple juice
- 3 tablespoons olive oil
- ¼ cup maple syrup
- 1 tablespoon thyme, chopped

Directions:

In your slow cooker, mix Brussels sprouts with onion, salt, pepper and apple juice, toss, cover and cook on Low for 3 hours. In a bowl, mix maple syrup with oil and thyme, whisk really well, add over Brussels sprouts, toss well, divide between plates and serve as a side dish.

Nutrition: calories 100, fat 4, fiber 4, carbs 14, protein 3

Beets and Carrots

Preparation time: 10 minutes | Cooking time: 7 hours | Servings: 8

Ingredients:
- 2 tablespoons stevia
- ¾ cup pomegranate juice
- 2 teaspoons ginger, grated
- 2 and ½ pounds beets, peeled and cut into wedges
- 12 ounces carrots, cut into medium wedges

Directions:

In your Slow cooker, mix beets with carrots, ginger, stevia and pomegranate juice, toss, cover and cook on Low for 7 hours. Divide between plates and serve as a side dish.

Nutrition: calories 125, fat 0, fiber 4, carbs 28, protein 3

Italian Veggie Mix

Preparation time: 10 minutes | Cooking time: 6 hours | Servings: 8

Ingredients:
- 38 ounces canned cannellini beans, drained
- 1 yellow onion, chopped
- ¼ cup basil pesto
- 19 ounces canned fava beans, drained
- 4 garlic cloves, minced
- 1 and ½ teaspoon Italian seasoning, dried and crushed
- 1 tomato, chopped
- 15 ounces already cooked polenta, cut into medium pieces
- 2 cups spinach
- 1 cup radicchio, torn

Directions:
In your Slow cooker, mix cannellini beans with fava beans, basil pesto, onion, garlic, Italian seasoning, polenta, tomato, spinach and radicchio, toss, cover and cook on Low for 6 hours. Divide between plates and serve as a side dish.

Nutrition: calories 364, fat 12, fiber 10, carbs 45, protein 21

Wild Rice and Barley Pilaf

Preparation time: 10 minutes | Cooking time: 7 hours | Servings: 12

Ingredients:
- ½ cup wild rice
- ½ cup barley
- 2/3 cup wheat berries
- 27 ounces veggie stock
- 2 cups baby lima beans
- 1 red bell pepper, chopped
- 1 yellow onion, chopped
- 1 tablespoon olive oil
- A pinch of salt and black pepper
- 1 teaspoon sage, dried and crushed
- 4 garlic cloves, minced

Directions:
In your Slow cooker, mix rice with barley, wheat berries, lima beans, bell pepper, onion, oil, salt, pepper, sage and garlic, stir, cover and cook on Low for 7 hours. Stir one more time, divide between plates and serve as a side dish.

Nutrition: calories 168, fat 5, fiber 4, carbs 25, protein 6

Apples and Potatoes

Preparation time: 10 minutes | Cooking time: 7 hours | Servings: 10

Ingredients:
- 2 green apples, cored and cut into wedges
- 3 pounds sweet potatoes, peeled and cut into medium wedges
- 1 cup coconut cream
- ½ cup dried cherries
- 1 cup apple butter
- 1 and ½ teaspoon pumpkin pie spice

Directions:
In your Slow cooker, mix sweet potatoes with green apples, cream, cherries, apple butter and spice, toss, cover and cook on Low for 7 hours. Toss, divide between plates and serve as a side dish.

Nutrition: calories 351, fat 8, fiber 5, carbs 48, protein 2

Asparagus and Mushroom Mix

Preparation time: 10 minutes | Cooking time: 5 hours | Servings: 4

Ingredients:
- 2 pounds asparagus spears, cut into medium pieces
- 1 cup mushrooms, sliced
- A drizzle of olive oil
- Salt and black pepper to the taste
- 2 cups coconut milk
- 1 teaspoon Worcestershire sauce
- 5 eggs, whisked

Directions:
Grease your Slow cooker with the oil and spread asparagus and mushrooms on the bottom. In a bowl, mix the eggs with milk, salt, pepper and Worcestershire sauce, whisk, pour into the slow cooker, toss everything, cover and cook on Low for 6 hours. Divide between plates and serve as a side dish.

Nutrition: calories 211, fat 4, fiber 4, carbs 6, protein 5

Asparagus Mix

Preparation time: 10 minutes | Cooking time: 6 hours | Servings: 4

Ingredients:
- 10 ounces cream of celery
- 12 ounces asparagus, chopped
- 2 eggs, hard-boiled, peeled and sliced
- 1 cup cheddar cheese, shredded
- 1 teaspoon olive oil

Directions:
Grease your Slow cooker with the oil, add cream of celery and cheese to the slow cooker and stir. Add asparagus and eggs, cover and cook on Low for 6 hours. Divide between plates and serve as a side dish.

Nutrition: calories 241, fat 5, fiber 4, carbs 5, protein 12

Chorizo and Cauliflower Mix

Preparation time: 10 minutes | Cooking time: 5 hours | Servings: 4

Ingredients:
- 1 pound chorizo, chopped
- 12 ounces canned green chilies, chopped
- 1 yellow onion, chopped
- ½ teaspoon garlic powder
- Salt and black pepper to the taste
- 1 cauliflower head, riced
- 2 tablespoons green onions, chopped

Directions:
Heat up a pan over medium heat, add chorizo and onion, stir brown for a few minutes and transfer to your Slow cooker. Add chilies, garlic powder, salt, pepper, cauliflower and green onions, toss, cover and cook on Low for 5 hours. Divide between plates and serve as a side dish.

Nutrition: calories 350, fat 12, fiber 4, carbs 6, protein 20

Easy and Veggies Mix

Preparation time: 10 minutes | Cooking time: 3 hours | Servings: 4

Ingredients:
- 1 and ½ cups red onion, cut into medium chunks
- 1 cup cherry tomatoes, halved
- 2 and ½ cups zucchini, sliced
- 2 cups yellow bell pepper, chopped
- 1 cup mushrooms, sliced
- 2 tablespoons basil, chopped
- 1 tablespoon thyme, chopped
- ½ cup olive oil
- ½ cup balsamic vinegar

Directions:
In your Slow cooker, mix onion pieces with tomatoes, zucchini, bell pepper, mushrooms, basil, thyme, oil and vinegar, toss to coat everything, cover and cook on High for 3 hours. Divide between plates and serve as a side dish.

Nutrition: calories 150, fat 2, fiber 2, carbs 6, protein 5

Okra Side Dish

Preparation time: 10 minutes | Cooking time: 3 hours | Servings: 4

Ingredients:
- 2 cups okra, sliced
- 1 and ½ cups red onion, roughly chopped
- 1 cup cherry tomatoes, halved
- 2 and ½ cups zucchini, sliced
- 2 cups red and yellow bell peppers, sliced
- 1 cup white mushrooms, sliced
- ½ cup olive oil
- ½ cup balsamic vinegar
- 2 tablespoons basil, chopped
- 1 tablespoon thyme, chopped

Directions:
In your Slow cooker, mix okra with onion, tomatoes, zucchini, bell peppers, mushrooms, basil and thyme. In a bowl mix oil with vinegar, whisk well, add to the slow cooker, cover and cook on High for 3 hours. Divide between plates and serve as a side dish.

Nutrition: calories 233, fat 12, fiber 4, carbs 8, protein 4

Okra Side Dish

Preparation time: 10 minutes | Cooking time: 4 hours | Servings: 4

Ingredients:
- 1 pound okra, sliced
- 1 tomato, chopped
- 6 ounces tomato sauce
- 1 cup water
- Salt and black pepper to the taste
- 1 yellow onion, chopped
- 2 garlic cloves, minced

Directions:
In your Slow cooker, mix okra with tomato, tomato sauce, water, salt, pepper, onion and garlic, stir, cover and cook on Low for 4 hours. Divide between plates and serve as a side dish.

Nutrition: calories 211, fat 4, fiber 6, carbs 17, protein 3

Okra Mix

Preparation time: 10 minutes | Cooking time: 8 hours | Servings: 4

Ingredients:
- 2 garlic cloves, minced
- 1 yellow onion, chopped
- 14 ounces tomato sauce
- 1 teaspoon sweet paprika
- 2 cups okra, sliced
- Salt and black pepper to the taste

Directions:
In your Slow cooker, mix garlic with the onion, tomato sauce, paprika, okra, salt and pepper, cover and cook on Low for 8 hours. Divide between plates and serve as a side dish.

Nutrition: calories 200, fat 6, fiber 5, carbs 10, protein 4

Stewed Okra

Preparation time: 10 minutes | Cooking time: 3 hours | Servings: 4

Ingredients:
- 2 cups okra, sliced
- 2 garlic cloves, minced
- 6 ounces tomato sauce
- 1 red onion, chopped
- A pinch of cayenne peppers
- 1 teaspoon liquid smoke
- Salt and black pepper to the taste

Directions:
In your Slow cooker, mix okra with garlic, onion, cayenne, tomato sauce, liquid smoke, salt and pepper, cover, cook on Low for 3 hours. Divide between plates and serve as a side dish.

Nutrition: calories 182, fat 3, fiber 6, carbs 8, protein 3

Okra and Corn

Preparation time: 10 minutes | Cooking time: 8 hours | Servings: 4

Ingredients:
- 3 garlic cloves, minced
- 1 small green bell pepper, chopped
- 1 small yellow onion, chopped
- 1 cup water
- 16 ounces okra, sliced
- 2 cups corn
- 1 and ½ teaspoon smoked paprika
- 28 ounces canned tomatoes, crushed
- 1 teaspoon oregano, dried
- 1 teaspoon thyme, dried
- 1 teaspoon marjoram, dried
- A pinch of cayenne pepper
- Salt and black pepper to the taste

Directions:
In your Slow cooker, mix garlic with bell pepper, onion, water, okra, corn, paprika, tomatoes, oregano, thyme, marjoram, cayenne, salt and pepper, cover, cook on Low for 8 hours, divide between plates and serve as a side dish.

Nutrition: calories 182, fat 3, fiber 6, carbs 8, protein 5

Roasted Beets

Preparation time: 10 minutes | Cooking time: 4 hours | Servings: 5

Ingredients:
- 10 small beets
- 5 teaspoons olive oil
- A pinch of salt and black pepper

Directions:
Divide each beet on a tin foil piece, drizzle oil, season them with salt and pepper, rub well, wrap beets, place them in your Slow cooker, cover and cook on High for 4 hours. Unwrap beets, cool them down a bit, peel, slice and serve them as a side dish.

Nutrition: calories 100, fat 2, fiber 2, carbs 4, protein 5

Thyme Beets

Preparation time: 10 minutes | Cooking time: 6 hours | Servings: 8

Ingredients:
- 12 small beets, peeled and sliced
- ¼ cup water
- 4 garlic cloves, minced
- 2 tablespoons olive oil
- 1 teaspoon thyme, dried
- Salt and black pepper to the taste
- 1 tablespoon fresh thyme, chopped

Directions:
In your Slow cooker, mix beets with water, garlic, oil, dried thyme, salt and pepper, cover and cook on Low for 6 hours. Divide beets on plates, sprinkle fresh thyme all over and serve as a side dish.

Nutrition: 66, fat 4, fiber 1, carbs 8, protein 1

Beets Side Salad

Preparation time: 10 minutes | Cooking time: 7 hours | Servings: 12

Ingredients:
- 5 beets, peeled and sliced
- ¼ cup balsamic vinegar
- 1/3 cup honey
- 1 tablespoon rosemary, chopped
- 2 tablespoons olive oil
- Salt and black pepper to the taste
- 2 garlic cloves, minced

Directions:
In your Slow cooker, mix beets with vinegar, honey, oil, salt, pepper, rosemary and garlic, cover and cook on Low for 7 hours. Divide between plates and serve as a side dish.

Nutrition: calories 70, fat 3, fiber 2, carbs 17, protein 3

Lemony Beets

Preparation time: 10 minutes | Cooking time: 8 hours | Servings: 6

Ingredients:
- 6 beets, peeled and cut into medium wedges
- 2 tablespoons honey
- 2 tablespoons olive oil
- 2 tablespoons lemon juice
- Salt and black pepper to the taste
- 1 tablespoon white vinegar
- ½ teaspoon lemon peel, grated

Directions:
In your Slow cooker, mix beets with honey, oil, lemon juice, salt, pepper, vinegar and lemon peel, cover and cook on Low for 8 hours. Divide between plates and serve as a side dish.

Nutrition: calories 80, fat 3, fiber 4, carbs 8, protein 4

Carrot and Beet Side Salad

Preparation time: 10 minutes | Cooking time: 7 hours | Servings: 6

Ingredients:
- ½ cup walnuts, chopped
- ¼ cup lemon juice
- ½ cup olive oil
- 1 shallot, chopped
- 1 teaspoon Dijon mustard
- 1 tablespoon brown sugar
- Salt and black pepper to the taste
- 2 beets, peeled and cut into wedges
- 2 carrots, peeled and sliced
- 1 cup parsley
- 5 ounces arugula

Directions:
In your Slow cooker, mix beets with carrots, salt, pepper, sugar, mustard, shallot, oil, lemon juice and walnuts, cover and cook on Low for 7 hours. Transfer everything to a bowl, add parsley and arugula, toss, divide between plates and serve as a side dish.

Nutrition: calories 100, fat 3, fiber 3, carbs 7, protein 3

Cauliflower and Carrot Gratin

Preparation time: 10 minutes | Cooking time: 7 hours | Servings: 12

Ingredients:
- 16 ounces baby carrots
- 6 tablespoons butter, soft
- 1 cauliflower head, florets separated
- Salt and black pepper to the taste
- 1 yellow onion, chopped
- 1 teaspoon mustard powder
- 1 and ½ cups milk
- 6 ounces cheddar cheese, grated
- ½ cup breadcrumbs

Directions:
Put the butter in your Slow cooker, add carrots, cauliflower, onion, salt, pepper, mustard powder and milk and toss. Sprinkle cheese and breadcrumbs all over, cover and cook on Low for 7 hours. Divide between plates and serve as a side dish.

Nutrition: calories 182, fat 4, fiber 7, carbs 9, protein 4

Herbed Beets

Preparation time: 10 minutes | Cooking time: 7 hours | Servings: 4

Ingredients:
- 6 medium assorted-color beets, peeled and cut into wedges
- 2 tablespoons balsamic vinegar
- 2 tablespoons olive oil
- 2 tablespoons chives, chopped
- 1 tablespoon tarragon, chopped
- Salt and black pepper to the taste
- 1 teaspoon orange peel, grated

Directions:

In your Slow cooker, mix beets with vinegar, oil, chives, tarragon, salt, pepper and orange peel, cover and cook on Low for 7 hours. Divide between plates and serve as a side dish.

Nutrition: calories 144, fat 3, fiber 1, carbs 17, protein 3

Summer Squash Mix

Preparation time: 10 minutes | Cooking time: 2 hours | Servings: 4

Ingredients:
- ¼ cup olive oil
- 2 tablespoons basil, chopped
- 2 tablespoons balsamic vinegar
- 2 garlic cloves, minced
- 2 teaspoons mustard
- Salt and black pepper to the taste
- 3 summer squash, sliced
- 2 zucchinis, sliced

Directions:

In your Slow cooker, mix squash with zucchinis, salt, pepper, mustard, garlic, vinegar, basil and oil, toss a bit, cover and cook on High for 2 hours. Divide between plates and serve as a side dish.

Nutrition: calories 179, fat 13, fiber 2, carbs 10, protein 4

Easy Veggie Side Salad

Preparation time: 10 minutes | Cooking time: 2 hours | Servings: 4

Ingredients:
- 2 garlic cloves, minced
- ½ cup olive oil
- ¼ cup basil, chopped
- Salt and black pepper to the taste
- 1 red bell pepper, chopped
- 1 eggplant, roughly chopped
- 1 summer squash, cubed
- 1 Vidalia onion, cut into wedges
- 1 zucchini, sliced
- 1 green bell pepper, chopped

Directions:

In your Slow cooker, mix red bell pepper with green one, squash, zucchini, eggplant, onion, salt, pepper, basil, oil and garlic, toss gently, cover and cook on High for 2 hours. Divide between plates and serve as a side dish.

Nutrition: calories 165, fat 11, fiber 3, carbs 15, protein 2

Italian Squash and Peppers Mix

Preparation time: 10 minutes | Cooking time: 1 hour 30 minutes | Servings: 4

Ingredients:
- 12 small squash, peeled and cut into wedges
- 2 red bell peppers, cut into wedges
- 2 green bell peppers, cut into wedges
- 1/3 cup Italian dressing
- 1 red onion, cut into wedges
- Salt and black pepper to the taste
- 1 tablespoon parsley, chopped

Directions:
In your Slow cooker, mix squash with red bell peppers, green bell peppers, salt, pepper and Italian dressing, cover and cook on High for 1 hour and 30 minutes. Add parsley, toss, divide between plates and serve as a side dish.

Nutrition: calories 80, fat 2, fiber 3, carbs 11, protein 2

Green Beans and Red Peppers

Preparation time: 10 minutes | Cooking time: 2 hours | Servings: 2

Ingredients:
- 2 cups green beans, halved
- 1 red bell pepper, cut into strips
- Salt and black pepper to the taste
- 1 tablespoon olive oil
- 1 and ½ tablespoon honey mustard

Directions:
In your Slow cooker, mix green beans with bell pepper, salt, pepper, oil and honey mustard, toss, cover and cook on High for 2 hours. Divide between plates and serve as a side dish.

Nutrition: calories 50, fat 0, fiber 4, carbs 8, protein 2

Garlic Butter Green Beans

Preparation time: 10 minutes | Cooking time: 2 hours | Servings: 6

Ingredients:
- 22 ounces green beans
- 2 garlic cloves, minced
- ¼ cup butter, soft
- 2 tablespoons parmesan, grated

Directions:
In your Slow cooker, mix green beans with garlic, butter and parmesan, toss, cover and cook on High for 2 hours. Divide between plates, sprinkle parmesan all over and serve as a side dish.

Nutrition: calories 60, fat 4, fiber 1, carbs 3, protein 1

Zucchini Casserole

Preparation time: 10 minutes | Cooking time: 2 hours | Servings: 10

Ingredients:
- 7 cups zucchini, sliced
- 2 cups crackers, crushed
- 2 tablespoons melted butter
- 1/3 cup yellow onion, chopped
- 1 cup cheddar cheese, shredded
- 1 cup chicken stock
- 1/3 cup sour cream
- Salt and black pepper to the taste
- 1 tablespoon parsley, chopped
- Cooking spray

Directions:
Grease your Slow cooker with cooking spray and arrange zucchini and onion in the pot. Add melted butter, stock, sour cream, salt and pepper and toss. Add cheese mixed with crackers, cover and cook on High for 2 hours. Divide zucchini casserole on plates, sprinkle parsley all over and serve as a side dish.

Nutrition: calories 180, fat 6, fiber 1, carbs 14, protein 4

Nut and Berry Side Salad

Preparation time: 10 minutes | Cooking time: 1 hours | Servings: 4

Ingredients:
- 2 cups strawberries, halved
- 2 tablespoons mint, chopped
- 1/3 cup raspberry vinegar
- 2 tablespoons honey
- 1 tablespoon canola oil
- Salt and black pepper to the taste
- 4 cups spinach, torn
- ½ cup blueberries
- ¼ cup walnuts, chopped
- 1 ounce goat cheese, crumbled

Directions:
In your Slow cooker, mix strawberries with mint, vinegar, honey, oil, salt, pepper, spinach, blueberries and walnuts, cover and cook on High for 1 hour. Divide salad on plates, sprinkle cheese on top and serve as a side dish.

Nutrition: calories 200, fat 12, fiber 4, carbs 17, protein 15

Blueberry and Spinach Salad

Preparation time: 10 minutes | Cooking time: 1 hours | Servings: 3

Ingredients:
- ¼ cup pecans, chopped
- ½ teaspoon sugar
- 2 teaspoons maple syrup
- 1 tablespoon white vinegar
- 2 tablespoons orange juice
- 1 tablespoon olive oil
- 4 cups spinach
- 2 oranges, peeled and cut into segments
- 1 cup blueberries

Directions:
In your Slow cooker, mix pecans with sugar, maple syrup, vinegar, orange juice, oil, spinach, oranges and blueberries, toss, cover and cook on High for 1 hour. Divide between plates and serve as a side dish.

Nutrition: calories 140, fat 4, fiber 3, carbs 10, protein 3

Rice and Farro Pilaf

Preparation time: 10 minutes | Cooking time: 5 hours | Servings: 12

Ingredients:
- 1 shallot, chopped
- 1 teaspoon garlic, minced
- A drizzle of olive oil
- 1 and ½ cups whole grain farro
- ¾ cup wild rice
- 6 cups chicken stock
- Salt and black pepper to the taste
- 1 tablespoon parsley and sage, chopped
- ½ cup hazelnuts, toasted and chopped
- ¾ cup cherries, dried

Directions:
In your Slow cooker, mix oil with garlic, shallot, farro, rice, stock, salt, pepper, sage and parsley, hazelnuts and cherries, toss, cover and cook on Low for 5 hours. Divide between plates and serve as a side dish.

Nutrition: calories 120, fat 2, fiber 7, carbs 20, protein 3

Pink Rice

Preparation time: 10 minutes | Cooking time: 5 hours | Servings: 8

Ingredients:
- 1 teaspoon salt
- 2 and ½ cups water
- 2 cups pink rice

Directions:
Put the rice in your Slow cooker add water and salt, stir, cover and cook on Low for 5 hours Stir rice a bit, divide it between plates and serve as a side dish.

Nutrition: calories 120, fat 3, fiber 3, carbs 16, protein 4

Pumpkin Rice

Preparation time: 10 minutes | Cooking time: 5 hours | Servings: 4

Ingredients:
- 2 ounces olive oil
- 1 small yellow onion, chopped
- 2 garlic cloves, minced
- 12 ounces risotto rice
- 4 cups chicken stock
- 6 ounces pumpkin puree
- ½ teaspoon nutmeg, ground
- 1 teaspoon thyme, chopped
- ½ teaspoon ginger, grated
- ½ teaspoon cinnamon powder
- ½ teaspoon allspice, ground
- 4 ounces heavy cream

Directions:
In your Slow cooker, mix oil with onion, garlic, rice, stock, pumpkin puree, nutmeg, thyme, ginger, cinnamon and allspice, stir, cover and cook on Low for 4 hours and 30 minutes. Add cream, stir, cover, cook on Low for 30 minutes more, divide between plates and serve as a side dish.

Nutrition: calories 251, fat 4, fiber 3, carbs 30, protein 5

Rice and Veggies

Preparation time: 6 minutes | Cooking time: 5 hours | Servings: 4

Ingredients:
- 2 cups basmati rice
- 1 cup mixed carrots, peas, corn and green beans
- 2 cups water
- ½ teaspoon green chili, minced
- ½ teaspoon ginger, grated
- 3 garlic cloves, minced
- 2 tablespoons butter
- 1 cinnamon stick
- 1 tablespoon cumin seeds
- 2 bay leaves
- 3 whole cloves
- 5 black peppercorns
- 2 whole cardamoms
- 1 tablespoon sugar
- Salt to the taste

Directions:
Put the water in your Slow cooker, add rice, mixed veggies, green chili, grated ginger, garlic, cinnamon stick, whole cloves, butter, cumin seeds, bay leaves, cardamoms, black peppercorns, salt and sugar, stir, cover and cook on Low for 5 hours. Discard cinnamon, divide between plates and serve as a side dish.

Nutrition: calories 300, fat 4, fiber 3, carbs 40, protein 13

Easy Farro

Preparation time: 10 minutes | Cooking time: 5 hours | Servings: 6

Ingredients:
- 1 tablespoon apple cider vinegar
- 1 cup whole grain farro
- 1 teaspoon lemon juice
- Salt to the taste
- 3 cups water
- 1 tablespoon olive oil
- ½ cup cherries, dried and chopped
- ¼ cup green onions, chopped
- 10 mint leaves, chopped
- 2 cups cherries, pitted and halved

Directions:
Put the water in your Slow cooker, add farro, stir, cover, cook on Low for 5 hours, drain and transfer to a bowl. Add salt, oil, lemon juice, vinegar, and dried cherries, fresh cherries, green onions and mint, toss, divide between plates and serve as a side dish.

Nutrition: calories 162, fat 3, fiber 6, carbs 12, protein 4

Mexican Rice

Preparation time: 10 minutes | Cooking time: 4 hours | Servings: 4

Ingredients:
- 1 cup long grain rice
- 1 and ¼ cups veggie stock
- ½ cup cilantro, chopped
- ½ avocado, pitted, peeled and chopped
- Salt and black pepper to the taste
- ¼ cup green hot sauce

Directions:
Put the rice in your Slow cooker, add stock, stir, cover, and cook on Low for 4 hours, fluff with a fork and transfer to a bowl. In your food processor, mix avocado with hot sauce and cilantro, blend well, pour over rice, toss well, add salt and pepper, divide between plates and serve as a side dish.

Nutrition: calories 100, fat 3, fiber 6, carbs 18, protein 4

Goat Cheese Rice

Preparation time: 10 minutes | Cooking time: 4 hours | Servings: 6

Ingredients:
- 2 garlic cloves, minced
- 2 tablespoons olive oil
- ¾ cup yellow onion, chopped
- 1 and ½ cups Arborio rice
- ½ cup white wine
- 12 ounces spinach, chopped
- 3 and ½ cups hot veggie stock
- Salt and black pepper to the taste
- 4 ounces goat cheese, soft and crumbled
- 2 tablespoons lemon juice
- 1/3 cup pecans, toasted and chopped

Directions:
In your Slow cooker, mix oil with garlic, onion, rice, wine, salt, pepper and stock, stir, cover and cook on Low for 4 hours. Add spinach, toss and leave aside for a few minutes Add lemon juice and goat cheese, stir, divide between plates and serve with pecans on top as a side dish.

Nutrition: calories 300, fat 12, fiber 4, carbs 20, protein 15

Rice and Artichokes

Preparation time: 10 minutes | Cooking time: 4 hours | Servings: 4

Ingredients:
- 1 tablespoon olive oil
- 5 ounces Arborio rice
- 2 garlic cloves, minced
- 1 and ¼ cups chicken stock
- 1 tablespoon white wine
- 6 ounces graham crackers, crumbled
- 1 and ¼ cups water
- 15 ounces canned artichoke hearts, chopped
- 16 ounces cream cheese
- 1 tablespoon parmesan, grated
- 1 and ½ tablespoons thyme, chopped
- Salt and black pepper to the taste

Directions:
In your Slow cooker, mix oil with rice, garlic, stock, wine, water, artichokes and crackers, stir, cover and cook on Low for 4 hours. Add cream cheese, salt, pepper, parmesan and thyme, toss, divide between plates and serve as a side dish.

Nutrition: calories 230, fat 3, fiber 5, carbs 30, protein 4

Green Beans and Mushrooms

Preparation time: 10 minutes | Cooking time: 3 hours | Servings: 4

Ingredients:
- 1 pound fresh green beans, trimmed
- 1 small yellow onion, chopped
- 6 ounces bacon, chopped
- 1 garlic clove, minced
- 1 cup chicken stock
- 8 ounces mushrooms, sliced
- Salt and black pepper to the taste
- A splash of balsamic vinegar

Directions:
In your Slow cooker, mix beans with onion, bacon, garlic, stock, mushrooms, salt, pepper and vinegar, stir, cover and cook on Low for 3 hours. Divide between plates and serve as a side dish.

Nutrition: calories 162, fat 4, fiber 5, carbs 8, protein 4

Black Beans Mix

Preparation time: 10 minutes | Cooking time: 7 hours | Servings: 8

Ingredients:
- 1 cup black beans, soaked overnight, drained and rinsed
- 1 cup water
- Salt and black pepper to the taste
- 1 spring onion, chopped
- 2 garlic cloves, minced
- ½ teaspoon cumin seeds

Directions:
In your Slow cooker, mix beans with water, salt, pepper, onion, garlic and cumin seeds, stir, cover and cook on Low for 7 hours. Divide everything between plates and serve as a side dish.

Nutrition: calories 300, fat 4, fiber 6, carbs 20, protein 15

Rice and Beans

Preparation time: 20 minutes | Cooking time: 5 hours | Servings: 6

Ingredients:
- 1 pound red kidney beans, soaked overnight and drained
- Salt to the taste
- 1 teaspoon olive oil
- 1 pound smoked sausage, roughly chopped
- 1 yellow onion, chopped
- 1 celery stalk, chopped
- 4 garlic cloves, chopped
- 1 green bell pepper, chopped
- 1 teaspoon thyme, dried
- 2 bay leaves
- 5 cups water
- Long grain rice, already cooked
- 2 green onions, minced
- 2 tablespoons parsley, minced
- Hot sauce for serving

Directions:
In your Slow cooker, mix red beans with salt, oil, sausage, onion, celery, garlic, bell pepper, thyme, bay leaves and water, cover and cook on Low for 5 hours. Divide the rice between plates, add beans, sausage and veggies on top, sprinkle green onions and parsley and serve as a side dish with hot sauce drizzled all over.

Nutrition: calories 200, fat 5, fiber 6, carbs 20, protein 5

Slow cooker Snack Recipes

Tamale Dip

Preparation time: 10 minutes | Cooking time: 2 hours | Servings: 8

Ingredients:
- 1 jalapeno, chopped
- 8 ounces cream cheese, cubed
- ¾ cup cheddar cheese, shredded
- ½ cup Monterey jack cheese, shredded
- 2 garlic cloves, minced
- 15 ounces enchilada sauce
- 1 cup canned corn, drained
- 1 cup rotisserie chicken, shredded
- 1 tablespoon chili powder
- Salt and black pepper to the taste
- 1 tablespoon cilantro, chopped

Directions:

In your Slow cooker, mix jalapeno with cream cheese, cheddar cheese, Monterey cheese, garlic, enchilada sauce, corn, chicken, chili powder, salt and pepper, stir, cover and cook on Low for 2 hours. Add cilantro, stir, divide into bowls and serve as a snack.

Nutrition: calories 200, fat 4, fiber 7, carbs 20, protein 4

BBQ Chicken Dip

Preparation time: 10 minutes | Cooking time: 1 hour 30 minutes | Servings: 10

Ingredients:
- 1 and ½ cups bbq sauce
- 1 small red onion, chopped
- 24 ounces cream cheese, cubed
- 2 cups rotisserie chicken, shredded
- 3 bacon slices, cooked and crumbled
- 1 plum tomato, chopped
- ½ cup cheddar cheese, shredded
- 1 tablespoon green onions, chopped

Directions:

In your Slow cooker, mix bbq sauce with onion, cream cheese, rotisserie chicken, bacon, tomato, cheddar and green onions, stir, cover and cook on Low for 1 hour and 30 minutes. Divide into bowls and serve.

Nutrition: calories 251, fat 4, fiber 6, carbs 10, protein 4

Mexican Dip

Preparation time: 10 minutes | Cooking time: 1 hour 30 minutes | Servings: 10

Ingredients:
- 24 ounces cream cheese, cubed
- 2 cups rotisserie chicken breast, shredded
- 3 ounces canned green chilies, chopped
- 1 and ½ cups Monterey jack cheese, shredded
- 1 and ½ cups salsa Verde
- 1 tablespoon green onions, chopped

Directions:

In your Slow cooker, mix cream cheese with chicken, chilies, cheese, salsa Verde and green onions, stir, cover and cook on Low for 1 hour and 30 minutes. Divide into bowls and serve.

Nutrition: calories 222, fat 4, fiber 5, carbs 15, protein 4

Tex Mex Dip

Preparation time: 10 minutes | Cooking time: 1 hour | Servings: 6

Ingredients:

- 15 ounces canned chili con carne
- 1 cup Mexican cheese, shredded
- 1 yellow onion, chopped
- 8 ounces cream cheese, cubed
- ½ cup beer
- A pinch of salt
- 12 ounces macaroni, cooked
- 1 tablespoons cilantro, chopped

Directions:

In your Slow cooker, mix chili con carne with cheese, onion, cream cheese, beer and salt, stir, cover and cook on High for 1 hour. Add macaroni and cilantro, stir, divide into bowls and serve.

Nutrition: calories 200, fat 4, fiber 6, carbs 17, protein 5

Artichoke Dip

Preparation time: 10 minutes | Cooking time: 2 hour | Servings: 6

Ingredients:

- 10 ounces spinach
- 30 ounces canned artichoke hearts
- 5 ounces boursin
- 1 and ½ cup cheddar cheese, shredded
- ½ cup parmesan, grated
- 2 garlic cloves, minced
- 1 teaspoon red pepper flakes, crushed
- A pinch of salt

Directions:

In your Slow cooker, mix spinach with artichokes, boursin, cheddar, parmesan, garlic, pepper flakes and salt, stir, cover and cook on High for 1 hour. Stir the dip, cover and cook on Low for 1 more hour. Divide into bowls and serve.

Nutrition: calories 251, fat 6, fiber 8, carbs 16, protein 5

Taco Dip

Preparation time: 10 minutes | Cooking time: 2 hours 30 minutes | Servings: 7

Ingredients:

- 1 rotisserie chicken, shredded
- 2 cups pepper jack, cheese, grated
- 15 ounces canned enchilada sauce
- 1 jalapeno, sliced
- 8 ounces cream cheese, soft
- 1 tablespoon taco seasoning

Directions:

In your Slow cooker, mix chicken with pepper jack, enchilada sauce, jalapeno, cream and taco seasoning, stir, cover and cook on High for 1 hour. Stir the dip, cover and cook on Low for 1 hour and 30 minutes more. Divide into bowls and serve as a snack.

Nutrition: calories 251, fat 5, fiber 8, carbs 17, protein 5

Lasagna Dip

Preparation time: 10 minutes | Cooking time: 1 hour | Servings: 10

Ingredients:
- 8 ounces cream cheese
- ¾ cup parmesan, grated
- 1 and ½ cups ricotta
- ½ teaspoon red pepper flakes, crushed
- 2 garlic cloves, minced
- 3 cups marinara sauce
- 1 and ½ cups mozzarella, shredded
- 1 and ½ teaspoon oregano, chopped

Directions:
In your Slow cooker, mix cream cheese with parmesan, ricotta, pepper flakes, garlic, marinara, mozzarella and oregano, stir, cover and cook on High for 1 hour. Stir, divide into bowls and serve as a dip.

Nutrition: calories 231, fat 4, fiber 7, carbs 21, protein 5

Beer and Cheese Dip

Preparation time: 10 minutes | Cooking time: 1 hour | Servings: 10

Ingredients:
- 12 ounces cream cheese
- 6 ounces beer
- 4 cups cheddar cheese, shredded
- 1 tablespoon chives, chopped

Directions:
In your Slow cooker, mix cream cheese with beer and cheddar, stir, cover and cook on Low for 1 hour. Stir your dip, add chives, divide into bowls and serve.

Nutrition: calories 212, fat 4, fiber 7, carbs 16, protein 5

Queso Dip

Preparation time: 10 minutes | Cooking time: 1 hour | Servings: 10

Ingredients:
- 16 ounces Velveeta
- 1 cup whole milk
- ½ cup cotija
- 2 jalapenos, chopped
- 2 teaspoons sweet paprika
- 2 garlic cloves, minced
- A pinch of cayenne pepper
- 1 tablespoon cilantro, chopped

Directions:
In your Slow cooker, mix Velveeta with milk, cotija, jalapenos, paprika, garlic and cayenne, stir, cover and cook on High for 1 hour. Stir the dip, add cilantro, divide into bowls and serve as a dip

Nutrition: calories 233, fat 4, fiber 7, carbs 10, protein 4

Crab Dip

*Preparation time: 10 minutes | **Cooking time:** 2 hours | **Servings:** 6*

Ingredients:
- 12 ounces cream cheese
- ½ cup parmesan, grated
- ½ cup mayonnaise
- ½ cup green onions, chopped
- 2 garlic cloves, minced
- Juice of 1 lemon
- 1 and ½ tablespoon Worcestershire sauce
- 1 and ½ teaspoons old bay seasoning
- 12 ounces crabmeat

Directions:
In your Slow cooker, mix cream cheese with parmesan, mayo, green onions, garlic, lemon juice, Worcestershire sauce, old bay seasoning and crabmeat, stir, cover and cook on Low for 2 hours. Divide into bowls and serve as a dip.

Nutrition: calories 200, fat 4, fiber 6, carbs 12, protein 3

Slow Cooked Dip

*Preparation time: 10 minutes | **Cooking time:** 3 hours | **Servings:** 12*

Ingredients:
- 9 cups corn, rice and wheat cereal
- 1 cup cheerios
- 2 cups pretzels
- 1 cup peanuts
- 6 tablespoons hot, melted butter
- 1 tablespoon salt
- ¼ cup Worcestershire sauce
- 1 teaspoon garlic powder

Directions:
In your Slow cooker, mix cereal with cheerios, pretzels, peanuts, butter, salt, Worcestershire sauce and garlic powder, toss well, cover and cook on Low for 3 hours. Divide into bowls and serve as a snack.

Nutrition: calories 182, fat 4, fiber 5, carbs 8, protein 8

Candied Pecans

*Preparation time: 10 minutes | **Cooking time:** 3 hours | **Servings:** 4*

Ingredients:
- 1 cup white sugar
- 1 and ½ tablespoons cinnamon powder
- ½ cup brown sugar
- 1 egg white, whisked
- 4 cups pecans
- 2 teaspoons vanilla extract
- ¼ cup water

Directions:
In a bowl, mix white sugar with cinnamon, brown sugar and vanilla and stir. Dip pecans in egg white, then in sugar mix and put them in your Slow cooker, also add the water, cover and cook on Low for 3 hours. Divide into bowls and serve as a snack.

Nutrition: calories 152, fat 4, fiber 7, carbs 16, protein 6

Chicken Bites

Preparation time: 10 minutes | Cooking time: 7 hours | Servings: 4

Ingredients:
- 1 pound chicken thighs, boneless and skinless
- 1 tablespoon ginger, grated
- 1 yellow onion, sliced
- 1 tablespoon garlic, minced
- 2 teaspoons cumin, ground
- 1 teaspoon cinnamon powder
- 2 tablespoons sweet paprika
- 1 and ½ cups chicken stock
- 2 tablespoons lemon juice
- ½ cup green olives, pitted and roughly chopped
- Salt to the taste
- 3 tablespoons olive oil
- 5 pita breads, cut in quarters and heated in the oven

Directions:
Heat up a pan with the olive oil over medium-high heat, add onions, garlic, ginger, salt and pepper, stir and cook for 2 minutes. Add cumin and cinnamon, stir well and take off heat. Put chicken pieces in your Slow cooker, add onions mix, lemon juice, olives and stock, stir, cover and cook on Low for 7 hours. Shred meat, stir the whole mixture again, divide it on pita chips and serve as a snack.

Nutrition: calories 265, fat 7, fiber 6, carbs 14, protein 6

Peanut Snack

Preparation time: 10 minutes | Cooking time: 1 hour 30 minutes | Servings: 4

Ingredients:
- 1 cup peanuts
- 1 cup chocolate peanut butter
-
- 12 ounces dark chocolate chips
- 12 ounces white chocolate chips

Directions:
In your Slow cooker, mix peanuts with peanut butter, dark and white chocolate chips, cover and cook on Low for 1 hour and 30 minutes. Divide this mix into small muffin cups, leave aside to cool down and serve as a snack.

Nutrition: calories 200, fat 4, fiber 6, carbs 10, protein 5

Apple Dip

Preparation time: 10 minutes | Cooking time: 1 hour 30 minutes | Servings: 8

Ingredients:
- 5 apples, peeled and chopped
- ½ teaspoon cinnamon powder
- 12 ounces jarred caramel sauce
- A pinch of nutmeg, ground

Directions:
In your Slow cooker, mix apples with cinnamon, caramel sauce and nutmeg, stir, cover and cook on High for 1 hour and 30 minutes. Divide into bowls and serve.

Nutrition: calories 200, fat 3, fiber 6, carbs 10, protein 5

Beef and Chipotle Dip

Preparation time: 10 minutes | Cooking time: 2 hours | Servings: 10

Ingredients:
- 8 ounces cream cheese, soft
- 2 tablespoons yellow onion, chopped
- 2 tablespoons mayonnaise
- 2 ounces hot pepper Monterey Jack cheese, shredded
- ¼ teaspoon garlic powder
- 2 chipotle chilies in adobo sauce, chopped
- 2 ounces dried beef, chopped
- ¼ cup pecans, chopped

Directions:
In your Slow cooker, mix cream cheese with onion, mayo, Monterey Jack cheese, garlic powder, chilies and dried beef, stir, cover and cook on Low for 2 hours. Add pecans, stir, divide into bowls and serve.

Nutrition: calories 130, fat 11, fiber 1, carbs 3, protein 4

Chicken Wings

Preparation time: 2 hours | Cooking time: 6 hours | Servings: 24

Ingredients:
- 1 teaspoon garlic powder
- ½ cup brown sugar
- ¾ cup white sugar
- 1 teaspoon ginger powder
- 1 cup soy sauce
- ¼ cup pineapple juice
- ¾ cup water
- ¼ cup olive oil
- 24 chicken wings

Directions:
In a bowl, mix chicken wings with garlic powder, brown sugar, white sugar, ginger powder, soy sauce, pineapple juice, water and oil, whisk well and leave aside for 2 hours in the fridge. Transfer chicken wings to your Slow cooker, add 1 cup of the marinade, cover and cook on Low for 6 hours. Serve chicken wings warm.

Nutrition: calories 140, fat 7, fiber 1, carbs 12, protein 6

Bean Dip

Preparation time: 10 minutes | Cooking time: 3 hours | Servings: 56

Ingredients:
- 16 ounces Mexican cheese
- 5 ounces canned green chilies
- 16 ounces canned refried beans
- 2 pounds tortilla chips
- Cooking spray

Directions:
Grease your Slow cooker with cooking spray, line it, add Mexican cheese, green chilies and refried beans, stir, cover and cook on Low for 3 hours. Divide into bowls and serve with tortilla chips on the side.

Nutrition: calories 120, fat 2, fiber 1, carbs 14, protein 3

Buffalo Meatballs

Preparation time: 10 minutes | Cooking time: 3 hours 10 minutes | Servings: 36

Ingredients:
- 1 cup breadcrumbs
- 2 pounds chicken, ground
- 2 eggs
- ¾ cup buffalo wings sauce
- ½ cup yellow onion, chopped
- 3 garlic cloves, minced
- Salt and black pepper to the taste
- 2 tablespoons olive oil
- ¼ cup butter, melted
- 1 cup blue cheese dressing

Directions:
In a bowl, mix chicken with breadcrumbs, eggs, onion, garlic, salt and pepper, stir and shape small meatballs out of this mix. Heat up a pan with the oil over medium-high heat, add meatballs, brown them for a few minutes on each side and transfer them to your Slow cooker. Add melted butter and Buffalo wings sauce, cover and cook on Low for 3 hours. Arrange meatballs on a platter and serve them with the blue cheese dressing on the side.

Nutrition: calories 100, fat 7, fiber 1, carbs 4, protein 4

Glazed Sausages

Preparation time: 10 minutes | Cooking time: 4 hours | Servings: 24

Ingredients:
- 10 ounces jarred red pepper jelly
- 1/3 cup bbq sauce
- ½ cup brown sugar
- 16 ounces pineapple chunks and juice
- 24 ounces cocktail-size sausages
- 1 tablespoons cornstarch
- 2 tablespoons water
- Cooking spray

Directions:
Grease your Slow cooker with cooking spray, add pepper jelly, bbq sauce, brown sugar, pineapple and sausages, stir, cover and cook on Low for 3 hours. Add cornstarch mixed with the water, whisk everything and cook on High for 1 more hour. Arrange sausages on a platter and serve them as a snack.

Nutrition: calories 170, fat 10, fiber 1, carbs 17, protein 4

Cheesy Mix

Preparation time: 10 minutes | Cooking time: 2 hours | Servings: 24

Ingredients:
- 2 cups small pretzels
- 2 cups wheat cereal
- 3 cups rice cereal
- 3 cups corn cereal
- 2 cups small cheese crackers
- 1/3 cup parmesan, grated
- 1/3 cup bacon flavor chips
- ½ cup melted butter
- 1/3 cup canola oil
- 1 ounce ranch dressing

Directions:
In your Slow cooker, mix pretzels with wheat cereal, rice cereal, corn cereal, crackers, chips and parmesan, cover and cook on High for 2 hours stirring every 20 minutes. In a bowl, mix butter with oil and ranch dressing and whisk well. Divide the mix from the slow cooker into bowls and serve them with the ranch dressing on the side.

Nutrition: calories 182, fat 2, fiber 6, carbs 12, protein 4

Cheeseburger Meatballs

Preparation time: 10 minutes | Cooking time: 3 hours | Servings: 12

Ingredients:
- 2 bacon slices, chopped
- 1 pound beef, ground
- ¼ cup milk
- ½ cup yellow onion, chopped
- ½ cup breadcrumbs
- 1 egg, whisked
- 1 tablespoon honey
- Salt and black pepper to the taste
- 3 ounces cheddar cheese, cubed
- 18 ounces bbq sauce
- 24 dill pickle slices

Directions:
In a bowl, mix beef with bacon, milk, onion, breadcrumbs, egg, honey, salt and pepper, stir well and shape medium meatballs out of this mix. Place a cheddar cube in each meatball, seal them well, put them in your Slow cooker, add bbq sauce, cover and cook on Low for 3 hours. Thread dill pickles on cocktail picks and serve them with your cheeseburger meatballs.

Nutrition: calories 200, fat 8, fiber 1, carbs 24, protein 10

Caramel Corn

Preparation time: 10 minutes | Cooking time: 2 hours | Servings: 13

Ingredients:
- ½ cup butter
- 1 teaspoon vanilla extract
- ¼ cup corn syrup
- 1 cup brown sugar
- 1 teaspoon baking soda
- 12 cups plain popcorn
- 1 cup mixed nuts
- Cooking spray

Directions:
Grease your Slow cooker with cooking spray, add butter, vanilla, corn syrup, brown sugar and baking soda, cover and cook on High for 1 hour, stirring after 30 minutes. Add popcorn, toss, cover and cook on Low for 1 hour more. Add nuts, toss, divide into bowls and serve as a snack.

Nutrition: calories 250, fat 14, fiber 1, carbs 20, protein 2

Bourbon Sausage Bites

Preparation time: 10 minutes | Cooking time: 3 hours | Servings: 12

Ingredients:
- 1/3 cup bourbon
- 1 pound smoked sausage, sliced
- 12 ounces chili sauce
- ¼ cup brown sugar
- 2 tablespoons yellow onion, grated

Directions:
Heat up a pan over medium-high heat, add sausage slices, brown them for 2 minutes on each side, drain them on paper towels and transfer to your Slow cooker. Add chili sauce, sugar, onion and bourbon, toss to coat, cover and cook on Low for 3 hours. Divide into bowls and serve as a snack.

Nutrition: calories 190, fat 11, fiber 1, carbs 12, protein 5

Curried Meatballs

Preparation time: 10 minutes | Cooking time: 4 hours | Servings: 40

Ingredients:
- 12 ounces pineapple preserves
- 8 ounces pineapple tidbits in juice
- 8 ounces Dijon mustard
- ½ cup brown sugar
- 1 teaspoon curry powder
- 2 and ½ pounds frozen meatballs

Directions:
In your Slow cooker, mix pineapple preserves with pineapple tidbits, mustard, sugar and curry powder and whisk well. Add meatballs, toss, cover and cook on High for 4 hours. Serve them hot.

Nutrition: calories 120, fat 5, fiber 1, carbs 13, protein 6

Pizza Dip

Preparation time: 10 minutes | Cooking time: 4 hours | Servings: 14

Ingredients:
- 14 ounces pizza sauce
- 1 cup turkey pepperoni, chopped
- ½ red bell pepper, chopped
- 8 green onions, chopped
- 2 ounces black olives, pitted and sliced
- 4 ounces mozzarella cheese, shredded
- 8 ounces cream cheese, cubed

Directions:
In your Slow cooker, mix pizza sauce with turkey pepperoni, bell pepper, green onions and black olives, stir, cover and cook on Low for 4 hours. Add mozzarella and cream cheese, stir, divide into bowls and serve as a snack.

Nutrition: calories 135, fat 12, fiber 1, carbs 3, protein 5

Sauerkraut Dip

Preparation time: 10 minutes | Cooking time: 2 hours | Servings: 12

Ingredients:
- 15 ounces canned sauerkraut, drained
- 8 ounces sour cream
- 4 ounces cream cheese
- 4 ounces corned beef, chopped
- 8 ounces Swiss cheese, shredded

Directions:
In your Slow cooker, mix sauerkraut with sour cream, cream cheese, beef and Swiss cheese, stir, cover and cook on Low for 2 hours. Divide into bowls and serve.

Nutrition: calories 166, fat 14, fiber 1, carbs 4, protein 7

Spicy Dip

Preparation time: 10 minutes | Cooking time: 3 hours | Servings: 10

Ingredients:
- 1 pound spicy sausage, chopped
- 8 ounces cream cheese, soft
- 8 ounces sour cream
- 20 ounces canned tomatoes and green chilies, chopped

Directions:
In your Slow cooker, mix sausage with cream cheese, sour cream and tomatoes and chilies, stir, cover and cook on Low for 3 hours. Divide into bowls and serve as a snack.

Nutrition: calories 300, fat 12, fiber 7, carbs 30, protein 34

Salsa Corn Dip

Preparation time: 10 minutes | Cooking time: 2 hours 30 minutes | Servings: 12

Ingredients:
- 2 teaspoons cumin, ground
- 16 ounces salsa Verde
- 12 ounces corn
- 1 yellow onion, chopped
- 4 garlic cloves, minced
- 8 ounces cream cheese, soft
- 1 cup Monterey jack cheese, shredded
- 1-pint cherry tomatoes, quartered
- ½ cup cilantro, chopped
- Cooking spray

Directions:
Grease your Slow cooker with cooking spray and mix salsa with cumin, corn, onion, garlic, cream cheese, Monterey Jack cheese, cherry tomatoes and cilantro. Stir, cover and cook on High for 2 hours and 30 minutes. Divide into bowls and serve as a snack.

Nutrition: calories 220, fat 4, fiber 7, carbs 12, protein 5

Cheesy Corn Dip

Preparation time: 10 minutes | Cooking time: 4 hours | Servings: 12

Ingredients:
- 3 cups corn
- 8 ounces cream cheese, soft
- 1 and ½ cup cheddar cheese, shredded
- ½ cup salsa Verde
- 2 ounces black olives, pitted and sliced
- 1 teaspoon chives, chopped
- Cooking spray

Directions:
Grease your Slow cooker with the cooking spray, add corn, cream cheese, cheddar, salsa Verde, olives and chives, stir, cover and cook on Low for 4 hours. Divide into bowls and serve as a snack.

Nutrition: calories 223, fat 4, fiber 7, carbs 17, protein 5

White Bean Spread

Preparation time: 10 minutes | Cooking time: 7 hours | Servings: 4

Ingredients:
- ½ cup white beans, dried
- 2 tablespoons cashews, chopped
- 1 teaspoon apple cider vinegar
- 1 cup veggie stock
- 1 tablespoon water

Directions:
In your Slow cooker, mix beans with cashews and stock, stir, cover and cook on Low for 6 hours. Drain, transfer to your food processor, add vinegar and water, pulse well, divide into bowls and serve as a spread.

Nutrition: calories 221, fat 6, fiber 5, carbs 19, protein 3

Lentils Rolls

Preparation time: 10 minutes | Cooking time: 8 hours | Servings: 4

Ingredients:
- 1 cup brown lentils, cooked
- 1 green cabbage head, leaves separated
- ½ cup onion, chopped
- 1 cup brown rice, already cooked
- 2 ounces white mushrooms, chopped
- ¼ cup pine nuts, toasted
- ¼ cup raisins
- 2 garlic cloves, minced
- 2 tablespoons dill, chopped
- 1 tablespoon olive oil
- 25 ounces marinara sauce
- A pinch of salt and black pepper
- ¼ cup water

Directions:
In a bowl, mix lentils with onion, rice, mushrooms, pine nuts, raisins, garlic, dill, salt and pepper and whisk well. Arrange cabbage leaves on a working surface, divide lentils mix and wrap them well. Add marinara sauce and water to your slow cooker and stir. Add cabbage rolls, cover and cook on Low for 8 hours. Arrange cabbage rolls on a platter and serve.

Nutrition: calories 281, fat 6, fiber 6, carbs 12, protein 3

Eggplant Salsa

Preparation time: 10 minutes | Cooking time: 7 hours | Servings: 4

Ingredients:
- 1 and ½ cups tomatoes, chopped
- 3 cups eggplant, cubed
- 2 teaspoons capers
- 6 ounces green olives, pitted and sliced
- 4 garlic cloves, minced
- 2 teaspoons balsamic vinegar
- 1 tablespoon basil, chopped
- Salt and black pepper to the taste

Directions:
In your Slow cooker, mix tomatoes with eggplant cubes, capers, green olives, garlic, vinegar, basil, salt and pepper, toss, cover and cook on Low for 7 hours. Divide salsa into bowls and serve.

Nutrition: calories 200, fat 6, fiber 5, carbs 9, protein 2

Veggie Spread

Preparation time: 10 minutes | Cooking time: 7 hours | Servings: 4

Ingredients:
- 1 cup carrots, sliced
- 1 and ½ cups cauliflower florets
- 1/3 cup cashews
- ½ cup turnips, chopped
- 2 and ½ cups water
- 1 cup almond milk
- 1 teaspoon garlic powder
- Salt and black pepper to the taste
- ¼ teaspoon smoked paprika
- ¼ teaspoon mustard powder
- A pinch of salt

Directions:
In your slow cooker, mix carrots with cauliflower, cashews, turnips and water, stir, cover and cook on Low for 7 hours. Drain, transfer to a blender, add almond milk, garlic powder, paprika, mustard powder, salt and pepper, blend well, divide into bowls and serve as a snack.

Nutrition: calories 291, fat 7, fiber 4, carbs 14, protein 3

Peas Dip

Preparation time: 10 minutes | Cooking time: 5 hours | Servings: 4

Ingredients:
- 1 and ½ cups black-eyed peas
- 3 cups water
- 1 teaspoon Cajun seasoning
- ½ cup pecans, toasted
- ½ teaspoon garlic powder
- ½ teaspoon jalapeno powder
- Salt and black pepper to the taste
- ¼ teaspoon liquid smoke
- ½ teaspoon Tabasco sauce

Directions:
In your slow cooker, mix black-eyed pea with Cajun seasoning, salt, pepper and water, stir, cover and cook on High for 5 hours. Drain, transfer to a blender, add pecans, garlic powder, jalapeno powder, Tabasco sauce, liquid smoke, more salt and pepper, pulse well and serve.

Nutrition: calories 221, fat 4, fiber 7, carbs 16, protein 4

Hummus

Preparation time: 10 minutes | Cooking time: 8 hours | Servings: 10

Ingredients:
- 1 cup chickpeas, dried
- 2 tablespoons olive oil
- 3 cups water
- A pinch of salt and black pepper
- 1 garlic clove, minced
- 1 tablespoon lemon juice

Directions:
In your slow cooker, mix chickpeas with water, salt and pepper, stir, cover and cook on Low for 8 hours. Drain chickpeas, transfer to a blender, add oil, more salt and pepper, garlic and lemon juice, blend well, divide into bowls and serve.

Nutrition: calories 211, fat 6, fiber 7, carbs 8, protein 4

Cashew Dip

Preparation time: 10 minutes | Cooking time: 3 hours | Servings: 10

Ingredients:
- 1 cup water
- 1 cup cashews
- 10 ounces hummus
- ¼ teaspoon garlic powder
- ¼ teaspoon onion powder
- A pinch of salt and black pepper
- ¼ teaspoon mustard powder
- 1 teaspoon apple cider vinegar

Directions:
In your slow cooker, mix water with cashews, salt and pepper, stir, cover and cook on High for 3 hours. Transfer to your blender, add hummus, garlic powder, onion powder, mustard powder and vinegar, pulse well, divide into bowls and serve.

Nutrition: calories 192, fat 7, fiber 7, carbs 12, protein 4

Potato Salsa

Preparation time: 10 minutes | Cooking time: 8 hours | Servings: 6

Ingredients:
- 1 sweet onion, chopped
- ¼ cup white vinegar
- 2 tablespoons mustard
- Salt and black pepper to the taste
- 1 and ½ pounds gold potatoes, cut into medium cubes
- ¼ cup dill, chopped
- 1 cup celery, chopped
- Cooking spray

Directions:
Spray your Slow cooker with cooking spray, add onion, vinegar, mustard, salt and pepper and whisk well. Add celery and potatoes, toss them well, cover and cook on Low for 8 hours. Divide salad into small bowls, sprinkle dill on top and serve.

Nutrition: calories 251, fat 6, fiber 7, carbs 12, protein 7

Black Bean Salsa Salad

Preparation time: 10 minutes | Cooking time: 4 hours | Servings: 6

Ingredients:
- 1 tablespoon soy sauce
- ½ teaspoon cumin, ground
- 1 cup canned black beans
- 1 cup salsa
- 6 cups romaine lettuce leaves
- ½ cup avocado, peeled, pitted and mashed

Directions:
In your slow cooker, mix black beans with salsa, cumin and soy sauce, stir, cover and cook on Low for 4 hours. In a salad bowl, mix lettuce leaves with black beans mix and mashed avocado, toss and serve.

Nutrition: calories 221, fat 4, fiber 7, carbs 12, protein 3

Mushroom Dip

Preparation time: 10 minutes | Cooking time: 4 hours | Servings: 6

Ingredients:

- 2 cups green bell peppers, chopped
- 1 cup yellow onion, chopped
- 3 garlic cloves, minced
- 1 pound mushrooms, chopped
- 28 ounces tomato sauce
- ½ cup goat cheese, crumbled
- Salt and black pepper to the taste

Directions:

In your Slow cooker, mix bell peppers with onion, garlic, mushrooms, tomato sauce, cheese, salt and pepper, stir, cover and cook on Low for 4 hours. Divide into bowls and serve.

Nutrition: calories 255, fat 4, fiber 7, carbs 9, protein 3

Beef Meatballs

Preparation time: 10 minutes | Cooking time: 8 hours | Servings: 8

Ingredients:

- 1 and ½ pounds beef, ground
- 1 egg, whisked
- 16 ounces canned tomatoes, crushed
- 14 ounces canned tomato puree
- ¼ cup parsley, chopped
- 2 garlic cloves, minced
- 1 yellow onion, chopped
- Salt and black pepper to the taste

Directions:

In a bowl, mix beef with egg, parsley, garlic, black pepper and onion, stir well and shape 16 meatballs. Place them in your slow cooker, add tomato puree and crushed tomatoes on top, cover and cook on Low for 8 hours. Arrange them on a platter and serve.

Nutrition: calories 160, fat 5, fiber 3, carbs 10, protein 7

Jalapeno Poppers

Preparation time: 10 minutes | Cooking time: 3 hours | Servings: 4

Ingredients:

- ½ pound chorizo, chopped
- 10 jalapenos, tops cut off and deseeded
- 1 small white onion, chopped
- ½ pound beef, ground
- ¼ teaspoon garlic powder
- 1 tablespoon maple syrup
- 1 tablespoon mustard
- 1/3 cup water

Directions:

In a bowl, mix beef with chorizo, garlic powder and onion and stir. Stuff your jalapenos with the mix, place them in your Slow cooker, add the water, cover and cook on High for 3 hours. Transfer jalapeno poppers to a lined baking sheet. In a bowl, mix maple syrup with mustard, whisk well, brush poppers with this mix, arrange on a platter and serve.

Nutrition: calories 214, fat 2, fiber 3, carbs 8, protein 3

Pecans Snack

Preparation time: 10 minutes | Cooking time: 2 hours 15 minutes | Servings: 5

Ingredients:
- 1 pound pecans, halved
- 2 tablespoons olive oil
- 1 teaspoon basil, dried
- 1 tablespoon chili powder
- 1 teaspoon oregano, dried
- ¼ teaspoon garlic powder
- 1 teaspoon thyme, dried
- ½ teaspoon onion powder
- A pinch of cayenne pepper

Directions:
In your slow cooker, mix pecans with oil, basil, chili powder, oregano, garlic powder, onion powder, thyme and cayenne and toss to coat. Cover, cook on High for 15 minutes and on Low for 2 hours. Divide into bowls and serve as a snack.

Nutrition: calories 78, fat 3, fiber 2, carbs 9, protein 2

Apple Jelly Sausage Snack

Preparation time: 10 minutes | Cooking time: 2 hours | Servings: 15

Ingredients:
- 2 pounds sausages, sliced
- 18 ounces apple jelly
- 9 ounces Dijon mustard

Directions:
Place sausage slices in your Slow cooker, add apple jelly and mustard, toss to coat well, cover and cook on Low for 2 hours. Divide into bowls and serve as a snack.

Nutrition: calories 200, fat 3, fiber 1, carbs 9, protein 10

Eggplant Dip

Preparation time: 10 minutes | Cooking time: 4 hours 10 minutes | Servings: 4

Ingredients:
- 1 eggplant
- 1 zucchini, chopped
- 2 tablespoons olive oil
- 2 tablespoons balsamic vinegar
- 1 tablespoon parsley, chopped
- 1 yellow onion, chopped
- 1 celery stick, chopped
- 1 tomato, chopped
- 2 tablespoons tomato paste
- 1 and ½ teaspoons garlic, minced
- A pinch of sea salt
- Black pepper to the taste

Directions:
Brush eggplant with the oil, place on preheated grill and cook over medium-high heat for 5 minutes on each side. Leave aside to cool down, chop it and put in your Slow cooker. Also, add zucchini, vinegar, onion, celery, tomato, parsley, tomato paste, garlic, salt and pepper and stir everything. Cover and cook on High for 4 hours. Stir your spread again very well, divide into bowls and serve.

Nutrition: calories 110, fat 1, fiber 2, carbs 7, protein 5

Lemon Peel Snack

Preparation time: 20 minutes | Cooking time: 4 hours | Servings: 10

Ingredients:
- 5 big lemons, sliced halves, pulp removed and peel cut into strips
- 2 and ¼ cups white sugar
- 5 cups water

Directions:
Put strips in your instant slow cooker, add water and sugar, stir cover and cook on Low for 4 hours. Drain lemon peel and keep in jars until serving.

Nutrition: calories 7, fat 1, fiber 1, carbs 2, protein 1

Fava Bean Dip

Preparation time: 10 minutes | Cooking time: 5 hours | Servings: 6

Ingredients:
- 1 pound fava bean, rinsed
- 1 cup yellow onion, chopped
- 4 and ½ cups water
- 1 bay leaf
- ¼ cup olive oil
- 1 garlic clove, minced
- 2 tablespoons lemon juice
- Salt to the taste

Directions:
Put fava beans in your Slow cooker, add 4 cups water, salt and bay leaf, cover and cook on Low for 3 hours. Drain beans, discard bay leaf, return beans to the slow cooker, and add ½-cup water, garlic and onion, stir, cover and cook on Low for 2 more hours. Transfer beans mix to your food processor, add olive oil and lemon juice and blend well. Divide into bowls and serve cold.

Nutrition: calories 300, fat 3, fiber 1, carbs 20, protein 6

Tamales

Preparation time: 10 minutes | Cooking time: 8 hours 30 minutes | Servings: 24

Ingredients:
- 8 ounces dried corn husks, soaked for 1 day and drained
- 4 cups water
- 3 pounds pork shoulder, boneless and chopped
- 1 yellow onion, chopped
- 2 garlic cloves, crushed
- 1 tablespoon chipotle chili powder
- 2 tablespoons chili powder
- Salt and black pepper to the taste
- 1 teaspoon cumin, ground
- 4 cups masa harina
- ¼ cup corn oil
- ¼ cup shortening
- 1 teaspoon baking powder

Directions:
In your Slow cooker, mix 2 cups water with salt, pepper, onion, garlic, chipotle powder, chili powder, cumin and pork, stir, cover the slow cooker and cook on Low for 7 hours. Transfer meat to a cutting board, shred it with2 forks, add to a bowl, mix with 1 tablespoon of cooking liquid, more salt and pepper, stir and leave aside. In another bowl, mix masa harina with salt, pepper, baking powder, shortening and oil and stir using a mixer. Add cooking liquid from the instant slow cooker and blend again well. Unfold cornhusks, place them on a work surface, add ¼-cup masa mix near the top of the husk, and press into a square and leaves 2 inches at the bottom. Add 1 tablespoon pork mix in the center of the masa, wrap the husk around the dough, place all of them in your Slow cooker, add the rest of the water, cover and cook on High for 1 hour and 30 minutes. Arrange tamales on a platter and serve.

Nutrition: calories 162, fat 4, fiber 3, carbs 10, protein 5

Tostadas

Preparation time: 10 minutes | Cooking time: 4 hours | Servings: 4

Ingredients:
- 4 pounds pork shoulder, boneless and cubed
- Salt and black pepper to the taste
- 2 cups coca cola
- 1/3 cup brown sugar
- ½ cup hot sauce
- 2 teaspoons chili powder
- 2 tablespoons tomato paste
- ¼ teaspoon cumin, ground
- 1 cup enchilada sauce
- Corn tortillas, toasted for a few minutes in the oven
- Mexican cheese, shredded for serving
- 4 shredded lettuce leaves, for serving
- Salsa
- Guacamole for serving

Directions:
In your Slow cooker, mix 1-cup coke with hot sauce, salsa, sugar, tomato paste, chili powder, cumin and pork, stir, cover and cook on Low for 4 hours. Drain juice from the slow cooker, transfer meat to a cutting board, shred it, return it to slow cooker, and add the rest of the coke and enchilada sauce and stir. Place tortillas on a working surface, divide pork mix, lettuce leaves, Mexican cheese and guacamole and serve as a snack.

Nutrition: calories 162, fat 3, fiber 6, carbs 12, protein 5

Mussels Salad

Preparation time: 10 minutes | Cooking time: 1 hour | Servings: 4

Ingredients:
- 2 pounds mussels, cleaned and scrubbed
- 1 radicchio, cut into thin strips
- 1 white onion, chopped
- 1 pound baby spinach
- ½ cup dry white wine
- 1 garlic clove, crushed
- ½ cup water
- A drizzle of olive oil

Directions:
Divide baby spinach and radicchio in salad bowls and leave aside for now. In your Slow cooker, mix mussels with onion, wine, garlic, water and oil, toss, cover and cook on High for 1 hour. Divide mussels on top of spinach and radicchio, add cooking liquid all over and serve.

Nutrition: calories 59, fat 4, fiber 1, carbs 1, protein 1

Italian Mussels Salad

Preparation time: 10 minutes | Cooking time: 1 hours | Servings: 4

Ingredients:
- 28 ounces canned tomatoes, crushed
- ½ cup white onion, chopped
- 2 jalapeno peppers, chopped
- ¼ cup dry white wine
- ¼ cup extra virgin olive oil
- ¼ cup balsamic vinegar
- 2 pounds mussels, cleaned and scrubbed
- 2 tablespoons red pepper flakes
- 2 garlic cloves, minced
- Salt to the taste
- ½ cup basil, chopped
- Lemon wedges for serving

Directions:
In your Slow cooker, mix tomatoes with onion, jalapenos, wine, oil, vinegar, garlic, pepper flakes, salt, basil and mussels, cover and cook on High for 1 hour. Discard unopened mussels, divide everything into bowls and serve with lemon wedges.

Nutrition: calories 100, fat 1, fiber 1, carbs 7, protein 2

Spicy Mussels

Preparation time: 10 minutes | Cooking time: 1 hours | Servings: 4

Ingredients:
- 2 pounds mussels, scrubbed and debearded
- 2 tablespoons olive oil
- 1 yellow onion, chopped
- ½ teaspoon red pepper flakes
- 14 ounces tomatoes, chopped
- 2 teaspoons garlic, minced
- ½ cup chicken stock
- 2 teaspoons oregano, dried

Directions:
In your Slow cooker, mix oil with onions, pepper flakes, garlic, stock, oregano, tomatoes and mussels, stir, cover and cook on High for 1 hour Divide between bowls and serve.

Nutrition: calories 83, fat 2, fiber 2, carbs 8, protein 3

Cheeseburger Dip

Preparation time: 10 minutes | Cooking time: 3 hours | Servings: 10

Ingredients:
- 1 pound beef, ground
- 1 teaspoon garlic powder
- Salt and black pepper to the taste
- 2 tablespoons Worcestershire sauce
- 8 bacon strips, chopped
- 3 garlic cloves, minced
- 1 yellow onion, chopped
- 12 ounces cream cheese, soft
- 1 cup sour cream
- 2 tablespoons ketchup
- 2 tablespoons mustard
- 10 ounces canned tomatoes and chilies, chopped
- 1 and ½ cup cheddar cheese, shredded
- 1 cup mozzarella, shredded

Directions:
In your Slow cooker, mix beef with garlic, salt, pepper, Worcestershire sauce, bacon, garlic, onion, cream cheese, sour cream, ketchup, mustard, tomatoes and chilies, cheddar and mozzarella, stir, cover and cook on Low for 3 hours. Divide into bowls and serve.

Nutrition: calories 251, fat 5, fiber 8, carbs 16, protein 4

Onion Dip

Preparation time: 10 minutes | Cooking time: 1 hours | Servings: 6

Ingredients:
- 8 ounces cream cheese, soft
- ¾ cup sour cream
- 1 cup cheddar cheese, shredded
- 10 bacon slices, cooked and chopped
- 2 yellow onions, chopped

Directions:
In your Slow cooker, mix cream cheese with sour cream, cheddar cheese, bacon and onion, stir, cover and cook on High for 1 hour. Divide into bowls and serve.

Nutrition: calories 222, fat 4, fiber 6, carbs 17, protein 4

Caramel Dip

Preparation time: 10 minutes | Cooking time: 2 hours | Servings: 4

Ingredients:
- 1 cup butter
- 12 ounces condensed milk
- 2 cups brown sugar
- 1 cup corn syrup

Directions:
In your Slow cooker, mix butter with condensed milk, sugar and corn syrup, cover and cook on High for 2 hours stirring often. Divide into bowls and serve.

Nutrition: calories 172, fat 2, fiber 6, carbs 12, protein 4

Chicken Cordon Bleu Dip

Preparation time: 10 minutes | Cooking time: 1 hour 30 minutes | Servings: 6

Ingredients:
- 16 ounces cream cheese
- 2 chicken breasts, baked and shredded
- 1 cup cheddar cheese, shredded
- 1 cup Swiss cheese, shredded
- 3 garlic cloves, minced
- 6 ounces ham, chopped
- 2 tablespoons green onions
- Salt and black pepper to the taste

Directions:
In your Slow cooker, mix cream cheese with chicken, cheddar cheese, Swiss cheese, garlic, ham, green onions, salt and pepper, stir, cover and cook on Low for 1 hour and 30 minutes. Divide into bowls and serve as a snack.

Nutrition: calories 243, fat 5, fiber 8, carbs 15, protein 3

Fajita Dip

Preparation time: 10 minutes | Cooking time: 4 hours | Servings: 6

Ingredients:
- 3 chicken breasts, skinless and boneless
- 8 ounces root beer
- 3 red bell peppers, chopped
- 1 yellow onion, chopped
- 8 ounces cream cheese
- 8 ounces pepper jack cheese, shredded
- 16 ounces sour cream
- 2 fajita seasoning mix packets
- 1 tablespoons olive oil
- Salt and black pepper to the taste

Directions:
In your Slow cooker, mix chicken with root beer, bell peppers, onion, cream cheese, pepper jack cheese, sour cream, fajita seasoning, oil, salt and pepper, stir, cover and cook on High for 4 hours. Shred meat using2 forks, divide into bowls and serve.

Nutrition: calories 261, fat 4, fiber 6, carbs 17, protein 5

Tomato Salsa

Preparation time: 10 minutes | Cooking time: 5 hours | Servings: 6

Ingredients:
- 7 cups tomatoes, chopped
- 1 green bell pepper, chopped
- 1 red bell pepper, chopped
- 2 yellow onions, chopped
- 4 jalapenos, chopped
- ¼ cup apple cider vinegar
- 1 teaspoon coriander, ground
- 1 tablespoon cilantro, chopped
- 3 tablespoons basil, chopped
- Salt and black pepper to the taste

Directions:
In your Slow cooker, mix tomatoes with green and red peppers, onions, jalapenos, vinegar, coriander, salt and pepper, stir, cover and cook on Low for 5 hours. Add basil and cilantro, stir, divide into bowls and serve.

Nutrition: calories 172, fat 3, fiber 5, carbs 8, protein 4

Salsa Snack

Preparation time: 10 minutes | Cooking time: 3 hours | Servings: 6

Ingredients:
- 10 roma tomatoes, chopped
- 2 jalapenos, chopped
- 1 sweet onion, chopped
- 28 ounces canned plum tomatoes
- 3 garlic cloves, minced
- 1 bunch cilantro, chopped
- Salt and black pepper to the taste

Directions:
In your Slow cooker, mix roma tomatoes with jalapenos, onion, plum tomatoes and garlic, stir, cover and cook on High for 3 hours. Add salt, pepper and cilantro, stir, divide into bowls and serve cold.

Nutrition: calories 162, fat 4, fiber 6, carbs 12, protein 3

Jalapeno Dip

Preparation time: 10 minutes | Cooking time: 4 hours | Servings: 6

Ingredients:
- 7 cups tomatoes, chopped
- 1 yellow onion, chopped
- 1 red onion, chopped
- 3 jalapenos, chopped
- 1 red bell pepper, chopped
- 1 green bell pepper, chopped
- ¼ cup apple cider vinegar
- 1 tablespoon cilantro, chopped
- 1 tablespoon sage, chopped
- 3 tablespoons basil, chopped
- Salt to the taste

Directions:
In your Slow cooker, mix tomatoes with onion, jalapenos, red bell pepper, green bell pepper, vinegar, sage, cilantro and basil, stir, cover and cook on Low for 4 hours. Transfer to your food processor, add salt, pulse well, divide into bowls and serve.

Nutrition: calories 162, fat 7, fiber 4, carbs 7, protein 3

Slow Cooker Poultry Recipes

Rotisserie Chicken
Preparation time: 10 minutes | Cooking time: 3 hours | Servings: 4

Ingredients:
- Cooking spray
- 1 tablespoons smoked paprika
- 2 tablespoons brown sugar
- 1 tablespoon chili powder
- 1 teaspoon thyme, chopped
- 1 whole chicken
- Salt and black pepper to the taste

Directions:
In a bowl, mix smoked paprika with sugar, chili powder, thyme, salt and pepper, stir and rub the chicken with this mix. Grease the Slow cooker with cooking spray, line it with tin foil, add chicken, cover and cook on High for 3 hours and 30 minutes. Serve right away.

Nutrition: calories 324, fat 4, fiber 7, carbs 16, protein 3

Chicken and Dumplings
Preparation time: 10 minutes | Cooking time: 4 hours | Servings: 4

Ingredients:
- 1 yellow onion, chopped
- 1 and ½ pounds chicken breast, skinless and boneless
- Salt and black pepper to the taste
- 1 teaspoon oregano, dried
- 2 cups cream of chicken soup
- 2 cups chicken stock
- 4 thyme springs, chopped
- 1 bay leaf
- 2 celery stalks, chopped
- 2 carrots, chopped
- 1 cup peas
- 3 garlic cloves, minced
- ½ cup parmesan, grated
- 1 biscuit dough tube, cut into small pieces
- 1 tablespoon parsley, chopped

Directions:
In your Slow cooker, mix onion with chicken, oregano, salt, pepper, cream of chicken soup, chicken stock, bay leaf and thyme, stir, cover and cook on High for 3 hours. Discard bay leaf, add celery, carrots, peas, garlic and biscuit pieces, stir, cover and cook on High for 1 hour. Add parmesan and parsley, divide into bowls and serve.

Nutrition: calories 311, fat 4, fiber 7, carbs 12, protein 5

Balsamic Chicken

Preparation time: 10 minutes | Cooking time: 5 hours | Servings: 4

Ingredients:
- 2 cups Brussels sprouts, halved
- 4 chicken breasts, skinless and boneless
- 2 cups red potatoes, halved
- ¼ cup balsamic vinegar
- ¼ cup honey
- 1/3 cup chicken stock
- 2 tablespoons Dijon mustard
- ½ teaspoon rosemary, dried
- 1 teaspoon thyme, dried
- ½ teaspoon oregano, dried
- ½ teaspoon red pepper flakes, crushed
- 2 garlic cloves, minced
- Salt and black pepper to the taste
- 1 tablespoon parsley, chopped

Directions:

In your Slow cooker, mix Brussels sprouts with chicken, potatoes, vinegar, honey, stock, mustard, rosemary, thyme, oregano, pepper flakes, garlic, salt and pepper, stir, cover and cook on Low for 5 hours. Add parsley, stir, divide between plates and serve.

Nutrition: calories 244, fat 4, fiber 6, carbs 12, protein 3

Buffalo Chicken

Preparation time: 10 minutes | Cooking time: 4 hours | Servings: 12

Ingredients:
- 2 pounds chicken breasts, skinless and boneless
- Salt and black pepper to the taste
- 2 garlic cloves, minced
- 1 cup cayenne sauce
- ½ cup chicken stock
- ½ packet ranch seasoning mix
- 1 tablespoon brown sugar

Directions:

In your Slow cooker, mix chicken with salt, pepper, garlic, cayenne sauce, stock, seasoning and sugar, toss, cover and cook on High for 4 hours. Divide between plates and serve.

Nutrition: calories 273, fat 6, fiber 7, carbs 17, protein 2

Alfredo Chicken

Preparation time: 10 minutes | Cooking time: 2 hours 30 minutes | Servings: 4

Ingredients:
- 1 pound chicken breasts, skinless and boneless
- 4 tablespoons soft butter
- 1 cup chicken stock
- 2 cups heavy cream
- Salt and black pepper to the taste
- ½ teaspoon Italian seasoning
- ½ teaspoon garlic powder
- 1/3 cup parmesan, grated
- ½ pound rigatoni

Directions:

In your Slow cooker, mix chicken with butter, stock, cream, salt, pepper, garlic powder and Italian seasoning, stir, cover and cook on High for 2 hours. Shred meat, return to slow cooker, also add rigatoni and parmesan, cover and cook on High for 30 minutes more. Divide between plates and serve.

Nutrition: calories 300, fat 7, fiber 7, carbs 17, protein 12

Slow Cooked Chicken

Preparation time: 10 minutes | *Cooking time:* 8 hours | *Servings:* 8

Ingredients:
- 1 big chicken
- 1 garlic head, peeled
- 1 yellow onion, chopped
- 1 lemon, sliced
- 1 tablespoons sweet paprika
- A pinch of sea salt
- Black pepper to the taste
- 1 teaspoon thyme, dried
- 2 carrots, chopped

Directions:

Stuff your chicken with half of the garlic and with half of the lemon slices and rub with salt, pepper, thyme and paprika both outside and inside. Put the carrots on the bottom of your Slow cooker, add the rest of the garlic, onion and lemon slices, place the bird on top, cover and cook on Low for 8 hours. Transfer chicken to a platter, carve and serve with a side salad.

Nutrition: calories 200, fat 4, fiber 3, carbs 8, protein 16

Slow Cooker Turkey Breast

Preparation time: 10 minutes | *Cooking time:* 8 hours | *Servings:* 4

Ingredients:
- 3 pounds turkey breast, bone in
- 1 cup black figs
- 3 sweet potatoes, cut into wedges
- ½ cup dried cherries, pitted
- 2 white onions, cut into wedges
- ½ cup dried cranberries
- 1/3 cup water
- 1 teaspoon onion powder
- 1 teaspoon garlic powder
- 1 teaspoon parsley flakes
- 1 teaspoon thyme, dried
- 1 teaspoon sage, dried
- 1 teaspoon paprika, dried
- A pinch of sea salt
- Black pepper to the taste

Directions:

Put the turkey breast in your Slow cooker, add sweet potatoes, figs, cherries, onions, cranberries, water, parsley, garlic and onion powder, thyme, sage, paprika, salt and pepper, toss, cover and cook on Low for 8 hours. Discard bone from turkey breast, slice meat, divide between plates and serve with the veggies, figs, cherries and berries on the side.

Nutrition: calories 320, fat 5, fiber 4, carbs 12, protein 15

Chicken Breasts

Preparation time: 10 minutes | *Cooking time:* 6 hours | *Servings:* 4

Ingredients:
- 2 red bell peppers, chopped
- 2 pounds chicken breasts, skinless and boneless
- 4 garlic cloves, minced
- 1 yellow onion, chopped
- 2 teaspoons paprika
- 1 cup low sodium chicken stock
- 2 teaspoons cinnamon powder
- ¼ teaspoon nutmeg, ground

Directions:

In a bowl, mix bell peppers with chicken breasts, garlic, onion, paprika, cinnamon and nutmeg, toss to coat, transfer everything to your Slow cooker, add stock, cover and cook on Low for 6 hours. Divide chicken and veggies between plates and serve.

Nutrition: calories 250, fat 3, fiber 5, carbs 12, protein 10

Turkey Breast and Cranberries

Preparation time: 10 minutes | Cooking time: 6 hours | Servings: 6

Ingredients:
- 6 pound turkey breast, skin and bone in
- 4 cups cranberries, rinsed
- 3 apples, peeled, cored and sliced
- ½ cup balsamic vinegar
- ½ cup maple syrup
- A pinch of sea salt
- Black pepper to the taste

Directions:
Put the turkey breast in your Slow cooker, add cranberries, apple slices, a pinch of salt, black pepper, vinegar and maple syrup, toss a bit, cover and cook on Low for 6 hours. Slice turkey breast and divide between plates, mash cranberries and apples a bit, add them on top of the meat and serve right away.

Nutrition: calories 360, fat 4, fiber 3, carbs 9, protein 20

Thyme Chicken

Preparation time: 10 minutes | Cooking time: 6 hours | Servings: 6

Ingredients:
- 1 whole chicken
- 5 thyme springs, chopped
- 2 celery stalks, chopped
- 3 garlic cloves, minced
- 2 carrots, chopped
- 1 yellow onion, chopped
- A pinch of white pepper
- Juice of 1 lemon

Directions:
Put half of the thyme, garlic, celery, onion and carrots in your Slow cooker, add the chicken on top and season with a pinch of white pepper. Add the rest of the thyme, onion, garlic, celery and carrots on top, drizzle the lemon juice, cover and cook on Low for 6 hours. Divide chicken between plates and serve.

Nutrition: calories 230, fat 4, fiber 2, carbs 16, protein 6

Mediterranean Chicken

Preparation time: 10 minutes | Cooking time: 4 hours | Servings: 4

Ingredients:
- 1 and ½ pounds chicken breast, skinless and boneless
- Juice of 2 lemons
- 1 rosemary spring, chopped
- ¼ cup olive oil
- 3 garlic cloves, minced
- A pinch of salt and black pepper
- 1 cucumber, chopped
- 1 cup kalamata olives, pitted and sliced
- ¼ cup red onions, chopped
- 2 tablespoons red vinegar

Directions:
In your Slow cooker, mix chicken with lemon juice, rosemary, oil, garlic, salt and pepper, stir, cover and cook on High for 4 hours. Transfer chicken to a cutting board, shred with 2 forks, and transfer to a bowl, add cucumber, olives, onion and vinegar, toss, divide between plates and serve.

Nutrition: calories 240, fat 3, fiber 3, carbs 12, protein 3

Chicken Chowder

Preparation time: 10 minutes | Cooking time: 6 hours | Servings: 4

Ingredients:
- 3 chicken breasts, skinless and boneless and cubed
- 4 cups chicken stock
- 1 sweet potato, cubed
- 8 ounces canned green chilies, chopped
- 1 yellow onion, chopped
- 15 ounces coconut cream
- 1 teaspoon garlic powder
- 4 bacon strips, cooked and crumbled
- A pinch of salt and black pepper
- 1 tablespoon parsley, chopped

Directions:
In your Slow cooker, mix chicken with stock, sweet potato, green chilies, onion, garlic powder, salt and pepper, stir, cover and cook on Low for 5 hours and 40 minutes. Add coconut cream and parsley, stir, cover and cook on Low for 20 minutes more. Ladle chowder into bowls, sprinkle bacon on top and serve.

Nutrition: calories 232, fat 3, fiber 7, carbs 14, protein 7

Chicken Thighs Delight

Preparation time: 10 minutes | Cooking time: 6 hours | Servings: 6

Ingredients:
- 2 pounds chicken thighs, boneless and skinless
- 1 yellow onion, chopped
- 3 carrots, chopped
- 1/3 cup prunes, dried and halved
- 3 garlic cloves, minced
- ½ cup green olives, pitted
- 2 teaspoon sweet paprika
- 1 teaspoon cinnamon, ground
- 2 teaspoons cumin, ground
- 2 teaspoons ginger, grated
- 1 cup chicken stock
- A pinch of salt and black pepper
- 1 tablespoon cilantro, chopped

Directions:
In your Slow cooker, mix chicken with onion, carrots, prunes, garlic, olives, paprika, cinnamon, cumin, ginger, stock, salt and pepper, stir, cover and cook on Low for 6 hours. Divide between plates, sprinkle cilantro on top and serve.

Nutrition: calories 384, fat 12, fiber 4, carbs 20, protein 34

Chicken with Peach and Orange Sauce

Preparation time: 10 minutes | Cooking time: 6 hours | Servings: 8

Ingredients:
- 6 chicken breasts, skinless and boneless
- 12 ounces orange juice
- 2 tablespoons lemon juice
- 15 ounces canned peaches and their juice
- 1 teaspoon soy sauce

Directions:
In your slow cooker, mix chicken with orange juice, lemon juice, peaches and soy sauce, toss, cover and cook on Low for 6 hours. Divide chicken breasts on plates, drizzle peach and orange sauce all over and serve.

Nutrition: calories 251, fat 4, fiber 6, carbs 18, protein 14

Flavored Chicken Thighs

Preparation time: 10 minutes | Cooking time: 4 hours | Servings: 4

Ingredients:
- 2 pounds chicken thighs
- Salt and black pepper to the taste
- ¾ cup sweet Bbq sauce
- A pinch of cayenne pepper
- 1 cup apple juice
- 1 teaspoon red pepper, crushed
- 2 teaspoons paprika
- ½ teaspoon basil, dried

Directions:
In your Slow cooker, mix chicken with salt, pepper, bbq sauce, cayenne, apple juice, red pepper, paprika and basil, stir, cover and cook on High for 4 hours. Divide everything between plates and serve.

Nutrition: calories 200, fat 3, fiber 6, carbs 10, protein 17

Classic Turkey Gumbo

Preparation time: 10 minutes | Cooking time: 7 hours | Servings: 4

Ingredients:
- 1 pound turkey wings
- Salt and black pepper to the taste
- 5 ounces water
- 1 yellow onion, chopped
- 1 yellow bell pepper, chopped
- 3 garlic cloves, chopped
- 2 tablespoons chili powder
- 1 and ½ teaspoons cumin, ground
- A pinch of cayenne pepper
- 2 cups veggies stock

Directions:
In your Slow cooker, mix turkey with salt, pepper, onion, bell pepper, garlic, chili powder, cumin, cayenne and stock, stir, cover and cook on Low for 7 hours. Divide everything between plates and serve.

Nutrition: calories 232, fat 4, fiber 7, carbs 17, protein 20

Chinese Duck

Preparation time: 10 minutes | Cooking time: 8 hours | Servings: 6

Ingredients:
- 1 duck, chopped in medium pieces
- 1 celery stalk, chopped
- 2 carrots, chopped
- 2 cups chicken stock
- Salt and black pepper to the taste
- 1 tablespoon ginger, grated

Directions:
In your Slow cooker, mix duck with celery, carrots, stock, salt, pepper and ginger, stir, cover and cook on Low for 8 hours. Divide duck, ginger sauce between plates, and serve.

Nutrition: calories 200, fat 3, fiber 6, carbs 19, protein 17

Turkey Wings and Veggies

Preparation time: 10 minutes | Cooking time: 8 hours | Servings: 4

Ingredients:

- 4 turkey wings
- 1 yellow onion, chopped
- 1 carrot, chopped
- 3 garlic cloves, minced
- 1 celery stalk, chopped
- 1 cup chicken stock
- Salt and black pepper to the taste
- 2 tablespoons olive oil
- A pinch of rosemary, dried
- 2 bay leaves
- A pinch of sage, dried
- A pinch of thyme, dried

Directions:

In your Slow cooker, mix turkey with onion, carrot, garlic, celery, stock, salt, pepper, oil, rosemary, sage, thyme and bay leaves, toss, cover and cook on Low for 8 hours. Divide between plates and serve hot.

Nutrition: calories 223, fat 5, fiber 7, carbs 18, protein 14

Turkey Wings and Sauce

Preparation time: 10 minutes | Cooking time: 8 hours | Servings: 4

Ingredients:

- 4 turkey wings
- 2 tablespoons butter, melted
- 2 tablespoons olive oil
- 1 and ½ cups cranberries, dried
- Salt and black pepper to the taste
- 1 yellow onion, roughly chopped
- 1 cup walnuts
- 1 cup orange juice
- 1 bunch thyme, chopped

Directions:

In your slow cooker mix butter with oil, turkey wings, cranberries, salt, pepper, onion, walnuts, orange juice and thyme, stir a bit, cover and cook on Low for 8 hours. Divide turkey and orange sauce between plates and serve.

Nutrition: calories 300, fat 12, fiber 4, carbs 17, protein 1

Chicken and Sauce

Preparation time: 10 minutes | Cooking time: 4 hours | Servings: 8

Ingredients:

- 1 whole chicken, cut into medium pieces
- 1 tablespoon olive oil
- 1 and ½ tablespoons lemon juice
- 1 cup chicken stock
- 1 tablespoon cilantro, chopped
- 1 teaspoon cinnamon powder
- Salt and black pepper to the taste
- 1 tablespoon sweet paprika
- 1 teaspoon onion powder

Directions:

In your Slow cooker, mix chicken with oil, lemon juice, stock, cilantro, cinnamon, salt, pepper, paprika and onion powder, stir, cover and cook on High for 4 hours. Divide chicken between plates and serve with cooking sauce drizzled on top.

Nutrition: calories 261, fat 4, fiber 6, carbs 12, protein 22

Chicken Wings and Mint Sauce

Preparation time: 20 minutes | *Cooking time:* 4 hours | *Servings:* 6

Ingredients:
- 18 chicken wings, cut into halves
- 1 tablespoon turmeric
- 1 tablespoon cumin, ground
- 1 tablespoon ginger, grated
- 1 tablespoon coriander, ground
- 1 tablespoon paprika
- A pinch of cayenne pepper
- Salt and black pepper to the taste
- 2 tablespoons olive oil

For the sauce:
- Juice of ½ lime
- 1 cup mint leaves
- 1 small ginger piece, chopped
- ¾ cup cilantro
- 1 tablespoon olive oil
- 1 tablespoon water
- 1 Serrano pepper

Directions:
In a bowl, mix 1-tablespoon ginger with cumin, coriander, paprika, turmeric, salt, pepper, cayenne and 2 tablespoons oil and stir well. Add chicken wings pieces to this mix, toss to coat well and keep in the fridge for 20 minutes. Add marinated wings to your Slow cooker, cook on High for 4 hours and transfer to a bowl. In your blender, mix mint with cilantro, 1 small ginger pieces, and juice of ½ lime, 1-tablespoon olive oil, salt, pepper, water and Serrano pepper and blend very well. Serve your chicken wings with this sauce on the side.

Nutrition: calories 230, fat 5, fiber 1, carbs 12, protein 9

Lemony Chicken

Preparation time: 10 minutes | *Cooking time:* 4 hours | *Servings:* 6

Ingredients:
- 1 whole chicken, cut into medium pieces
- Salt and black pepper to the taste
- Zest of 2 lemons
- Juice of 2 lemons
- Lemon rinds from 2 lemons

Directions:
Put chicken pieces in your Slow cooker, season with salt and pepper to the taste, drizzle lemon juice, add lemon zest and lemon rinds, cover and cook on High for 4 hours. Discard lemon rinds, divide chicken between plates, drizzle sauce from the slow cooker over it and serve.

Nutrition: calories 334, fat 24, fiber 2, carbs 4.5, protein 27

Chicken and Paprika Sauce

Preparation time: 10 minutes | *Cooking time:* 4 hours | *Servings:* 5

Ingredients:
- 1 tablespoon coconut oil
- 3 and ½ pounds chicken breasts
- 1 cup chicken stock
- 1 and ¼ cups yellow onion, chopped
- 1 tablespoon lime juice
- ¼ cup coconut milk
- 2 teaspoons sweet paprika
- 1 teaspoon red pepper flakes
- 2 tablespoons green onions, chopped
- Salt and black pepper to the taste

Directions:
Heat up a pan with the oil over medium-high heat, add chicken, cook for 2 minutes on each side and transfer to your Slow cooker. Add stock, onion, lime juice, coconut milk, sweet paprika, pepper flakes, salt, pepper and green onions, toss, cover and cook on High for 4 hours. Divide everything between plates and serve.

Nutrition: calories 250, fat 4, fiber 3, carbs 12, protein 6

Chicken Thighs and Mushrooms

Preparation time: 10 minutes | Cooking time: 4 hours | Servings: 4

Ingredients:
- 4 chicken thighs
- 2 cups mushrooms, sliced
- ¼ cup butter, melted
- Salt and black pepper to the taste
- ½ teaspoon onion powder
- ½ teaspoon garlic powder
- ½ cup water
- 1 teaspoon Dijon mustard
- 1 tablespoon tarragon, chopped

Directions:
In your Slow cooker, mix chicken with butter, mushrooms, salt, pepper, onion powder, garlic powder, water, mustard and tarragon, toss, cover and cook on High for 4 hours. Divide between plates and serve.

Nutrition: calories 453, fat 32, fiber 6, carbs 15, protein 36

Creamy Duck Breast

Preparation time: 10 minutes | Cooking time: 4 hours | Servings: 1

Ingredients:
- 1 medium duck breast, skin scored
- 1 tablespoon sugar
- 1 tablespoon heavy cream
- 2 tablespoons butter, melted
- ½ teaspoon orange extract
- Salt and black pepper to the taste
- 1 cup baby spinach
- ¼ teaspoon sage, dried

Directions:
In your Slow cooker, mix butter with duck breast, cream, sugar, orange extract, salt, pepper and sage, stir, cover and cook on High for 4 hours. Add spinach, toss, leave aside for a few minutes, transfer to a plate and serve.

Nutrition: calories 567, fat 56, fiber 1, carbs 22, protein 35

Duck Breast and Veggies

Preparation time: 10 minutes | Cooking time: 4 hours | Servings: 2

Ingredients:
- 2 duck breasts, skin on and thinly sliced
- 2 zucchinis, sliced
- 1 tablespoon olive oil
- 1 spring onion stack, chopped
- 1 radish, chopped
- 2 green bell peppers, chopped
- Salt and black pepper to the taste

Directions:
In your Slow cooker, mix duck with oil, salt and pepper and toss. Add zucchinis, onion, radish and bell peppers, cover and cook on High for 4 hours. Divide everything between plates and serve.

Nutrition: calories 450, fat 23, fiber 3, carbs 14, protein 50

Turkey Soup

Preparation time: 10 minutes | Cooking time: 3 hours | Servings: 4

Ingredients:

- 3 celery stalks, chopped
- 1 yellow onion, chopped
- 1 tablespoon olive oil
- 6 cups turkey stock
- Salt and black pepper to the taste
- ¼ cup parsley, chopped
- 3 cups baked spaghetti squash, chopped
- 3 cups turkey, cooked and shredded

Directions:

In your Slow cooker, mix oil with celery, onion, stock, salt, pepper, squash, turkey and parsley, stir, cover, cook on High for 3 hours, ladle into bowls and serve.

Nutrition: calories 250, fat 4, fiber 1, carbs 13, protein 10

Slow Cooked Turkey Delight

Preparation time: 10 minutes | Cooking time: 4 hours | Servings: 8

Ingredients:

- 4 cups zucchinis, cut with a spiralizer
- 1 egg, whisked
- 3 cups cabbage, shredded
- 3 cups turkey meat, cooked and shredded
- ½ cup turkey stock
- ½ cup cream cheese
- 1 teaspoon poultry seasoning
- 2 cup cheddar cheese, grated
- ½ cup parmesan cheese, grated
- Salt and black pepper to the taste
- ¼ teaspoon garlic powder

Directions:

In your Slow cooker, mix the egg, stock, cream, parmesan, cheddar cheese, salt, pepper, poultry seasoning and garlic powder and stir. Add turkey meat, cabbage and zucchini noodles, cover and cook on High for 4 hours. Divide between plates and serve.

Nutrition: calories 240, fat 15, fiber 1, carbs 13, protein 25

Turkey Curry

Preparation time: 10 minutes | Cooking time: 4 hours | Servings: 4

Ingredients:

- 18 ounces turkey meat, minced
- 3 ounces spinach
- 20 ounces canned tomatoes, chopped
- 2 tablespoons coconut oil
- 2 tablespoons coconut cream
- 2 garlic cloves, minced
- 2 yellow onions, sliced
- 1 tablespoon coriander, ground
- 2 tablespoons ginger, grated
- 1 tablespoons turmeric powder
- 1 tablespoon cumin, ground
- Salt and black pepper to the taste
- 2 tablespoons chili powder

Directions:

In your Slow cooker, mix turkey with spinach, tomatoes, oil, cream, garlic, onion, coriander, ginger, turmeric, cumin, chili, salt and pepper, stir, cover and cook on High for 4 hours. Divide into bowls and serve.

Nutrition: calories 240, fat 4, fiber 3, carbs 13, protein 12

Chicken and Mustard Sauce

Preparation time: 10 minutes | Cooking time: 4 hours | Servings: 3

Ingredients:
- 8 bacon strips, cooked and chopped
- 1/3 cup Dijon mustard
- Salt and black pepper to the taste
- 1 cup yellow onion, chopped
- 1 tablespoon olive oil
- 1 and ½ cups chicken stock
- 3 chicken breasts, skinless and boneless
- ¼ teaspoon sweet paprika

Directions:
In a bowl, mix paprika with mustard, salt and pepper and stir well. Spread this on chicken breasts and massage. Heat up a pan with the oil over medium-high heat, add chicken breasts, cook for 2 minutes on each side and transfer to your Slow cooker. Add stock, bacon and onion, stir, cover and cook on High for 4 hours. Divide chicken between plates, drizzle mustard sauce all over and serve.

Nutrition: calories 223, fat 8, fiber 1, carbs 13, protein 26

Chicken Casserole

Preparation time: 10 minutes | Cooking time: 4 hours | Servings: 8

Ingredients:
- 1 and ½ pounds chicken breast, skinless and boneless and cubed
- Salt and black pepper to the taste
- 1 egg
- 1 cup flour
- ¼ cup parmesan, grated
- ½ teaspoon garlic powder
- 1 and ½ teaspoons parsley, dried
- ½ teaspoon basil, dried
- 4 tablespoons olive oil
- 4 cups spaghetti squash, already cooked
- 6 ounces mozzarella, shredded
- 1 and ½ cups marinara sauce

Directions:
In a bowl, mix flour with parmesan, salt, pepper, garlic powder and 1 teaspoon parsley and stir. In another bowl, whisk the egg with a pinch of salt and pepper. Dip chicken in egg and then in flour mix. Heat up a pan with 3 tablespoons oil over medium-high heat, add chicken, cook until they are golden on both sides and transfer to your Slow cooker. In a bowl, mix spaghetti squash with salt, pepper, dried basil, 1 tablespoon oil and the rest of the parsley and stir. Spread this over chicken, add marinara sauce, top with mozzarella, cover and cook on High for 4 hours. Leave casserole aside to cool down a bit, divide between plates and serve.

Nutrition: calories 300, fat 6, fiber 3, carbs 15, protein 28

Chicken and Broccoli Casserole

Preparation time: 10 minutes | Cooking time: 4 hours | Servings: 4

Ingredients:
- 3 cups cheddar cheese, grated
- 10 ounces broccoli florets
- 3 chicken breasts, skinless, boneless, cooked and cubed
- 1 cup mayonnaise
- 1 tablespoon olive oil
- 1/3 cup chicken stock
- Salt and black pepper to the taste
- Juice of 1 lemon

Directions:
Grease your Slow cooker with the oil and arrange chicken pieces on the bottom. Spread broccoli florets and then half of the cheese. In a bowl, mix mayo with stock, salt, pepper and lemon juice. Pour this over chicken, sprinkle the rest of the cheese, cover and cook on High for 4 hours. Serve hot.

Nutrition: calories 320, fat 5, fiber 4, carbs 16, protein 25

Red Chicken Soup

Preparation time: 10 minutes | Cooking time: 3 hours | Servings: 4

Ingredients:
- 3 tablespoons butter, melted
- 4 ounces cream cheese
- 2 cups chicken meat, cooked and shredded
- 1/3 cup red sauce
- 4 cups chicken stock
- Salt and black pepper to the taste
- ½ cup sour cream
- ¼ cup celery, chopped

Directions:

In your blender, mix stock with red sauce, cream cheese, butter, salt, pepper and sour cream, pulse well and transfer to your Slow cooker. Add celery and chicken, stir, cover and cook on High for 3 hours. Divide into bowls and serve.

Nutrition: calories 400, fat 23, fiber 5, carbs 15, protein 30

Citrus Chicken

Preparation time: 10 minutes | Cooking time: 4 hours | Servings: 4

Ingredients:
- 2 pounds chicken thighs, skinless, boneless and cut into pieces
- Salt and black pepper to the taste
- 3 tablespoons olive oil
- ¼ cup flour

For the sauce:
- 2 tablespoons fish sauce
- 1 and ½ teaspoons orange extract
- 1 tablespoon ginger, grated
- ¼ cup orange juice
- 1 tablespoon orange zest
- ¼ teaspoon sesame seeds
- 2 tablespoons scallions, chopped
- ½ teaspoon coriander, ground
- 1 cup water
- ¼ teaspoon red pepper flakes
- 2 tablespoons soy sauce

Directions:

In a bowl, mix flour, salt, and pepper, stir, add chicken pieces and toss to coat well. Heat up a pan with the oil over medium heat, add chicken, cook until they are golden on both sides and transfer to your Slow cooker. In your blender, mix orange juice with ginger, fish sauce, soy sauce, stevia, orange extract, water and coriander and blend well. Pour this over the chicken, sesame seeds, orange zest, scallions and pepper flakes, stir, cover and cook on High for 4 hours. Divide between plates and serve.

Nutrition: calories 423, fat 20, fiber 5, carbs 12, protein 45

Chicken and Creamy Mushroom Sauce

Preparation time: 10 minutes | Cooking time: 4 hours | Servings: 4

Ingredients:
- 8 chicken thighs
- Salt and black pepper to the taste
- 1 yellow onion, chopped
- 1 tablespoon olive oil
- 4 bacon strips, cooked and chopped
- 4 garlic cloves, minced
- 10 ounces cremini mushrooms, halved
- 2 cups white chardonnay wine
- 1 cup whipping cream
- A handful parsley, chopped

Directions:

Heat up a pan with the oil over medium heat, add chicken pieces, season them with salt and pepper, cook until they brown and transfer to your Slow cooker. Add onions, garlic, bacon, mushrooms, wine, parsley and cream, stir, cover and cook on High for 4 hours. Divide between plates and serve.

Nutrition: calories 340, fat 10, fiber 7, carbs 14, protein 24

Slow Cooker Chicken Breasts

Preparation time: 10 minutes | Cooking time: 4 hours | Servings: 4

Ingredients:
- 6 chicken breasts, skinless and boneless
- Salt and black pepper to the taste
- ¼ cup jalapenos, chopped
- 5 bacon slices, chopped
- 8 ounces cream cheese
- ¼ cup yellow onion, chopped
- ½ cup mayonnaise
- ½ cup parmesan, grated
- 1 cup cheddar cheese, grated

Directions:
Arrange chicken breasts in your Slow cooker add salt, pepper, jalapenos, bacon, cream cheese, onion, mayo, parmesan and cheddar, cover and cook on High for 4 hours. Divide between plates and serve.

Nutrition: calories 340, fat 12, fiber 2, carbs 15, protein 20

Chicken and Sour Cream

Preparation time: 10 minutes | Cooking time: 4 hours | Servings: 4

Ingredients:
- 4 chicken thighs
- Salt and black pepper to the taste
- 1 teaspoon onion powder
- ¼ cup sour cream
- 2 tablespoons sweet paprika

Directions:
In a bowl, mix paprika with salt, pepper and onion powder and stir. Season chicken pieces with this paprika mix, place them in your Slow cooker, add sour cream, toss, cover and cook on High for 4 hours. Divide everything between plates and serve.

Nutrition: calories 384, fat 31, fiber 2, carbs 11, protein 33

Chicken Stroganoff

Preparation time: 10 minutes | Cooking time: 4 hours | Servings: 4

Ingredients:
- 2 garlic cloves, minced
- 8 ounces mushrooms, roughly chopped
- ¼ teaspoon celery seeds, ground
- 1 cup chicken stock
- 1 cup coconut milk
- 1 yellow onion, chopped
- 1 pound chicken breasts, cut into medium pieces
- 1 and ½ teaspoons thyme, dried
- 2 tablespoons parsley, chopped
- Salt and black pepper to the tasted
- Already cooked pasta for serving

Directions:
Put chicken in your Slow cooker, add salt, pepper, onion, garlic, mushrooms, coconut milk, celery seeds, stock, half of the parsley and thyme, stir, cover and cook on High for 4 hours. Add the rest of the parsley and pasta, toss, divide between plates and serve.

Nutrition: calories 364, fat 22, fiber 2, carbs 14, protein 24

Pepperoni Chicken

Preparation time: 10 minutes | *Cooking time:* 6 hours | *Servings:* 6

Ingredients:

- 14 ounces pizza sauce
- 1 tablespoon olive oil
- 4 medium chicken breasts, skinless and boneless
- Salt and black pepper to the taste
- 1 teaspoon oregano, dried
- 6 ounces mozzarella, sliced
- 1 teaspoon garlic powder
- 2 ounces pepperoni, sliced

Directions:

Put the chicken in your Slow cooker, add pizza sauce, oil, salt, pepper, garlic powder, pepperoni and mozzarella, cover and cook on Low for 6 hours. Toss everything, divide between plates and serve.

Nutrition: calories 320, fat 10, fiber 6, carbs 14, protein 27

Chicken and Green Onion Sauce

Preparation time: 10 minutes | *Cooking time:* 4 hours | *Servings:* 4

Ingredients:

- 2 tablespoons butter, melted
- 4 green onions, chopped
- 4 chicken breast halves, skinless and boneless
- Salt and black pepper to the taste
- 8 ounces sour cream

Directions:

In your Slow cooker, mix chicken with melted butter, green onion, salt, pepper and sour cream, cover and cook on High for 4 hours. Divide chicken between plates, drizzle green onions sauce all over and serve.

Nutrition: calories 200, fat 7, fiber 2, carbs 11, protein 20

Mushrooms Stuffed With Chicken

Preparation time: 10 minutes | *Cooking time:* 3 hours | *Servings:* 6

Ingredients:

- 16 ounces button mushroom caps
- 4 ounces cream cheese
- ¼ cup carrot, chopped
- 1 teaspoon ranch seasoning mix
- 4 tablespoons hot sauce
- ¾ cup blue cheese, crumbled
- ¼ cup red onion, chopped
- ½ cup chicken meat, ground
- Salt and black pepper to the taste
- Cooking spray

Directions:

In a bowl, mix cream cheese with blue cheese, hot sauce, ranch seasoning, salt, pepper, chicken, carrot and red onion, stir and stuff mushrooms with this mix. Grease your Slow cooker with cooking spray, add stuffed mushrooms, cover and cook on High for 3 hours. Divide mushrooms between plates and serve.

Nutrition: calories 240, fat 4, fiber 1, carbs 12, protein 7

Creamy Spinach and Artichoke Chicken

Preparation time: 10 minutes | Cooking time: 4 hours | Servings: 4

Ingredients:

- 4 ounces cream cheese
- 4 chicken breasts, boneless and skinless
- 10 ounces canned artichoke hearts, chopped
- 10 ounces spinach
- ½ cup parmesan, grated
- 1 tablespoon dried onion
- 1 tablespoon garlic, dried
- Salt and black pepper to the taste
- 4 ounces mozzarella, shredded

Directions:

Place chicken breasts in your Slow cooker season with salt and pepper, add artichokes, cream cheese, spinach, onion, garlic, spinach and top with mozzarella. Cover slow cooker, cook on High for 4 hours, toss, divide everything between plates and serve.

Nutrition: calories 450, fat 23, fiber 1, carbs 14, protein 39

Chicken Meatloaf

Preparation time: 10 minutes | Cooking time: 4 hours 20 minutes | Servings: 8

Ingredients:

- 1 cup marinara sauce
- 2 pound chicken meat, ground
- 2 tablespoons parsley, chopped
- 4 garlic cloves, minced
- 2 teaspoons onion powder
- 2 teaspoons Italian seasoning
- Salt and black pepper to the taste
-
- Cooking spray

For the filling:

- ½ cup ricotta cheese
- 1 cup parmesan, grated
- 1 cup mozzarella, shredded
- 2 teaspoons chives, chopped
- 2 tablespoons parsley, chopped
- 1 garlic clove, minced

Directions:

In a bowl, mix chicken with half of the marinara sauce, salt, pepper, Italian seasoning, 4 garlic cloves, onion powder and 2 tablespoons parsley and stir well. In another bowl, mix ricotta with half of the parmesan, half of the mozzarella, chives, 1 garlic clove, salt, pepper and 2 tablespoons parsley and stir well. Grease your Slow cooker with cooking spray, add half of the chicken mix into the slow cooker and spread evenly. Add cheese filling, spread, top with the rest of the meat, spread again, cover and cook on High for 4 hours. Spread the rest of the marinara sauce, the rest of the parmesan and the mozzarella over the meatloaf, cover slow cooker and cook on High for 20 minutes more. Leave meatloaf to cool down, slice, divide between plates and serve.

Nutrition: calories 273, fat 14, fiber 1, carbs 14, protein 28

Thai Peanut Chicken

Preparation time: 10 minutes | Cooking time: 4 hours | Servings: 8

Ingredients:
- 2 and ½ pounds chicken thighs and drumsticks
- 1 tablespoon soy sauce
- 1 tablespoon apple cider vinegar
- A pinch of red pepper flakes
- Salt and black pepper to the taste
- ½ teaspoon ginger, ground
- 1/3 cup peanut butter
- 1 garlic clove, minced
- ½ cup warm water

Directions:
In your blender mix peanut butter with water, soy sauce, salt, pepper, pepper flakes, ginger, garlic and vinegar and blend well. Pat dry chicken pieces arrange them in your Slow cooker, cover and cook on High for 4 hours. Divide between plates and serve.

Nutrition: calories 375, fat 12, fiber 1, carbs 10, protein 42

Flavored Chicken Drumsticks

Preparation time: 10 minutes | Cooking time: 4 hours | Servings: 4

Ingredients:
- 1 bunch lemongrass, bottom removed and trimmed
- 1-inch piece ginger root, chopped
- 4 garlic cloves, minced
- 2 tablespoons fish sauce
- 3 tablespoons soy sauce
- 1 teaspoon Chinese five spice
- 10 chicken drumsticks
- 1 cup coconut milk
- Salt and black pepper to the taste
- 1 teaspoon butter, melted
- ¼ cup cilantro, chopped
- 1 yellow onion, chopped
- 1 tablespoon lime juice

Directions:
In your food processor, mix lemongrass with ginger, garlic, soy sauce, fish sauce, five spice and coconut milk and pulse well. In your Slow cooker, mix chicken with butter, onion, salt, pepper, lime juice and lemongrass mix, cover and cook on High for 4 hours. Toss chicken, divide everything between plates and serve with cilantro sprinkled on top.

Nutrition: calories 400, fat 12, fiber 3, carbs 6, protein 20

Chicken Thighs and Romano Cheese Mix

Preparation time: 10 minutes | Cooking time: 4 hours | Servings: 4

Ingredients:
- 6 chicken things, boneless and skinless and cut into medium chunks
- Salt and black pepper to the taste
- ½ cup white flour
- 2 tablespoons olive oil
- 10 ounces tomato sauce
- 1 teaspoon white wine vinegar
- 4 ounces mushrooms, sliced
- 1 tablespoon sugar
- 1 tablespoon oregano, dried
- 1 teaspoon garlic, minced
- 1 teaspoon basil, dried
- 1 yellow onion, chopped
- 1 cup Romano cheese, grated

Directions:
Grease your Slow cooker with the oil, add chicken pieces, onion, garlic, salt, pepper and flour and toss. Add tomato sauce, vinegar, mushrooms, sugar, oregano, basil and cheese, cover and cook on High for 4 hours. Divide between plates and serve.

Nutrition: calories 430, fat 12, fiber 6, carbs 25, protein 60

Slow Cooker Chicken Thighs

Preparation time: 10 minutes | Cooking time: 4 hours | Servings: 6

Ingredients:
- 5 pounds chicken thighs
- Salt and black pepper to the taste
- ½ cup white vinegar
- 1 teaspoon black peppercorns
- 4 garlic cloves, minced
- 3 bay leaves
- ½ cup soy sauce

Directions:

In your Slow cooker mix chicken, vinegar, soy sauce, salt, pepper, garlic, peppercorns and bay leaves, stir, cover and cook on High for 4 hours. Discard bay leaves, stir, divide chicken mix between plates and serve.

Nutrition: calories 430, fat 12, fiber 3, carbs 10, protein 36

Chicken and Tomatillos

Preparation time: 10 minutes | Cooking time: 4 hours | Servings: 6

Ingredients:
- 1 pound chicken thighs, skinless and boneless
- 2 tablespoons olive oil
- 1 yellow onion, chopped
- 1 garlic clove, minced
- 4 ounces canned green chilies, chopped
- A handful cilantro, chopped
- Salt and black pepper to the taste
- 15 ounces canned tomatillos, chopped
- 5 ounces canned garbanzo beans, drained
- 15 ounces rice, cooked
- 5 ounces tomatoes, chopped
- 15 ounces cheddar cheese, grated
- 4 ounces black olives, pitted and chopped

Directions:

In your Slow cooker, mix oil with onions, garlic, chicken, chilies, salt, pepper, cilantro and tomatillos, stir, cover the slow cooker and cook on High for 3 hours Take chicken out of the slow cooker, shred, return to slow cooker, add rice, beans, cheese, tomatoes and olives, cover and cook on High for 1 more hour. Divide between plates and serve.

Nutrition: calories 300, fat 11, fiber 3, carbs 14, protein 30

Duck and Potatoes

Preparation time: 10 minutes | Cooking time: 6 hours | Servings: 4

Ingredients:
- 1 duck, cut into small chunks
- Salt and black pepper to the taste
- 1 potato, cut into cubes
- 1-inch ginger root, sliced
- 4 garlic cloves, minced
- 4 tablespoons sugar
- 4 tablespoons soy sauce
- 2 green onions, chopped
- 4 tablespoons sherry wine
- ¼ cup water

Directions:

In your Slow cooker mix duck pieces with garlic, ginger, green onions, soy sauce, sugar, wine, a pinch of salt, black pepper, potatoes and water, stir, cover and cook on Low for 6 hours. Divide between plates and serve right away,

Nutrition: calories 245, fat 12, fiber 1, carbs 6, protein 16

Chicken Salad

Preparation time: 55 minutes | Cooking time: 3 hours | Servings: 2

Ingredients:
- 1 chicken breast, skinless and boneless
- 1 cup chicken stock
- 2 cups water
- Salt and black pepper to the taste
- 1 tablespoon mustard
- 3 garlic cloves, minced
- 1 tablespoon balsamic vinegar
- 1 tablespoon honey
- 3 tablespoons olive oil
- Mixed salad greens
- A handful cherry tomatoes, halved

Directions:
In a bowl, mix water with salt to the taste, add chicken, stir, cover and keep in the fridge for 45 minutes. Drain chicken, add to your Slow cooker, add stock, salt and pepper, cover and cook on High for 3 hours. Transfer chicken breast to a cutting board and cut into thin strips. In a bowl, mix garlic with salt and pepper to the taste, mustard, honey, vinegar and olive oil and whisk very well. In a salad bowl, mix chicken strips with salad greens and tomatoes. Drizzle the vinaigrette on top and serve.

Nutrition: calories 200, fat 4, fiber 6, carbs 15, protein 12

Hot Chicken Wings

Preparation time: 10 minutes | Cooking time: 4 hours | Servings: 6

Ingredients:
- 12 chicken wings, cut into 24 pieces
- 1 pound celery, cut into thin matchsticks
- ¼ cup honey
- 4 tablespoons hot sauce
- Salt to the taste
- ¼ cup tomato puree
- 1 cup yogurt
- 1 tablespoon parsley, chopped

Directions:
In your Slow cooker, mix chicken with celery, honey, hot sauce, salt, tomato puree and parsley, stir, cover and cook on High for 3 hours and 30 minutes. Add yogurt, toss, cover, cook on High for 30 minutes more, divide between plates and serve

Nutrition: calories 300, fat 4, fiber 4, carbs 14, protein 22

Coca Cola Chicken

Preparation time: 10 minutes | Cooking time: 4 hours | Servings: 4

Ingredients:
- 1 yellow onion, minced
- 4 chicken drumsticks
- 1 tablespoon balsamic vinegar
- 1 chili pepper, chopped
- 15 ounces coca cola
- Salt and black pepper to the taste
- 2 tablespoons olive oil

Directions:
Heat up a pan with the oil over medium-high heat, add chicken pieces, stir and brown them on all sides and then transfer them to your Slow cooker. Add vinegar, chili, coca cola, salt and pepper, cover and cook on High for 4 hours. Divide chicken mix between plates and serve.

Nutrition: calories 372, fat 14, fiber 3, carbs 20, protein 15

Duck Chili

Preparation time: 10 minutes | *Cooking time:* 7 hours | *Servings:* 4

Ingredients:
- 1 pound northern beans, soaked and rinsed
- 1 yellow onion, cut into half
- 1 garlic heat, top trimmed off
- Salt and black pepper to the taste
- 2 cloves
- 1 bay leaf
- 6 cups water

For the duck:
- 1 pound duck, ground
- 1 tablespoon vegetable oil
- 1 yellow onion, minced
- 2 carrots, chopped
- Salt and black pepper to the taste
- 4 ounces canned green chilies and their juice
- 1 teaspoon brown sugar
- 15 ounces canned tomatoes and their juices, chopped
- A handful cilantro, chopped

Directions:
Put the beans in your Slow cooker, add the whole onion, garlic head, cloves, bay leaf, the water and salt to the taste, stir, cover, cook on High for 4 hours, drain them and put them in a bowl. Clean the slow cooker, add oil, carrots, chopped onion, season with salt and pepper, duck, chilies, tomatoes and sugar, stir, cover and cook on High for 3 hours more. Divide on duck and beans mix plates and serve with cilantro sprinkled on top.

Nutrition: calories 283, fat 15, fiber 2, carbs 16, protein 22

Cuban Chicken

Preparation time: 10 minutes | *Cooking time:* 4 hours | *Servings:* 4

Ingredients:
- 4 gold potatoes, cut into medium chunks
- 1 yellow onion, thinly sliced
- 4 big tomatoes, cut into medium chunks
- 1 chicken, cut into 8 pieces
- Salt and black pepper to the taste
- 2 bay leaves
- Salt and black pepper to the taste

Directions:
In your instant slow cooker, mix potatoes with onion, chicken, tomato, bay leaves, salt and pepper, stir well, cover and cook on High for 4 hours. Add more salt and pepper, discard bay leaves, divide chicken mix between plates and serve.

Nutrition: calories 263, fat 2, fiber 1, carbs 27, protein 14

Chicken and Lentils

Preparation time: 10 minutes | *Cooking time:* 4 hours | *Servings:* 4

Ingredients:
- 8 ounces bacon, cooked and chopped
- 2 tablespoons olive oil
- 1 cup yellow onion, chopped
- 8 ounces lentils, dried
- 2 carrots, chopped
- 12 parsley springs, chopped
- Salt and black pepper to the taste
- 2 bay leaves
- 2 and ½ pounds chicken pieces
- 1 quart chicken stock
- 2 teaspoons sherry vinegar

Directions:
Grease your Slow cooker with the oil, add bacon, onions, lentils, carrots, chicken pieces, parsley, bay leaves, stock, salt and pepper to the taste, stir, cover and cook at High for 4 hours Transfer chicken to a cutting board, discard skin and bones, shred meat and return to the slow cooker, add vinegar, stir, divide between plates and serve.

Nutrition: calories 321, fat 3, fiber 12, carbs 29, protein 16

Chicken and Chickpeas

Preparation time: 10 minutes | Cooking time: 4 hours | Servings: 4

Ingredients:
- 1 yellow onion, chopped
- 2 tablespoons butter
- 4 garlic cloves, minced
- 1 tablespoon ginger, grated
- 1 and ½ teaspoon paprika
- 1 tablespoon cumin, ground
- 1 and ½ teaspoons coriander, ground
- 1 teaspoon turmeric, ground
- Salt and black pepper to the taste
- A pinch of cayenne pepper
- 15 ounces canned tomatoes, crushed
- ¼ cup lemon juice
- 1 pound spinach, chopped
- 3 pounds chicken drumsticks and thighs
- ½ cup cilantro, chopped
- ½ cup chicken stock
- 15 ounces canned chickpeas, drained
- ½ cup heavy cream

Directions:
Grease your Slow cooker with the butter, add onion, garlic, ginger, paprika, cumin, coriander, turmeric, salt, pepper, cayenne, tomatoes, lemon juice, spinach, chicken, stock, chickpeas and heavy cream, cover and cook on High for 4 hours. Add cilantro, stir everything, divide between plates and serve.

Nutrition: calories 300, fat 4, fiber 6, carbs 30, protein 17

Chicken and Sauce

Preparation time: 10 minutes | Cooking time: 5 hours | Servings: 4

Ingredients:
- 1 chicken, cut into medium pieces
- Salt and black pepper to the taste
- 1 tablespoon olive oil
- ½ teaspoon sweet paprika
- ¼ cup white wine
- ½ teaspoon marjoram, dried
- ¼ cup chicken stock
- 2 tablespoons white vinegar
- ¼ cup apricot preserves
- 1 and ½ teaspoon ginger, grated
- 2 tablespoons honey

Directions:
In your Slow cooker, mix chicken with salt, pepper, oil, paprika, wine, marjoram, stock, vinegar, apricots preserves, ginger and honey, stir, cover and cook on Low for 5 hours. Divide between plates and serve.

Nutrition: calories 230, fat 3, fiber 5, carbs 12, protein 22

Goose Mix

Preparation time: 10 minutes | Cooking time: 5 hours | Servings: 5

Ingredients:
- 1 goose breast, fat trimmed off and cut into pieces
- 1 goose leg, skinless
- 1 goose thigh, skinless
- Salt and black pepper to the taste
- 3 and ½ cups water
- 2 teaspoons garlic, minced
- 1 yellow onion, chopped
- 12 ounces canned mushroom cream

Directions:
In your Slow cooker mix goose breast, leg and thigh with onion, salt, pepper, water, garlic, and mushroom cream, stir, cover and cook on Low for 5 hours. Divide into bowls and serve.

Nutrition: calories 272, fat 4, fiber 7, carbs 16, protein 22

Goose and Sauce

Preparation time: 10 minutes | Cooking time: 5 hours | Servings: 4

Ingredients:
- 1 goose breast half, skinless, boneless and cut into thin slices
- ¼ cup olive oil
- 1 sweet onion, chopped
- 2 teaspoons garlic, chopped
- Salt and black pepper to the taste
- ¼ cup sweet chili sauce

Directions:

In your Slow cooker, mix goose with oil, onion, garlic, salt, pepper and chili sauce, stir, cover and cook on Low for 5 hours. Divide between plates and serve.

Nutrition: calories 192, fat 4, fiber 8, carbs 12, protein 22

Chicken Liver Stew

Preparation time: 5 minutes | Cooking time: 2 hours | Servings: 8

Ingredients:
- 1 teaspoon olive oil
- ¾ pound chicken livers
- 1 yellow onion, chopped
- ¼ cup tomato sauce
- 1 bay leaf
- 1 tablespoons capers
- 1 tablespoon butter
- A pinch of salt and black pepper

Directions:

In your Slow cooker, mix oil with chicken livers, onion, tomato sauce, bay leaf, capers, butter, salt and pepper, stir, cover and cook on High for 1 hour and 30 minutes. Divide between plates and serve

Nutrition: calories 152, fat 4, fiber 2, carbs 5, protein 7

Slow cooker Meat Recipes

Beef Roast

Preparation time: 10 minutes | *Cooking time:* 8 hours | *Servings:* 8

Ingredients:

- 2 and ½ pounds beef chuck roast
- 2 cups carrots, chopped
- 1 tablespoon olive oil
- 2 cup yellow onion, chopped
- 1 cup celery, chopped
- ¾ cup dill pickle, chopped
- ½ cup dry red wine
- 1/3 cup German mustard
- A pinch of salt and black pepper
- ¼ teaspoon cloves, ground
- 2 tablespoons flour
- 2 bay leaves
- 2 tablespoons beef stock

Directions:

In your Slow cooker, mix beef with carrots, oil, onion, celery, pickle, wine, mustard, salt, pepper, cloves, flour, bay leaves and stock, toss well, cover and cook on Low for 8 hours. Slice roast, divide between plates, drizzle cooking juices all over and serve.

Nutrition: calories 256, fat 7, fiber 2, carbs 10, protein 31

Fennel Short Ribs

Preparation time: 10 minutes | *Cooking time:* 10 hours | *Servings:* 6

Ingredients:

- 3 pounds beef short ribs
- 1 fennel bulb, cut into wedges
- 2 yellow onions, cut into wedges
- 1 cup carrot, sliced
- 14 ounces canned tomatoes, chopped
- 1 cup dry red wine
- 2 tablespoons tapioca, crushed
- 2 tablespoons tomato paste
- 1 teaspoon rosemary, dried
- Salt and black pepper to the taste
- 4 garlic cloves, minced

Directions:

In your Slow cooker, mix short ribs with fennel, onions, carrots, tomatoes, wine, tapioca, tomato paste, salt, pepper, rosemary and garlic, cover and cook on Low for 10 hours. Divide everything between plates and serve.

Nutrition: calories 432, fat 14, fiber 6, carbs 25, protein 42

Apple Pork Ribs

Preparation time: 12 minutes | Cooking time: 6 hours | Servings: 4

Ingredients:
- 4 cups vinegar
- 4 pounds pork ribs
- 2 tablespoons apple cider vinegar
- 2 cups water
- 3 tablespoons soy sauce
- Salt and black pepper to the taste
- A pinch of garlic powder
- A pinch of Chinese 5 spice

Directions:

Put your ribs in a big bowl, add white vinegar and water, toss, cover and keep in the fridge for 12 hours. Drain ribs, season with salt and black pepper to the taste, garlic powder and Chinese 5 spice, rub well, transfer them to your slow cooker and add apple cider vinegar and soy sauce as well. Toss to coat well, cover slow cooker and cook on High for 6 hours. Divide ribs between plates and serve.

Nutrition: calories 300, fat 6, fiber 3, carbs 15, protein 15

Beef Chuck Roast

Preparation time: 10 minutes | Cooking time: 8 hours 30 minutes | Servings: 6

Ingredients:
- 4 pounds beef chuck roast
- 1 cup veggie stock
- 1 tablespoon coconut oil
- 1 bay leaf
- 10 thyme springs
- 4 garlic cloves, minced
- 1 carrot, roughly chopped
- 1 yellow onion, roughly chopped
- 2 celery ribs, roughly chopped
- 1 cauliflower head, florets separated
- Salt and black pepper to the taste

Directions:

Season beef with salt and some black pepper. Heat up a pan with the oil over medium-high heat, add beef roast, brown for 5 minutes on each side, transfer to your slow cooker, add thyme springs, stock, bay leaf, garlic, celery, onion and carrot, cover and cook on Low for 8 hours. Add cauliflower, cover slow cooker again, cook on High for 20 minutes more, divide everything between plates and serve.

Nutrition: calories 340, fat 5, fiber 3, carbs 14, protein 22

Pork Chops and Pineapple Mix

Preparation time: 10 minutes | Cooking time: 6 hours | Servings: 4

Ingredients:
- 2 pounds pork chops
- 1/3 cup sugar
- ¼ cup ketchup
- 15 ounces pineapple, cubed
- 3 tablespoons apple cider vinegar
- 5 tablespoons soy sauce
- 2 teaspoons garlic, minced
- 3 tablespoons flour

Directions:

In a bowl, mix ketchup with sugar, vinegar, soy sauce and tapioca, whisk well, add pork chops, toss well and transfer everything to your Slow cooker Add pineapple and garlic, toss again, cover, cook on Low for 6 hours, divide everything between plates and serve.

Nutrition: calories 345, fat 5, fiber 6, carbs 13, protein 14

Mexican Pork Roast

Preparation time: 10 minutes | Cooking time: 8 hours | Servings: 6

Ingredients:
- 1 yellow onion, chopped
- 2 tablespoons sweet paprika
- 15 ounces canned tomato, roasted and chopped
- 1 teaspoon cumin, ground
- 1 teaspoon coconut oil
- Salt and black pepper to the taste
- A pinch of nutmeg, ground
- 5 pounds pork roast
- Juice of 1 lemon
- ¼ cup apple cider vinegar

Directions:
Heat up a pan with the oil over medium-high heat, add onions, brown them for a couple of minutes, transfer them to your slow cooker, add paprika, tomato, cumin, nutmeg, lemon juice, vinegar, salt, pepper and pork, toss coat and cook on Low for 8 hours. Slice roast, arrange on plates and serve with tomatoes and onions mix.

Nutrition: calories 350, fat 5, fiber 2, carbs 13, protein 24

Pork Tenderloin and Apples

Preparation time: 10 minutes | Cooking time: 8 hours | Servings: 4

Ingredients:
- A pinch of nutmeg, ground
- 2 pounds pork tenderloin
- 4 apples, cored and sliced
- 2 tablespoons maple syrup

Directions:
Place apples in your Slow cooker, sprinkle nutmeg over them, add pork tenderloin, sprinkle some more nutmeg, drizzle the maple syrup, cover and cook on Low for 8 hours. Slice pork tenderloin, divide it between plates and serve with apple slices and cooking juices.

Nutrition: calories 400, fat 4, fiber 5, carbs 12, protein 20

Lamb Leg and Sweet Potatoes

Preparation time: 10 minutes | Cooking time: 8 hours | Servings: 4

Ingredients:
- 2 tablespoons olive oil
- 1 lamb leg, bone in
- 1 garlic head, peeled and cloves separated
- 5 sweet potatoes, cubed
- 5 rosemary springs
- 2 cups chicken stock
- Salt and black pepper to the taste

Directions:
Rub your lamb leg with the oil, salt and pepper. Place the potatoes and the garlic cloves on the bottom of your slow cooker, add lamb leg, rosemary springs and stock, cover and cook lamb on Low for 8 hours. Divide lamb and potatoes between plates and serve.

Nutrition: calories 350, fat 6, fiber 5, carbs 12, protein 22

Lamb Shanks

Preparation time: 10 minutes | *Cooking time:* 8 hours 10 minutes | *Servings:* 4

Ingredients:
- 4 lamb shanks, trimmed
- 3 tablespoons olive oil
- 1 onion, chopped
- 2 carrots, chopped
- 15 ounces canned tomatoes, chopped
- 2 garlic cloves, minced
- 2 celery stalks, chopped
- 2 tablespoons tomato paste
- 2 cups veggie stock
- 1 tablespoon rosemary, dried
- 1 tablespoon thyme, dried
- 1 tablespoon oregano, dried
- Salt and black pepper to the taste

Directions:

Heat up a pan with 2 tablespoons oil over medium-high heat, add lamb shanks, brown them for 5 minutes on each side and transfer to your Slow cooker. Add the rest of the oil, onion, carrots, tomatoes, garlic, celery, tomato paste, stock, rosemary, thyme, salt and pepper, stir, cover and cook on Low for 8 hours. Divide everything between plates and serve.

Nutrition: calories 350, fat 5, fiber 4, carbs 12, protein 20

Flavored Pork Roast

Preparation time: 10 minutes | *Cooking time:* 4 hours | *Servings:* 6

Ingredients:
- 1 pound sweet potatoes, chopped
- 3 and ½ pounds pork roast
- 8 medium carrots, chopped
- Salt and black pepper to the taste
- 15 ounces canned tomatoes, chopped
- 1 yellow onion, chopped
- Grated zest and juice of 1 lemon
- 4 garlic cloves, minced
- 3 bay leaves
- Black pepper to the taste
- ½ cup kalamata olives, pitted

Directions:

Put potatoes in your Slow cooker, add carrots, tomatoes, onions, lemon juice and zest, pork, bay leaves, salt, black pepper and garlic, stir, cover and cook on High for 4 hours. Transfer meat to a cutting board, slice it and divide between plates. Discard bay leaves, transfer veggies to a bowl, mash them, mix with olives, add next to the meat and serve right away!

Nutrition: calories 250, fat 4, fiber 3, carbs 6, protein 13

Beef and Onions

Preparation time: 10 minutes | *Cooking time:* 6 hours 5 minutes | *Servings:* 6

Ingredients:
- 3 pounds beef roast, trimmed and boneless
- 1 tablespoon Italian seasoning
- Salt and black pepper to the taste
- 1 garlic clove, minced
- 1/3 cup sun-dried tomatoes, chopped
- ½ cup beef stock
- ½ cup kalamata olives pitted and halved
- 1 cup yellow onions chopped
- 1 tablespoon olive oil

Directions:

Heat up a pan with the oil over medium-high heat, add beef, brown for 5 minutes, season with black pepper and Italian seasoning, transfer to your slow cooker, add tomatoes, onions and stock, cover and cook on Low for 6 hours. Transfer meat to a cutting board, slice, divide between plates, add onions and tomatoes on the side and serve with cooking juices on top.

Nutrition: calories 300, fat 5, fiber 5, carbs 12, protein 25

Artichoke Lamb Shoulder

Preparation time: 10 minutes | Cooking time: 8 hours 10 minutes | Servings: 6

Ingredients:
- 3 pounds lamb shoulder, boneless
- 3 onions, roughly chopped
- 1 tablespoon olive oil
- 1 tablespoon oregano, chopped
- 6 garlic cloves, minced
- 1 tablespoon lemon zest, grated
- Salt and black pepper to the taste
- ½ teaspoon allspice
- 1 and ½ cups veggie stock
- 14 ounces canned artichoke hearts, chopped
- ¼ cup tomato paste
- 2 tablespoons parsley, chopped

Directions:
Heat up a pan with the oil over medium-high heat, add lamb, brown for 5 minutes on each side, transfer to your Slow cooker, add onion, lemon zest, garlic, a pinch of salt, pepper, oregano, allspice, stock and tomato paste, cover and cook on Low for 7 hours and 45 minutes. Add artichokes and parsley, stir gently, cover, cook on Low for 15 more minutes, divide into bowls and serve hot.

Nutrition: calories 370, fat 4, fiber 5, carbs 12, protein 16

Chinese Pork Shoulder

Preparation time: 10 minutes | Cooking time: 7 hours | Servings: 4

Ingredients:
- 2 and ½ pounds pork shoulder
- 4 cups chicken stock
- ½ cup soy sauce
- ¼ cup white vinegar
- 2 tablespoons chili sauce
- Juice of 1 lime
- 1 tablespoon ginger, grated
- 1 tablespoon Chinese 5 spice
- 2 cups portabella mushrooms, sliced
- Salt and black pepper to the taste
- 1 zucchini, sliced

Directions:
In your Slow cooker, mix pork with stock, soy sauce, vinegar, chili sauce, lime juice, ginger, 5 spice, mushrooms, zucchini, salt and pepper, toss a bit, cover and cook on Low for 7 hours. Transfer pork shoulder to a cutting board, shred using 2 forks, return to Slow cooker, toss with the rest of the ingredients, and divide between plates and serve.

Nutrition: calories 342, fat 6, fiber 8, carbs 27, protein 18

Roast and Pepperoncinis

Preparation time: 10 minutes | Cooking time: 8 hours | Servings: 4

Ingredients:
- 5 pounds beef chuck roast
- 1 tablespoon soy sauce
- 10 pepperoncinis
- 1 cup beef stock
- 2 tablespoons butter, melted

Directions:
In your Slow cooker, mix beef roast with soy sauce, pepperoncinis, stock and butter, toss well, cover and cook on Low for 8 hours. Transfer roast to a cutting board, shred using 2 forks, return to slow cooker, toss, divide between plates and serve.

Nutrition: calories 362, fat 4, fiber 8, carbs 17, protein 17

Balsamic Beef Cheeks

Preparation time: 10 minutes | Cooking time: 4 hours | Servings: 4

Ingredients:
- 4 beef cheeks, halved
- 2 tablespoons olive oil
- Salt and black pepper to the taste
- 1 white onion, chopped
- 4 garlic cloves, minced
- 2 cup beef stock
- 5 cardamom pods
- 1 tablespoon balsamic vinegar
- 3 bay leaves
- 7 cloves
- 2 vanilla beans, split
- 1 and ½ tablespoons tomato paste
- 1 carrot, sliced

Directions:
In your Slow cooker, mix beef cheeks with the oil, salt, pepper, onion, garlic, stock, cardamom, vinegar, bay leaves, cloves, vanilla beans, tomato paste and carrot, toss, cover, cook on High for 4 hours, divide between plates and serve.

Nutrition: calories 321, fat 5, fiber 7, carbs 18, protein 12

Seasoned Beef

Preparation time: 10 minutes | Cooking time: 8 hours | Servings: 6

Ingredients:
- 4 pounds beef roast
- 2 cups beef stock
- 2 sweet potatoes, cubed
- 6 carrots, sliced
- 7 celery stalks, chopped
- 1 yellow onion, chopped
- 1 tablespoon onion powder
- 1 tablespoon garlic powder
- 1 tablespoon sweet paprika
- Salt and black pepper to the taste

Directions:
In your Slow cooker, beef with stock, sweet potatoes, carrots, celery, onion, onion powder, garlic powder, paprika, salt and pepper, stir, cover, cook on Low for 8 hours, slice roast, divide between plates, drizzle sauce from the slow cooker all and serve with the veggies on the side.

Nutrition: calories 372, fat 6, fiber 12, carbs 19, protein 11

Beef Soup

Preparation time: 10 minutes | Cooking time: 6 hours | Servings: 4

Ingredients:
- 1 pound beef, ground
- 2 cups cauliflower, chopped
- 1 cup yellow onion, chopped
- 2 red bell peppers, chopped
- 15 ounces tomato sauce
- 15 ounces tomatoes, chopped
- 3 cups beef stock
- ½ teaspoon basil, dried
- ½ teaspoon oregano, dried
- 3 garlic cloves, minced
- Salt and black pepper to the taste

Directions:
In your Slow cooker, mix beef with cauliflower, onion, bell peppers, tomato sauce, tomatoes, stock, basil, oregano, garlic, salt and pepper, stir, cover, cook on Low for 6 hours, ladle into bowls and serve.

Nutrition: calories 214, fat 6, fiber 6, carbs 18, protein 7

Thai Cocoa Pork

Preparation time: 10 minutes | Cooking time: 7 hours | Servings: 4

Ingredients:
- 2 tablespoons olive oil
- 2 pounds pork butt, boneless and cubed
- Salt and black pepper to the taste
- 6 eggs, hard-boiled, peeled and sliced
- 1 tablespoon cilantro, chopped
- 1 tablespoon coriander seeds
- 1 tablespoon ginger, grated
- 1 tablespoon black peppercorns
- 2 tablespoons garlic, chopped
- 2 tablespoons five spice powder
- 1 and ½ cup soy sauce
- 2 tablespoons cocoa powder
- 1 yellow onion, chopped
- 8 cups water

Directions:
In your Slow cooker, mix oil with pork, salt, pepper, cilantro, coriander, ginger, peppercorns, garlic, five spice, soy sauce, cocoa, onion and water, toss, cover and cook on Low for 7 hours. Divide stew into bowls, add egg slices on top and serve.

Nutrition: calories 400, fat 10, fiber 9, carbs 28, protein 22

Herbed and Cinnamon Beef

Preparation time: 10 minutes | Cooking time: 5 hours | Servings: 6

Ingredients:
- 4 pounds beef brisket
- 2 oranges, sliced
- 2 garlic cloves, minced
- 2 yellow onions, thinly sliced
- 11 ounces celery, thinly sliced
- 1 tablespoon dill, dried
- 3 bay leaves
- 4 cinnamon sticks, cut into halves
- Salt and black pepper to the taste
- 17 ounces veggie stock

Directions:
In your Slow cooker, mix beef with orange slices, garlic, onion, celery, dill, bay leaves, cinnamon, salt, pepper and stock, stir, cover and cook on High for 5 hours. Divide beef mix between plates and serve.

Nutrition: calories 300, fat 5, fiber 7, carbs 12, protein 4

Beef Brisket and Turnips Mix

Preparation time: 10 minutes | Cooking time: 8 hours | Servings: 6

Ingredients:
- 2 and ½ pounds beef brisket
- 4 cups veggie stock
- 2 bay leaves
- 3 garlic cloves, chopped
- 4 carrots, chopped
- 1 cabbage head cut into 6 wedges
- Salt and black pepper to the taste
- 3 turnips, cut into quarters

Directions:
In your Slow cooker, mix beef with stock, bay leaves, garlic, carrots, cabbage, salt, pepper and turnips, stir, cover and cook on Low for 8 hours. Divide beef brisket and turnips mix between plates and serve.

Nutrition: calories 321, fat 15, fiber 4, carbs 18, protein 19

Veggie Lamb Shanks

Preparation time: 10 minutes | Cooking time: 7 hours | Servings: 4

Ingredients:
- 4 lamb shanks
- 2 tablespoons olive oil
- 1 yellow onion, finely chopped
- 3 carrots, roughly chopped
- 2 garlic cloves, minced
- 2 tablespoons tomato paste
- 1 teaspoon oregano, dried
- 1 tomato, roughly chopped
- 4 ounces chicken stock
- Salt and black pepper to the taste

Directions:
In your Slow cooker, mix lamb with oil, onion, garlic, carrots, tomato paste, tomato, oregano, stock, salt and pepper, stir, cover and cook on Low for 7 hours. Divide into bowls and serve hot.

Nutrition: calories 400, fat 13, fiber 4, carbs 17, protein 24

Lamb Leg and Mushrooms Mix

Preparation time: 10 minutes | Cooking time: 8 hours | Servings: 8

Ingredients:
- 1 and ½ pounds lamb leg, bone-in
- 2 carrots, sliced
- ½ pounds mushrooms, sliced
- 4 tomatoes, chopped
- 1 small yellow onion, chopped
- 6 garlic cloves, minced
- 2 tablespoons tomato paste
- 1 teaspoon olive oil
- Salt and black pepper to the taste
- A handful parsley, chopped

Directions:
In your Slow cooker, mix lamb with carrots, mushrooms, tomatoes, onion, garlic, tomato paste, oil, salt, pepper and parsley, toss, cover, cook on Low for 8 hours, divide between plates and serve.

Nutrition: calories 372, fat 12, fiber 7, carbs 18, protein 22

Smoky Lamb

Preparation time: 10 minutes | Cooking time: 7 hours | Servings: 4

Ingredients:
- 4 lamb chops
- 1 teaspoon liquid smoke
- 1 cup green onions, chopped
- 2 cups canned tomatoes, chopped
- 1 teaspoon smoked paprika
- 2 tablespoons garlic, minced
- Salt and black pepper to the taste
- 3 cups beef stock

Directions:
In your Slow cooker, mix lamb with liquid smoke, green onions, tomatoes, paprika, garlic, salt, pepper and stock, stir, cover and cook on Low for 7 hours. Divide everything between plates and serve.

Nutrition: calorie 364, fat 12, fiber 7, carbs 29, protein 28

Sausage and Onion Jam

Preparation time: 15 minutes | Cooking time: 3 hours | Servings: 6

Ingredients:
- 6 pork sausages
- 2 tablespoons olive oil
- ½ cup onion jam
- 3 ounces beef stock
- 3 ounces water
- Salt and black pepper to the taste
- 1 tablespoon flour

Directions:
In your slow cooker, mix sausages with oil, onion jam, stock, water, salt, pepper and flour, toss, cover, cook on High for 3 hours, divide everything between plates and serve.

Nutrition: calories 431, fat 15, fiber 4, carbs 29, protein 13

French Lamb

Preparation time: 10 minutes | Cooking time: 8 hours | Servings: 4

Ingredients:
- 4 lamb chops
- 1 cup onion, chopped
- 2 cups canned tomatoes, chopped
- 1 cup leek, chopped
- 2 tablespoons garlic, minced
- 1 teaspoon herbs de Provence
- Salt and black pepper to the taste
- 3 cups water

Directions:
In your Slow cooker mix, lamb chops with onion, tomatoes, leek, garlic, herbs de Provence, salt, pepper and water, stir, cover and cook on Low for 8 hours. Divide lamb and veggies between plates and serve.

Nutrition: calories 430, fat 12, fiber 8, carbs 20, protein 18

Jamaican Pork

Preparation time: 10 minutes | Cooking time: 7 hours | Servings: 12

Ingredients:
- ½ cup beef stock
- 1 tablespoon olive oil
- ¼ cup keto Jamaican spice mix
- 4 pounds pork shoulder

Directions:
In your Slow cooker, mix pork with oil and Jamaican spice mix, rub well, add stock, cover and cook on Low for 7 hours. Slice roast and serve.

Nutrition: calories 400, fat 6, fiber 7, carbs 10, protein 25

Pork Sirloin Salsa Mix

Preparation time: 10 minutes | Cooking time: 8 hours | Servings: 4

Ingredients:
- 2 pounds pork sirloin roast, cut into thick slices
- Salt and black pepper to the taste
- 2 teaspoons garlic powder
- 2 teaspoons cumin, ground
- 1 tablespoon olive oil
- 16 ounces green chili tomatillo salsa

Directions:

In your Slow cooker, mix pork with cumin, salt, pepper and garlic powder and rub well. Add oil and salsa, toss, cover and cook on Low for 8 hours. Divide between plates and serve hot.

Nutrition: calories 400, fat 7, fiber 6, carbs 10, protein 25

Beef Meatloaf

Preparation time: 10 minutes | Cooking time: 4 hours | Servings: 4

Ingredients:
- 2 pounds beef, ground
- ¼ cup parmesan, grated
- ¼ cup yellow onion, chopped
- 1 egg, whisked
- Salt and black pepper to the taste
- 1 tablespoon garlic, minced
- ½ teaspoon thyme, dried
- 1 tablespoon olive oil
- 1 yellow onion, chopped
- 1 cup ketchup
- ½ cup beef stock

Directions:

In a bowl mix beef, cheese, ¼ cup onion, egg, thyme, salt and pepper, stir and shape a meatloaf. Heat up a pan with the oil over medium-high heat, add onion, stock and ketchup, stir, bring to a simmer and transfer to your Slow cooker. Add meatloaf, cover and cook on High for 4 hours. Slice meatloaf, divide between plates and serve with the sauce drizzled all over.

Nutrition: calories 363, fat 6, fiber 3, carbs 12, protein 14

Pork Loin and Cauliflower Rice

Preparation time: 10 minutes | Cooking time: 8 hours | Servings: 6

Ingredients:
- 3 bacon slices, cooked and chopped
- 3 carrots, chopped
- 2 pounds pork loin roast
- 1 rhubarb stalk, chopped
- 2 bay leaves
- ¼ cup red wine vinegar
- 4 garlic cloves, minced
- Salt and black pepper to the taste
- ¼ cup olive oil
- 1 tablespoon garlic powder
- 1 tablespoon Italian seasoning
- 24 ounces cauliflower rice
- 1 teaspoon turmeric powder
- 1 cup beef stock

Directions:

In your Slow cooker, mix bacon with carrots, pork, rhubarb, bay leaves, vinegar, salt, pepper, oil, garlic powder, Italian seasoning, stock and turmeric, toss, cover and cook on Low for 7 hours. Add cauliflower rice, cover, cook on Low for 1 more hour, divide between plates and serve.

Nutrition: calories 310, fat 6, fiber 3, carbs 14, protein 10

Lamb and Spinach Salad

Preparation time: 10 minutes | Cooking time: 7 hours | Servings: 4

Ingredients:
- 1 tablespoon olive oil
- 2 garlic cloves, minced
- 2 cups veggie stock
- 3 pounds leg of lamb, bone discarded
- Salt and black pepper to the taste
- 1 teaspoon cumin, ground
- ¼ teaspoon thyme, dried

For the salad:
- 4 ounces feta cheese, crumbled
- ½ cup pecans, toasted
- 2 cups spinach
- 1 and ½ tablespoons lemon juice
- ¼ cup olive oil
- 1 cup mint, chopped

Directions:
In your Slow cooker, mix 1 tablespoon oil with garlic, stock, lamb, salt, pepper, cumin and thyme, cover and cook on Low for 7 hours. Leave leg of lamb aside to cool down, slice and divide between plates. In a bowl, mix spinach with mint, feta cheese, ¼ cup olive oil, lemon juice, pecans, salt and pepper, toss and divide next to lamb slices. Serve right away.

Nutrition: calories 234, fat 20, fiber 3, carbs 12, protein 32

Lamb Stew

Preparation time: 10 minutes | Cooking time: 7 hours | Servings: 4

Ingredients:
- 1 yellow onion, chopped
- 2 pounds lamb meat, cubed
- 2 tablespoons butter, melted
- 3 carrots, chopped
- 2 cups beef stock
- 1 tomato, chopped
- 1 garlic clove, minced
- Salt and black pepper to the taste
- 2 rosemary springs, chopped
- 1 teaspoon thyme, chopped

Directions:
In your Slow cooker, mix butter with onion, lamb, carrots, tomato, garlic, thyme, rosemary, salt, pepper and stock, stir, cover and cook on Low for 7 hours. Divide into bowls and serve.

Nutrition: calories 260, fat 12, fiber 6, carbs 10, protein 36

Sausages and Celeriac Mash

Preparation time: 15 minutes | Cooking time: 6 hours | Servings: 6

Ingredients:

For the mash
- 2 celeriac, peeled and cut into cubes
- Salt and black pepper to the taste
- 1 teaspoon mustard powder
- 1 tablespoon butter, melted
- 4 ounces warm coconut milk
- 6 ounces water
- 1 tablespoon cheddar cheese, grated

For the sausages:
- 6 pork sausages
- 2 tablespoons olive oil
- ½ cup onion jam
- 2 ounces veggie stock
- 3 ounces water
- Salt and black pepper to the taste

Directions:
Put celeriac cubes in your Slow cooker, add 6 ounces water, salt and pepper, stir, cover and cook on High for 2 hours. Add mustard powder, butter, milk and cheese, stir really well and leave aside for now. Clean the Slow cooker, add oil, sausages, onion jam, 3 ounces water, stock, salt and pepper, cover and cook on High for 3 hours. Divide sausages on plates, add mashed celeriac on the side and serve with some of the cooking juices from the slow cooker drizzled all over.

Nutrition: calories 421, fat 12, fiber 4, carbs 7, protein 15

Pork Belly and Applesauce

Preparation time: 10 minutes | Cooking time: 8 hours | Servings: 6

Ingredients:
- 2 tablespoons sugar
- 1 tablespoon lemon juice
- 1 quart water
- 17 ounces apples, cored and cut into wedges
- 2 pounds pork belly, scored
- Salt and black pepper to the taste
- A drizzle of olive oil

Directions:
In your blender, mix water with apples, lemon juice and sugar and pulse well Put the pork belly in your Slow cooker, add oil, salt, pepper and applesauce, toss, cover and cook on Low for 8 hours. Slice pork roast, divide between plates and serve with the applesauce on top.

Nutrition: calories 456, fat 34, fiber 4, carbs 10, protein 25

Stuffed Pork

Preparation time: 2 minutes | Cooking time: 8 hours | Servings: 4

Ingredients:
- Zest of 2 limes
- Juice of 1 orange
- Zest of 1 orange
- Juice of 2 limes
- 4 teaspoons garlic, minced
- ¾ cup olive oil
- 1 cup cilantro, chopped
- 1 cup mint, chopped
- 1 teaspoon oregano, dried
- Salt and black pepper to the taste
- 2 teaspoons cumin, ground
- 4 pork loin steaks
- 2 pickles, chopped
- 4 ham slices
- 6 Swiss cheese slices
- 2 tablespoons mustard

Directions:
In your food processor, mix lime zest and juice with orange zest and juice, garlic, oil, cilantro, mint, oregano, cumin, salt and pepper and blend well. Season steaks with salt and pepper, place them in a bowl, add marinade you've made, toss to coat and leave aside for a couple of hours. Place steaks on a working surface, divide pickles, cheese, mustard and ham on them, roll, secure with toothpicks, put them in your Slow cooker, cover and cook on Low for 7 hours. Divide between plates and serve.

Nutrition: calories 270, fat 7, fiber 2, carbs 13, protein 20

Pork Rolls

Preparation time: 10 minutes | Cooking time: 8 hours | Servings: 6

Ingredients:
- 6 prosciutto slices
- 2 tablespoons parsley, chopped
- 1 pound pork cutlets, thinly sliced and flattened
- 1/3 cup ricotta cheese
- 1 tablespoon coconut oil
- ¼ cup yellow onion, chopped
- 3 garlic cloves, minced
- 2 tablespoons parmesan, grated
- 15 ounces canned tomatoes, chopped
- 1/3 cup chicken stock
- Salt and black pepper to the taste
- ½ teaspoon Italian seasoning

Directions:
Place prosciutto slices on top of each pork cutlet, then divide ricotta, parsley and parmesan, roll each pork piece and secure with a toothpick. In your Slow cooker, mix oil with onion, garlic, tomatoes, stock, Italian seasoning, salt, pepper and pork rolls, cover and cook on Low for 8 hours. Divide between plates and serve.

Nutrition: calories 280, fat 17, fiber 1, carbs 14, protein 34

Pork Chops

Preparation time: 10 minutes | Cooking time: 8 hours | Servings: 4

Ingredients:
- 2 yellow onions, chopped
- 6 bacon slices, chopped
- ½ cup chicken stock
- Salt and black pepper to the taste
- 4 pork chops

Directions:
In your Slow cooker, mix onions with bacon, stock, salt, pepper and pork chops, cover and cook on Low for 8 hours. Divide pork chops on plates, drizzle cooking juices all over and serve.

Nutrition: calories 325, fat 18, fiber 1, carbs 12, protein 36

Worcestershire Pork Chops

Preparation time: 10 minutes | Cooking time: 7 hours 23 minutes | Servings: 4

Ingredients:
- 4 medium pork chops
- 1 teaspoon Dijon mustard
- 1 tablespoon Worcestershire sauce
- 1 teaspoon lemon juice
- 1 tablespoon water
- Salt and black pepper to the taste
- 1 teaspoon lemon pepper
- 1 tablespoon olive
- 1 tablespoon chives, chopped

Directions:
In a bowl, mix water with Worcestershire sauce, mustard and lemon juice and whisk well. Heat up a pan with the oil over medium heat, add pork chops, season with salt, pepper and lemon pepper, cook them for 6 minutes, flip and cook for 6 more minutes and transfer to your Slow cooker. Add Worcestershire sauce mix, toss, cover and cook on Low for 7 hours. Divide pork chops on plates, sprinkle chives on top and serve.

Nutrition: calories 132, fat 5, fiber 1, carbs 12, protein 18

Rosemary Pork

Preparation time: 10 minutes | Cooking time: 7 hours | Servings: 4

Ingredients:
- 4 pork chops, bone in
- 1 cup chicken stock
- Salt and black pepper to the taste
- 1 teaspoon rosemary, dried
- 3 garlic cloves, minced

Directions:
Season pork chops with salt and pepper and place in your Slow cooker. Add rosemary, garlic and stock, cover and cook on Low for 7 hours. Divide pork between plates and drizzle cooking juices all over.

Nutrition: calories 165, fat 2, fiber 1, carbs 12, protein 26

Oregano Pork Chops

Preparation time: 10 minutes | Cooking time: 8 hours | Servings: 4

Ingredients:
- 4 pork chops
- 1 tablespoon oregano, chopped
- 2 garlic cloves, minced
- 1 tablespoon olive oil
- 15 ounces canned tomatoes, chopped
- 1 tablespoon tomato paste
- Salt and black pepper to the taste
- ¼ cup tomato juice

Directions:
In your Slow cooker, mix pork with oregano, garlic, oil, tomatoes, tomato paste, salt, pepper and tomato juice, cover and cook on Low for 8 hours. Divide everything between plates and serve.

Nutrition: calories 210, fat 10, fiber 2, carbs 15, protein 25

Spicy Pork

Preparation time: 4 hours 10 minutes | Cooking time: 7 hours | Servings: 4

Ingredients:
- ¼ cup lime juice
- 4 pork rib chops
- 1 tablespoon olive
- 2 garlic cloves, minced
- 1 tablespoon chili powder
- 1 teaspoon cinnamon, ground
- 2 teaspoons cumin, ground
- Salt and black pepper to the taste
- ½ teaspoon hot pepper sauce
- Sliced mango for serving

Directions:
In a bowl, mix lime juice with oil, garlic, cumin, cinnamon, chili powder, salt, pepper and hot pepper sauce, whisk well, add pork chops, toss to coat and leave aside in the fridge for 4 hours. Transfer pork and marinade to your Slow cooker, cover and cook on Low for 7 hours. Divide between plates and serve with mango slices on the side.

Nutrition: calories 200, fat 8, fiber 1, carbs 12, protein 26

Beef Meatballs Casserole

Preparation time: 10 minutes | Cooking time: 7 hours | Servings: 8

Ingredients:
- 1/3 cup flour
- 2 eggs
- 1 pound beef sausage, chopped
- 1 pound beef, ground
- Salt and black pepper to taste
- 1 tablespoons parsley, dried
- ¼ teaspoon red pepper flakes
- ¼ cup parmesan, grated
- ¼ teaspoon onion powder
- ½ teaspoon garlic powder
- ¼ teaspoon oregano, dried
- 1 cup ricotta cheese
- 2 cups marinara sauce
- 1 and ½ cups mozzarella cheese, shredded

Directions:
In a bowl, mix sausage with beef, salt, pepper, almond flour, parsley, pepper flakes, onion powder, garlic powder, oregano, parmesan and eggs, stir well and shape meatballs out of this mix. Arrange meatballs in your Slow cooker, add half of the marinara sauce, ricotta cheese and top with the rest of the marinara. Add mozzarella at the end, cover and cook on Low for 7 hours. Divide between plates and serve.

Nutrition: calories 456, fat 35, fiber 3, carbs 12, protein 32

Beef Stuffed Squash

Preparation time: 10 minutes | Cooking time: 7 hours | Servings: 2

Ingredients:
- 2 pounds spaghetti squash, halved
- 1 cup chicken stock
- Salt and black pepper to the taste
- 3 garlic cloves, minced
- 1 yellow onion, chopped
- 1 Portobello mushroom, sliced
- 28 ounces canned tomatoes, chopped
- 1 teaspoon oregano, dried
- ¼ teaspoon cayenne pepper
- ½ teaspoon thyme, dried
- 1 pound beef, ground
- 1 green bell pepper, chopped

Directions:
Heat up a pan over medium-high heat, add meat, garlic, onion and mushroom, stir and cook until meat browns. Add salt, pepper, thyme, oregano, cayenne, tomatoes and green pepper, stir and cook for 10 minutes. Stuff squash halves with this beef mix, return to the slow cooker, cover and cook on High for 4 hours. Divide between 2 plates and serve.

Nutrition: calories 260, fat 7, fiber 2, carbs 14, protein 10

Beef and Tzatziki

Preparation time: 10 minutes | Cooking time: 7 hours | Servings: 6

Ingredients:
- ¼ cup milk
- 17 ounces beef, ground
- 1 yellow onion, grated
- 5 bread slices, torn
- 1 egg, whisked
- ¼ cup parsley, chopped
- Salt and black pepper to the taste
- 2 garlic cloves, minced
- ¼ cup mint, chopped
- 2 and ½ teaspoons oregano, dried
- ¼ cup olive oil
- 7 ounces cherry tomatoes, cut into halves
- 1 cucumber, thinly sliced
- 1 cup baby spinach
- 1 and ½ tablespoons lemon juice
- 7 ounces jarred tzatziki

Directions:
Put torn bread in a bowl, add milk and leave aside for 3 minutes. Squeeze bread, chop, put into a bowl, add beef, egg, salt, pepper, oregano, mint, parsley, garlic and onion, stir well, shape balls from this mix and place them in your Slow cooker. Add tzatziki, cover and cook on Low for 7 hours. In a salad bowl, mix spinach with cucumber, tomatoes, oil, meatballs, salt, pepper and lemon juice, toss and serve.

Nutrition: calories 200, fat 4, fiber 1, carbs 12, protein 7

German Beef Soup

Preparation time: 10 minutes | Cooking time: 6 hours | Servings: 8

Ingredients:
- 3 teaspoons olive oil
- 1 pound beef, ground
- 14 ounces beef stock
- 2 cups chicken stock
- 14 ounces canned tomatoes and juice
- 1 tablespoon sugar
- 14 ounces sauerkraut, chopped
- 1 tablespoon Worcestershire sauce
- 4 bay leaves
- Salt and black pepper to the taste
- 3 tablespoons parsley, chopped
- 1 onion, chopped
- 1 teaspoon sage, dried
- 1 tablespoon garlic, minced
- 2 cups water

Directions:
Heat up a pan with the oil over medium heat, add beef, stir, brown for 10 minutes and transfer to your Slow cooker. Add chicken and beef stock, sauerkraut, sugar, canned tomatoes, Worcestershire sauce, parsley, sage, bay leaves, onions, garlic, water, salt and pepper, stir, cover and cook on Low for 6 hours. Divide into bowls and serve.

Nutrition: calories 250, fat 5, fiber 1, carbs 12, protein 23

Paprika Lamb

Preparation time: 10 minutes | Cooking time: 7 hours | Servings: 4

Ingredients:
- 2 teaspoons paprika
- 2 garlic cloves, minced
- 2 teaspoons oregano, dried
- 2 tablespoons sumac
- 12 lamb cutlets
- ¼ cup olive oil
- 2 tablespoons water
- 2 teaspoons cumin, ground
- 4 carrots, sliced
- ¼ cup parsley, chopped
- 2 teaspoons harissa
- 1 tablespoon red wine vinegar
- Salt and black pepper to the taste
- 2 tablespoons black olives, pitted and sliced
- 6 radishes, thinly sliced

Directions:
In a bowl, mix cutlets with paprika, garlic, oregano, sumac, salt, pepper, half of the oil and the water and rub well. Put carrots in your Slow cooker and add olives and radishes. In another bowl, mix harissa with the rest of the oil, parsley, cumin, vinegar and a splash of water and stir well. Add this over carrots mix, season with salt and pepper and toss to coat. Add lamb cutlets, cover, cook on Low for 7 hours, divide everything between plates and serve.

Nutrition: calories 245, fat 32, fiber 6, carbs 12, protein 34

Lamb Casserole

Preparation time: 10 minutes | Cooking time: 7 hours | Servings: 2

Ingredients:
- 2 garlic cloves, minced
- 1 red onion, chopped
- 1 tablespoon olive oil
- 1 celery stick, chopped
- 10 ounces lamb fillet, cut into medium pieces
- Salt and black pepper to the taste
- 1 and ¼ cups lamb stock
- 2 carrots, chopped
- ½ tablespoon rosemary, chopped
- 1 leek, chopped
- 1 tablespoon mint sauce
- 1 teaspoon sugar
- 1 tablespoon tomato puree
- ½ cauliflower, florets separated
- ½ celeriac, chopped
- 2 tablespoons butter

Directions:
Heat up a slow cooker with the oil over medium heat, add garlic, onion and celery, stir and cook for 5 minutes. Add lamb pieces, stir, brown for 3 minutes and transfer everything to your Slow cooker. Add carrot, leek, rosemary, stock, tomato puree, mint sauce, sugar, cauliflower, celeriac, butter, salt and black pepper, cover and cook on Low for 7 hours. Divide lamb and all the veggies between plates and serve.

Nutrition: calories 324, fat 4, fiber 5, carbs 12, protein 20

Lavender and Orange Lamb

Preparation time: 2 hours | Cooking time: 7 hours | Servings: 4

Ingredients:
- 2 tablespoons rosemary, chopped
- 1 and ½ pounds lamb chops
- Salt and black pepper to the taste
- 1 tablespoon lavender, chopped
- 2 garlic cloves, minced
- 1 red orange, cut into halves
- 2 red oranges, peeled and cut into segments
- 2 small pieces of orange peel
- 1 teaspoon butter

Directions:
In a bowl, mix lamb chops with salt, pepper, rosemary, lavender, garlic and orange peel, toss to coat and leave aside for a couple of hours in the fridge. Put the butter in your Slow cooker, add lamb chops, squeeze 1 orange over them, add the rest of the oranges over the lamb, cover slow cooker and cook on Low for 7 hours. Divide lamb and sauce all over and serve.

Nutrition: calories 250, fat 5, fiber 7, carbs 15, protein 20

Lamb and Orange Sauce

Preparation time: 10 minutes | Cooking time: 4 hours | Servings: 4

Ingredients:
- 2 lamb shanks
- Salt and black pepper to the taste
- 1 garlic head, peeled
- 4 tablespoons olive oil
- Zest of ½ orange
- Juice of ½ orange
- ½ teaspoon oregano, dried

Directions:
In your Slow cooker, mix lamb with salt, pepper and garlic, cover and cook on High for 4 hours. In a bowl, mix orange juice with orange zest, salt, pepper, olive oil and oregano and whisk very well. Shred lamb meat, discard bone, divide meat between plates. Drizzle the orange sauce all over and serve.

Nutrition: calories 260, fat 7, fiber 3, carbs 15, protein 12

Lamb and Mint Pesto

Preparation time: 1 minutes | Cooking time: 7 hours | Servings: 4

Ingredients:
- 1 cup parsley
- 1 cup mint
- 1 small yellow onion, roughly chopped
- 1/3 cup pistachios
- 1 teaspoon lemon zest
- 5 tablespoons avocado oil
- Salt to the taste
- 2 pounds lamb riblets
- ½ onion, chopped
- 5 garlic cloves, minced
- Juice of 1 orange

Directions:
In your food processor, mix parsley with mint, 1 small onion, pistachios, and lemon zest, salt and avocado oil and blend very well. Rub lamb with this mix, place in a bowl, cover and leave in the fridge for 1 hour. Transfer lamb and pesto to your Slow cooker, add garlic and ½ onion, drizzle orange juice, cover, cook on Low for 7 hours. Divide everything between plates and serve.

Nutrition: calories 200, fat 4, fiber 1, carbs 15, protein 16

Lamb and Fennel Mix

Preparation time: 10 minutes | Cooking time: 7 hours | Servings: 4

Ingredients:
- 12 ounces lamb racks
- 2 fennel bulbs, sliced
- Salt and black pepper to the taste
- 2 tablespoons olive oil
- 4 figs, cut into halves
- 1/8 cup apple cider vinegar
- 1 tablespoon sugar

Directions:
In a bowl, mix fennel with figs, vinegar, sugar and oil, toss to coat well and transfer to your Slow cooker. Add lamb, salt and pepper, cover and cook on Low for 7 hours. Divide between plates and serve.

Nutrition: calories 230, fat 3, fiber 3, carbs 5, protein 10

Beef and Pancetta

Preparation time: 10 minutes | Cooking time: 4 hours 10 minutes | Servings: 4

Ingredients:
- 8 ounces pancetta, chopped
- 4 pounds beef, cubed
- 4 garlic cloves, minced
- 2 brown onions, chopped
- 2 tablespoons olive oil
- 4 tablespoons red vinegar
- 4 cups beef stock
- 2 tablespoons tomato paste
- 2 cinnamon sticks
- 3 lemon peel strips
- A handful parsley, chopped
- 4 thyme springs
- 2 tablespoons butter
- Salt and black pepper to the taste

Directions:
Heat up a pan with the oil over medium-high heat, add pancetta, onion and garlic, stir, cook for 5 minutes, add beef, stir and brown for a few minutes Add vinegar, salt, pepper, stock, tomato paste, cinnamon, lemon peel, thyme and butter, stir, cook for 3 minutes more, transfer everything to your Slow cooker, cook on High for 4 hours, discard cinnamon, lemon peel and thyme, add parsley, stir, divide between plates and serve.

Nutrition: calories 250, fat 6, fiber 1, carbs 17, protein 33

Veal Stew

Preparation time: 10 minutes | Cooking time: 8 hours | Servings: 12

Ingredients:
- 2 tablespoons avocado oil
- 3 pounds veal, cubed
- 1 yellow onion, chopped
- 1 small garlic clove, minced
- Salt and black pepper to the taste
- 1 cup water
- 1 and ½ cups marsala wine
- 10 ounces canned tomato paste
- 1 carrot, chopped
- 7 ounces mushrooms, chopped
- 3 egg yolks
- ½ cup heavy cream
- 2 teaspoons oregano, dried

Directions:
Heat up a slow cooker with the oil over medium-high heat, add veal, stir, brown for a few minutes, transfer to your Slow cooker, add garlic, onion, wine, water, oregano, tomato paste, mushrooms, carrots, salt and pepper, stir, cover and cook on Low for 7 hours and 30 minutes In a bowl, mix cream with egg yolks and whisk well. Pour this over the meat, cover and cook on Low for 30 minutes more. Divide between plates and serve hot.

Nutrition: calories 254, fat 15, fiber 6, carbs 13, protein 23

Veal and Tomatoes

Preparation time: 10 minutes | Cooking time: 7 hours | Servings: 4

Ingredients:
- 4 medium veal leg steaks
- 1 teaspoon avocado oil
- 2 garlic cloves, minced
- 1 red onion, chopped
- Salt and black pepper to the taste
- 2 teaspoons sage, chopped
- 15 ounces canned tomatoes, chopped
- 2 tablespoons parsley, chopped
- 1 ounce bocconcini, sliced

Directions:
Heat up a pan with the oil over medium-high heat, add veal, brown for 2 minutes on each side and transfer to your Slow cooker. Add onion, sage, garlic, tomatoes, parsley, bocconcini, salt and pepper, cover and cook on Low for 7 hours. Divide between plates and serve.

Nutrition: calories 276, fat 6, fiber 4, carbs 15, protein 36

Wine Piccata

Preparation time: 10 minutes | Cooking time: 7 hours | Servings: 2

Ingredients:
- 2 tablespoons butter
- ¼ cup white wine
- ¼ cup chicken stock
- 1 and ½ tablespoons capers
- 1 garlic clove, minced
- 8 ounces veal cutlets
- Salt and black pepper to the taste

Directions:
Heat up a pan with half of the butter over medium-high heat, add veal cutlets, season with salt and pepper, cook for 1 minute on each side and transfer to your Slow cooker. Add garlic, wine, stock, capers and the rest of the butter, cover and cook on Low for 7 hours. Divide between plates and serve right away.

Nutrition: calories 204, fat 12, fiber 1, carbs 15, protein 29

Onion Sausage Mix

Preparation time: 5 minutes | Cooking time: 4 hours | Servings: 4

Ingredients:
- 1 cup yellow onion, chopped
- 1 and ½ pound Italian pork sausage, sliced
- ½ cup red bell pepper, chopped
- Salt and black pepper to the taste
- 5 pounds kale, chopped
- 1 teaspoon garlic, minced
- ¼ cup red hot chili pepper, chopped
- 1 cup water

Directions:

In your Slow cooker, mix onion with sausage, bell pepper, salt, pepper, garlic, chili pepper and water, cover and cook on High for 3 hours. Add kale, toss a bit, cover and cook on High for 1 more hour. Divide between plates and serve.

Nutrition: calories 250, fat 4, fiber 1, carbs 12, protein 20

Cheesy Sausage Casserole

Preparation time: 10 minutes | Cooking time: 4 hours | Servings: 4

Ingredients:
- 2 tablespoons olive oil
- 2 pounds Italian pork sausage, chopped
- 1 onion, sliced
- 4 sun-dried tomatoes, thinly sliced
- Salt and black pepper to the taste
- ½ pound gouda cheese, grated
- 3 yellow bell peppers, chopped
- 3 orange bell peppers, chopped
- A pinch of red pepper flakes
- 1 tablespoon parsley, chopped

Directions:

Heat up a pan with the oil over medium-high heat, add sausage slices, stir, and cook for 3 minutes on each side and transfer to your Slow cooker. Add onion, tomatoes, salt, pepper, orange bell pepper, red bell pepper, pepper flakes and sprinkle Gouda cheese at the end. Cover slow cooker, cook on High for 4 hours, sprinkle parsley on top, divide between plates and serve.

Nutrition: calories 260, fat 5, fiber 3, carbs 16, protein 14

Sausage Soup

Preparation time: 10 minutes | Cooking time: 6 hours | Servings: 6

Ingredients:
- 1 tablespoon avocado oil
- 32 ounces pork sausage meat, ground
- 10 ounces canned tomatoes and jalapenos, chopped
- 10 ounces spinach
- 1 green bell pepper, chopped
- 4 cups beef stock
- 1 teaspoon onion powder
- Salt and black pepper to the taste
- 1 tablespoon cumin
- 1 tablespoon chili powder
- 1 teaspoon garlic powder
- 1 teaspoon Italian seasoning

Directions:

Heat up a pan with the oil over medium heat; add sausage, stir, and brown for a couple of minutes on all sides and transfer to your Slow cooker. Add green bell pepper, canned tomatoes and jalapenos, stock, onion powder, salt, pepper, cumin, chili powder, garlic powder, Italian seasoning and stock, stir, cover and cook on Low for 5 hours and 30 minutes. Add spinach, cover, cook on Low for 30 minutes more, stir soup, ladle it into bowls and serve.

Nutrition: calories 524, fat 43, fiber 2, carbs 15, protein 26

Italian Sausage Soup

Preparation time: 10 minutes | Cooking time: 6 hours | Servings: 12

Ingredients:
- 64 ounces chicken stock
- 1 teaspoon olive oil
- 1 cup heavy cream
- 10 ounces spinach
- 6 bacon slices, chopped
- 1 pound radishes, chopped
- 2 garlic cloves, minced
- Salt and black pepper to the taste
- A pinch of red pepper flakes, crushed
- 1 yellow onion, chopped
- 1 and ½ pounds hot pork sausage, chopped

Directions:
Heat up a pan with the oil over medium-high heat, add sausage, onion and garlic, stir brown for a few minutes and transfer to your Slow cooker. Add stock, spinach, radishes, bacon, cream, salt, pepper and red pepper flakes, stir, cover and cook on Low for 6 hours. Ladle soup into bowls and serve.

Nutrition: calories 291, fat 22, fiber 2, carbs 14, protein 17

Beef Curry

Preparation time: 10 minutes | Cooking time: 8 hours | Servings: 4

Ingredients:
- 2 pounds beef steak, cubed
- 2 tablespoons olive oil
- 3 potatoes, diced
- 1 tablespoon mustard
- 2 and ½ tablespoons curry powder
- 2 yellow onions, chopped
- 2 garlic cloves, minced
- 10 ounces canned coconut milk
- 2 tablespoons tomato sauce
- Salt and black pepper to the taste

Directions:
In your Slow cooker, mix oil with steak, potatoes, mustard, curry powder, garlic, coconut milk, tomato sauce, salt and pepper, toss, cover and cook on Low for 8 hours. Stir curry one more time, divide into bowls and serve.

Nutrition: calories 432, fat 12, fiber 5, carbs 15, protein 26

Spicy Beef Mix

Preparation time: 10 minutes | Cooking time: 8 hours | Servings: 6

Ingredients:
- 1 and ½ pounds beef, ground
- 1 sweet onion, chopped
- Salt and black pepper to the taste
- 16 ounces mixed beans, soaked overnight and drained
- 28 ounces canned tomatoes, chopped
- 17 ounces beef stock
- 12 ounces pale ale
- 6 garlic cloves, chopped
- 7 jalapeno peppers, diced
- 2 tablespoons vegetable oil
- 4 carrots, chopped
- 3 tablespoons chili powder
- 1 bay leaf
- 1 teaspoon chipotle powder

Directions:
In your Slow cooker, mix oil with beef, onion, salt, pepper, beans, tomatoes, stock, garlic, jalapenos, carrots, chili powder, bay leaf, chipotle powder and pale ale, toss, cover and cook on Low for 8 hours. Divide into bowls and serve.

Nutrition: calories 300, fat 4, fiber 5, carbs 20, protein 16

Slow Cooker Fish Recipes

Salmon and Green Onions Mix
Preparation time: 10 minutes | Cooking time: 2 hours | Servings: 4

Ingredients:
- 1 green onions bunch, halved
- 10 tablespoons lemon juice
- 4 salmon fillets, boneless
- Salt and black pepper to the taste
- 2 tablespoons avocado oil

Directions:
Grease your Slow cooker with the oil, add salmon, top with onion, lemon juice, salt and pepper, cover, cook on High for 2 hours, divide everything between plates and serve.

Nutrition: calories 260, fat 3, fiber 1, carbs 14, protein 14

Seafood Chowder
Preparation time: 10 minutes | Cooking time: 8 hours 30 minutes | Servings: 4

Ingredients:
- 2 cups water
- ½ fennel bulb, chopped
- 2 sweet potatoes, cubed
- 1 yellow onion, chopped
- 2 bay leaves
- 1 tablespoon thyme, dried
- 1 celery rib, chopped
- Salt and black pepper to the taste
- 1 bottle clam juice
- 2 tablespoons tapioca powder
- 1 cup coconut milk
- 1 pounds salmon fillets, cubed
- 5 sea scallops, halved
- 24 shrimp, peeled and deveined
- ¼ cup parsley, chopped

Directions:
In your Slow cooker, mix water with fennel, potatoes, onion, bay leaves, thyme, celery, clam juice, salt, pepper and tapioca, stir, cover and cook on Low for 8 hours. Add salmon, coconut milk, scallops, shrimp and parsley, cook on Low for 30 minutes more, ladle chowder into bowls and serve.

Nutrition: calories 354, fat 10, fiber 2, carbs 10, protein 12

Asian Salmon Mix
Preparation time: 10 minutes | Cooking time: 3 hours | Servings: 2

Ingredients:
- 2 medium salmon fillets, boneless
- Salt and black pepper to the taste
- 2 tablespoons soy sauce
- 2 tablespoons maple syrup
- 16 ounces mixed broccoli and cauliflower florets
- 2 tablespoons lemon juice
- 1 teaspoon sesame seeds

Directions:
Put the cauliflower and broccoli florets in your Slow cooker and top with salmon fillets. In a bowl, mix maple syrup with soy sauce and lemon juice, whisk well, and pour this over salmon fillets, season with salt, pepper, sprinkle sesame seeds on top and cook on Low for 3 hours. Divide everything between plates and serve.

Nutrition: calories 230, fat 4, fiber 2, carbs 12, protein 6

Shrimp Mix

Preparation time: 10 minutes | Cooking time: 1 hour 30 minutes | Servings: 4

Ingredients:
- 2 tablespoons olive oil
- 1 pound shrimp, peeled and deveined
- ¼ cup chicken stock
- 1 tablespoon garlic, minced
- 2 tablespoons parsley, chopped
- Juice of ½ lemon
- Salt and black pepper to the taste

Directions:
Put the oil in your Slow cooker, add stock, garlic, parsley, lemon juice, salt and pepper and whisk really well. Add shrimp, stir, cover, and cook on High for 1 hour and 30 minutes, divide into bowls and serve.

Nutrition: calories 240, fat 4, fiber 3, carbs 9, protein 3

Asian Steamed Fish

Preparation time: 10 minutes | Cooking time: 1 hours | Servings: 4

Ingredients:
- 2 tablespoons sugar
- 4 salmon fillets, boneless
- 2 tablespoons soy sauce
- ¼ cup olive oil
- ¼ cup veggie stock
- 1 small ginger piece, grated
- 6 garlic cloves, minced
- 2 tablespoons Worcestershire sauce
- 1 bunch leeks, chopped
- 1 bunch cilantro, chopped

Directions:
Put the oil in your slow cooker, add leeks and top with the fish. In a bowl, mix stock with ginger, sugar, garlic, cilantro and soy sauce, stir, add this over fish, cover and cook on High for 1 hour. Divide fish between plates and serve with the sauce drizzled on top.

Nutrition: calories 300, fat 8, fiber 2, carbs 12, protein 6

Poached Cod and Pineapple Mix

Preparation time: 10 minutes | Cooking time: 4 hours | Servings: 2

Ingredients:
- 1 pound cod, boneless
- 6 garlic cloves, minced
- 1 small ginger pieces, chopped
- ½ tablespoon black peppercorns
- 1 cup pineapple juice
- 1 cup pineapple, chopped
- ¼ cup white vinegar
- 4 jalapeno peppers, chopped
- Salt and black pepper to the taste

Directions:
Put the fish in your cooker, season with salt and pepper. Add garlic, ginger, peppercorns, pineapple juice, pineapple chunks, vinegar and jalapenos. Stir gently, cover and cook on Low for 4 hours. Divide fish between plates, top with the pineapple mix and serve.

Nutrition: calories 240, fat 4, fiber 4, carbs 14, protein 10

Chili Catfish

Preparation time: 10 minutes | Cooking time: 6 hours | Servings: 4

Ingredients:
- 1 catfish, boneless and cut into 4 pieces
- 3 red chili peppers, chopped
- ½ cup sugar
- ¼ cup water
- 1 tablespoon soy sauce
- 1 shallot, minced
- A small ginger piece, grated
- 1 tablespoon coriander, chopped

Directions:
Put catfish pieces in your Slow cooker. Heat up a pan with the sugar over medium-high heat and stir until it caramelizes. Add soy sauce, shallot, ginger, water and chili pepper, stir, pour over the fish, add coriander, cover and cook on Low for 6 hours. Divide fish between plates and serve with the sauce from the slow cooker drizzled on top.

Nutrition: calories 200, fat 4, fiber 4, carbs 8, protein 10

Tuna Loin Mix

Preparation time: 10 minutes | Cooking time: 4 hours 10 minutes | Servings: 2

Ingredients:
- ½ pound tuna loin, cubed
- 1 garlic clove, minced
- 4 jalapeno peppers, chopped
- 1 cup olive oil
- 3 red chili peppers, chopped
- 2 teaspoons black peppercorns, ground
- Salt and black pepper to the taste

Directions:
Put the oil in your Slow cooker, add chili peppers, jalapenos, peppercorns, salt, pepper and garlic, whisk, cover and cook on Low for 4 hours. Add tuna, stir again, cook on High for 10 minutes more, divide between plates and serve.

Nutrition: calories 200, fat 4, fiber 3, carbs 10, protein 4

Creamy Sea Bass

Preparation time: 10 minutes | Cooking time: 1 hour 30 minutes | Servings: 2

Ingredients:
- 1 pound sea bass
- 2 scallion stalks, chopped
- 1 small ginger piece, grated
- 1 tablespoon soy sauce
- 2 cups coconut cream
- 4 bok choy stalks, chopped
- 3 jalapeno peppers, chopped
- Salt and black pepper to the taste

Directions:
Put the cream in your Slow cooker, add ginger, soy sauce, scallions, a pinch of salt, black pepper, jalapenos, stir, top with the fish and bok choy, cover and cook on High for 1 hour and 30 minutes. Divide the fish mix between plates and serve.

Nutrition: calories 270, fat 3, fiber 3, carbs 18, protein 17

Flavored Cod Fillets

Preparation time: 10 minutes | Cooking time: 2 hours | Servings: 4

Ingredients:
- 4 medium cod fillets, boneless
- ¼ teaspoon nutmeg, ground
- 1 teaspoon ginger, grated
- Salt and black pepper to the taste
- 1 teaspoon onion powder
- ¼ teaspoon sweet paprika
- 1 teaspoon cayenne pepper
- ½ teaspoon cinnamon powder

Directions:
In a bowl, mix cod fillets with nutmeg, ginger, salt, pepper, onion powder, paprika, cayenne black pepper and cinnamon, toss, transfer to your Slow cooker, cover and cook on Low for 2 hours. Divide between plates and serve with a side salad.

Nutrition: calories 200, fat 4, fiber 2, carbs 14, protein 4

Shrimp and Baby Carrots Mix

Preparation time: 10 minutes | Cooking time: 4 hours minutes | Servings: 2

Ingredients:
- 1 small yellow onion, chopped
- 15 baby carrots
- 2 garlic cloves, minced
- 1 small green bell pepper, chopped
- 8 ounces canned coconut milk
- 3 tablespoons tomato paste
- ½ teaspoon red pepper, crushed
- ¾ tablespoons curry powder
- ¾ tablespoon tapioca flour
- 1 pound shrimp, peeled and deveined

Directions:
In your food processor, mix onion with garlic, bell pepper, tomato paste, coconut milk, red pepper and curry powder, blend well, add to your Slow cooker, also add baby carrots, stir, cover and cook on Low for 4 hours. Add tapioca and shrimp, stir, cover and cook on Low for 30 minutes more. Divide into bowls and serve.

Nutrition: calories 230, fat 4, fiber 3, carbs 14, protein 5

Dill Trout

Preparation time: 10 minutes | Cooking time: 2 hours | Servings: 4

Ingredients:
- 2 lemons, sliced
- ¼ cup chicken stock
- Salt and black pepper to the taste
- 2 tablespoons dill, chopped
- 12 ounces spinach
- 4 medium trout

Directions:
Put the stock in your Slow cooker, add the fish inside, season with salt and pepper, top with lemon slices, dill and spinach, cover and cook on High for 2 hours. Divide fish, lemon and spinach between plates and drizzle some of the juice from the slow cooker all over.

Nutrition: calories 240, fat 5, fiber 4, carbs 9, protein 14

Fish Pie

Preparation time: 10 minutes | Cooking time: 2 hours 30 minutes | Servings: 4

Ingredients:
- 1 red onion, chopped
- 2 salmon fillets, skinless and cut into medium pieces
- 2 mackerel fillets, skinless and cut into medium pieces
- 3 haddock fillets and cut into medium pieces
- 2 bay leaves
- ¼ cup butter+ 2 tablespoons
- 1 cauliflower head, florets separated and riced
- 4 eggs, hard-boiled, peeled and sliced
- 4 cloves
- 1 cup whipping cream
- ½ cup water
- A pinch of nutmeg, ground
- 1 cup cheddar cheese, shredded+ ½ cup
- 1 tablespoon parsley, chopped
- Salt and black pepper to the taste
- 4 tablespoons chives, chopped

Directions:
Put cream and ½ cup water in your Slow cooker,, add salmon, mackerel and haddock, onion, cloves and bay leaves, cover and cook on High for 1 hour and 30 minutes Add nutmeg, eggs, 1 cup cheese, ¼ cup butter, cauliflower rice, the rest of the cheddar, chives, parsley, salt, pepper and the rest of the butter, cover and cook on High for 1 more hour. Slice pie, divide between plates and serve.

Nutrition: calories 300, fat 45, fiber 3, carbs 5, protein 26

Slow Cooked Haddock

Preparation time: 10 minutes | Cooking time: 2 hours | Servings: 4

Ingredients:
- 1 pound haddock
- 3 teaspoons water
- 2 tablespoons lemon juice
- Salt and black pepper to the taste
- 2 tablespoons mayonnaise
- 1 teaspoon dill, chopped
- Cooking spray
- ½ teaspoon old bay seasoning

Directions:
Spray your Slow cooker with the cooking spray; add lemon juice, water, fish, salt, pepper, mayo, dill and old bay seasoning, cover, cook on High for 2 hours. Divide between plates and serve.

Nutrition: calories 274, fat 12, fiber 1, carbs 6, protein 20

Buttery Trout

Preparation time: 10 minutes | Cooking time: 2 hours | Servings: 4

Ingredients:
- 4 trout fillets, boneless
- Salt and black pepper to the taste
- 3 teaspoons lemon zest, grated
- 3 tablespoons chives, chopped
- 6 tablespoons butter, melted
- 2 tablespoons olive oil
- 2 teaspoons lemon juice

Directions:
Put the butter in your Slow cooker, add trout fillets, season with salt, pepper, lemon zest, chives, oil and lemon juice, rub fish a bit, cover and cook on High for 2 hours. Divide fish between plates and serve with the butter sauce drizzled on top.

Nutrition: calories 320, fat 12, fiber 6, carbs 12, protein 24

Salmon and Kimchi Sauce

Preparation time: 10 minutes | Cooking time: 2 hours | Servings: 4

Ingredients:
- 2 tablespoons butter, soft
- 1 and ¼ pound salmon fillet
- 2 ounces Kimchi, finely chopped
- Salt and black pepper to the taste

Directions:
In your food processor, mix butter with Kimchi, blend well, and rub salmon with salt, pepper and Kimchi mix, place in your Slow cooker, cover and cook on High for 2 hours. Divide between plates and serve with a side salad.

Nutrition: calories 270, fat 12, fiber 5, carbs 13, protein 21

Salmon Meatballs and Sauce

Preparation time: 10 minutes | Cooking time: 2 hours | Servings: 4

Ingredients:
- 2 tablespoons butter
- 2 garlic cloves, minced
- 1/3 cup onion, chopped
- 1 pound wild salmon, boneless and minced
- ¼ cup chives, chopped
- 1 egg
- 2 tablespoons Dijon mustard
- 1 tablespoon flour
- Salt and black pepper to the taste

For the sauce:
- 4 garlic cloves, minced
- 2 tablespoons butter, melted
- 2 tablespoons Dijon mustard
- Juice and Zest of 1 lemon
- 2 cups coconut cream
- 2 tablespoons chives, chopped

Directions:
Heat up a pan with 2 tablespoons butter over medium heat, add onion and 2-garlic cloves stir, cook for 3 minutes and transfer to a bowl. In another bowl, mix onion and garlic with salmon, chives, flour, salt, pepper, 2 tablespoons mustard and egg and stir well. Shape meatballs from the salmon mix and put them in your Slow cooker. Add 2 tablespoons butter, 4 garlic cloves, coconut cream, 2 teaspoons mustard, lemon juice, lemon zest and chives, cover and cook on High for 2 hours. Divide meatballs on plates, drizzle the sauce all over and serve.

Nutrition: calories 271, fat 5, fiber 1, carbs 6, protein 23

Salmon and Caper Sauce

Preparation time: 10 minutes | Cooking time: 20 hours | Servings: 5

Ingredients:
- 3 salmon fillets, boneless
- Salt and black pepper to the taste
- 1 tablespoon olive oil
- 1 tablespoon Italian seasoning
- 2 tablespoons capers
- 3 tablespoons lemon juice
- 4 garlic cloves, minced
- 2 tablespoons butter

Directions:
Put the butter in your Slow cooker, add salmon fillets, salt, pepper, oil, seasoning, capers, lemon juice and garlic, cover and cook on High for 2 hours. Divide fish and sauce between plates and serve.

Nutrition: calories 245, fat 12, fiber 1, carbs 13, protein 23

Tabasco Halibut

Preparation time: 10 minutes | Cooking time: 3 hours | Servings: 4

Ingredients:
- ½ cup parmesan, grated
- ¼ cup butter, melted
- ¼ cup mayonnaise
- 2 tablespoons green onions, chopped
- 6 garlic cloves, minced
- ½ teaspoon Tabasco sauce
- 4 halibut fillets, boneless
- Salt and black pepper to the taste
- Juice of ½ lemon

Directions:
Season halibut with salt, pepper and some of the lemon juice, place in your Slow cooker, add butter, mayo, green onions, garlic, and Tabasco sauce and lemon juice, toss a bit, cover and cook on High for 2 hours. Add parmesan, leave fish mix aside for a few more minutes, divide between plates and serve.

Nutrition: calories 240, fat 12, fiber 1, carbs 15, protein 23

Creamy Salmon

Preparation time: 10 minutes | Cooking time: 2 hours | Servings: 4

Ingredients:
- 4 salmon fillets, boneless
- 1 tablespoon olive oil
- Salt and black pepper to the taste
- 1/3 cup parmesan, grated
- 1 and ½ teaspoon mustard
- ½ cup sour cream

Directions:
Place salmon in your Slow cooker, season with salt and pepper, drizzle the oil and rub. In a bowl, mix sour cream with parmesan, mustard, salt and pepper, stir well, spoon this over the salmon fillets, cover and cook on High for 2 hours. Divide between plates and serve.

Nutrition: calories 263, fat 6, fiber 1, carbs 14, protein 20

Chinese Cod

Preparation time: 10 minutes | Cooking time: 2 hours | Servings: 4

Ingredients:
- 1 pound cod, cut into medium pieces
- Salt and black pepper to the taste
- 2 green onions, chopped
- 3 garlic cloves, minced
- 3 tablespoons soy sauce
- 1 cup fish stock
- 1 tablespoons balsamic vinegar
- 1 tablespoon ginger, grated
- ½ teaspoon chili pepper, crushed

Directions:
In your Slow cooker, mix fish with salt, pepper green onions, garlic, soy sauce, fish stock, vinegar, ginger and chili pepper, toss, cover and cook on High for 2 hours. Divide everything between plates and serve.

Nutrition: calories 204, fat 3, fiber 6, carbs 14, protein 24

Mustard Fish Mix

Preparation time: 10 minutes | Cooking time: 2 hours 30 minutes | Servings: 4

Ingredients:
- 4 white fish fillets, skinless and boneless
- ½ teaspoon mustard seeds
- Salt and black pepper to the taste
- 2 green chilies, chopped
- 1 teaspoon ginger, grated
- 1 teaspoon curry powder
- ¼ teaspoon cumin, ground
- 2 tablespoons olive oil
- 1 small red onion, chopped
- 1-inch turmeric root, grated
- ¼ cup cilantro, chopped
- 1 and ½ cups coconut cream
- 3 garlic cloves, minced

Directions:
Heat up a slow cooker with half of the oil over medium heat, add mustard seeds, ginger, onion, garlic, turmeric, chilies, curry powder and cumin, stir and cook for 3-4 minutes. Add the rest of the oil to your Slow cooker, add spice mix, fish, coconut milk, salt and pepper, cover and cook on High for 2 hours and 30 minutes. Divide into bowls and serve with the cilantro sprinkled on top.

Nutrition: calories 500, fat 34, fiber 7, carbs 13, protein 44

Italian Barramundi and Tomato Relish

Preparation time: 10 minutes | Cooking time: 2 hours | Servings: 4

Ingredients:
- 2 barramundi fillets, skinless
- 2 teaspoon olive oil
- 2 teaspoons Italian seasoning
- ¼ cup green olives, pitted and chopped
- ¼ cup cherry tomatoes, chopped
- ¼ cup black olives, chopped
- 1 tablespoon lemon zest
- 2 tablespoons lemon zest
- Salt and black pepper to the taste
- 2 tablespoons parsley, chopped
- 1 tablespoon olive oil

Directions:
Rub fish with salt, pepper, Italian seasoning and 2 teaspoons olive oil and put into your Slow cooker. In a bowl, mix tomatoes with all the olives, salt, pepper, lemon zest and lemon juice, parsley and 1-tablespoon olive oil, toss, add over fish, cover and cook on High for 2 hours. Divide fish between plates, top with tomato relish and serve.

Nutrition: calories 140, fat 4, fiber 2, carbs 11, protein 10

Spicy Creole Shrimp

Preparation time: 10 minutes | Cooking time: 1 hour 30 minutes | Servings: 2

Ingredients:
- ½ pound big shrimp, peeled and deveined
- 2 teaspoons Worcestershire sauce
- 2 teaspoons olive oil
- Juice of 1 lemon
- Salt and black pepper to the taste
- 1 teaspoon Creole seasoning

Directions:
In your Slow cooker, mix shrimp with Worcestershire sauce, oil, lemon juice, salt, pepper and Creole seasoning, toss, cover and cook on High for 1 hour and 30 minutes. Divide into bowls and serve.

Nutrition: calories 140, fat 3, fiber 1, carbs 6, protein 6

Sriracha Shrimp

Preparation time: 10 minutes | Cooking time: 1 hour 30 minutes | Servings: 6

Ingredients:
- ¼ cup yellow onion, chopped
- 2 tablespoons olive oil
- 1 garlic clove, minced
- 1 and ½ pounds shrimp, peeled and deveined
- ¼ cup red pepper, roasted and chopped
- 14 ounces canned tomatoes, chopped
- ¼ cup cilantro, chopped
- 2 tablespoons sriracha sauce
- 1 cup coconut milk
- Salt and black pepper to the taste
- 2 tablespoons lime juice

Directions:

Put the oil in your Slow cooker, add onion, garlic, shrimp, red pepper, tomatoes, cilantro, sriracha sauce, milk, salt, pepper and lime juice, toss, cover and cook on High for 1 hour and 30 minutes. Divide into bowls and serve.

Nutrition: calories 250, fat 12, fiber 3, carbs 5, protein 20

Shrimp and Peas Soup

Preparation time: 10 minutes | Cooking time: 1 hours | Servings: 4

Ingredients:
- 4 scallions, chopped
- 1 tablespoon olive oil
- 1 small ginger root, grated
- 8 cups chicken stock
- ¼ cup soy sauce
- 5 ounces canned bamboo shoots, sliced
- Black pepper to the taste
- ¼ teaspoon fish sauce
- 1 pound shrimp, peeled and deveined
- ½ pound snow peas
- 1 tablespoon sesame oil
- ½ tablespoon chili oil

Directions:

In your Slow cooker, mix olive oil with scallions, ginger, stock, soy sauce, bamboo, black pepper, fish sauce, shrimp, peas, sesame oil and chili oil, cover and cook on High for 1 hour. Stir soup, ladle into bowls and serve.

Nutrition: calories 240, fat 3, fiber 2, carbs 12, protein 14

Calamari and Sauce

Preparation time: 10 minutes | Cooking time: 2 hours 20 mizutes | Servings: 4

Ingredients:
- 1 squid, cut into medium rings
- A pinch of cayenne pepper
- 2 tablespoons flour
- Salt and black pepper to the taste
- ¼ cup fish stock
- 1 tablespoons lemon juice
- 4 tablespoons mayo
- 1 teaspoon sriracha sauce

Directions:

Season squid rings with salt, pepper and cayenne and put them in your Slow cooker. Add flour, stock, lemon juice and sriracha sauce, toss, cover and cook on High for 2 hour and 20 minutes. Add mayo, toss, divide between plates and serve.

Nutrition: calories 345, fat 32, fiber 3, carbs 12, protein 13

Calamari and Shrimp

Preparation time: 10 minutes | Cooking time: 2 hours 30 minutes | Servings: 2

Ingredients:
- 8 ounces calamari, cut into medium rings
- 7 ounces shrimp, peeled and deveined
- 3 tablespoons flour
- 1 tablespoon olive oil
- 2 tablespoons avocado, chopped
- 1 teaspoon tomato paste
- 1 tablespoon mayonnaise
- 1 teaspoon Worcestershire sauce
- 1 teaspoon lemon juice
- 2 lemon slices
- Salt and black pepper to the taste
- ½ teaspoon turmeric powder

Directions:
In your Slow cooker, mix calamari with flour, oil, tomato paste, mayo, Worcestershire sauce, lemon juice, lemon slices, salt, pepper and turmeric, cover and cook on High for 2 hours. Add shrimp, cover and cook on High for 30 minutes more. Divide between plates and serve.

Nutrition: calories 368, fat 23, fiber 3, carbs 10, protein 34

Clam Chowder

Preparation time: 10 minutes | Cooking time: 2 hours | Servings: 4

Ingredients:
- 1 cup celery stalks, chopped
- Salt and black pepper to the taste
- 1 teaspoon thyme, ground
- 2 cups chicken stock
- 14 ounces canned baby clams
- 2 cups whipping cream
- 1 cup onion, chopped
- 13 bacon slices, chopped

Directions:
Heat up a pan over medium heat, add bacon slices, brown them and transfer to a bowl. Heat up the same pan over medium heat, add celery and onion, stir and cook for 5 minutes. Transfer everything to your Slow cooker, also add bacon, baby clams, salt, pepper, stock, thyme and whipping cream, stir and cook on High for 2 hours. Divide into bowls and serve.

Nutrition: calories 420, fat 22, fiber 0, carbs 5, protein 25

Shrimp Salad

Preparation time: 10 minutes | Cooking time: 1 hours | Servings: 4

Ingredients:
- 2 tablespoons olive oil
- 1 pound shrimp, peeled and deveined
- Salt and black pepper to the taste
- 2 tablespoons lime juice
- 3 endives, leaves separated
- 3 tablespoons parsley, chopped
- 2 teaspoons mint, chopped
- 1 tablespoon tarragon, chopped
- 1 tablespoon lemon juice
- 2 tablespoons mayonnaise
- 1 teaspoon lime zest
- ½ cup sour cream

Directions:
In a bowl, mix shrimp with salt, pepper and the olive oil, toss to coat and spread into the Slow cooker, Add lime juice, endives, parsley, mint, tarragon, lemon juice, lemon zest, mayo and sour cream, toss, cover and cook on High for 1 hour. Divide into bowls and serve.

Nutrition: calories 200, fat 11, fiber 2, carbs 11, protein 13

Italian Clams

Preparation time: 10 minutes | Cooking time: 2 hours | Servings: 6

Ingredients:
- ½ cup butter, melted
- 36 clams, scrubbed
- 1 teaspoon red pepper flakes, crushed
- 1 teaspoon parsley, chopped
- 5 garlic cloves, minced
- 1 tablespoon oregano, dried
- 2 cups white wine

Directions:
In your Slow cooker, mix butter with clams, pepper flakes, parsley, garlic, oregano and wine, stir, cover and cook on High for 2 hours. Divide into bowls and serve.

Nutrition: calories 224, fat 15, fiber 2, carbs 7, protein 4

Orange Salmon

Preparation time: 10 minutes | Cooking time: 2 hours | Servings: 2

Ingredients:
- 2 lemons, sliced
- 1 pound wild salmon, skinless and cubed
- ¼ cup balsamic vinegar
- ¼ cup red orange juice
- 1 teaspoon olive oil
- 1/3 cup orange marmalade

Directions:
Heat up a slow cooker over medium heat, add vinegar, orange juice and marmalade, stir well, bring to a simmer for 1 minute and transfer to your Slow cooker. Add salmon, lemon slices and oil, toss, cover and cook on High for 2 hours. Divide salmon plates and serve with a side salad.

Nutrition: calories 260, fat 3, fiber 2, carbs 16, protein 8

Tuna and Chimichurri

Preparation time: 10 minutes | Cooking time: 1 hour 15 minutes | Servings: 4

Ingredients:
- ½ cup cilantro, chopped
- 1/3 cup olive oil
- 1 small red onion, chopped
- 3 tablespoon balsamic vinegar
- 2 tablespoons parsley, chopped
- 2 tablespoons basil, chopped
- 1 jalapeno pepper, chopped
- 1 pound tuna steak, boneless, skinless and cubed
- Salt and black pepper to the taste
- 1 teaspoon red pepper flakes
- 2 garlic cloves, minced
- 1 teaspoon thyme, chopped
- A pinch of cayenne pepper
- 2 avocados, pitted, peeled and sliced
- 6 ounces baby arugula

Directions:
In a bowl, mix the oil with jalapeno, vinegar, onion, cilantro, basil, garlic, parsley, pepper flakes, thyme, cayenne, salt and pepper, whisk well, transfer to your Slow cooker, cover and cook on High for 1 hour. Add tuna, cover and cook on High for 15 minutes more. Divide arugula on plates, top with tuna slices, drizzle the chimichurri sauce and serve with avocado slices on the side.

Nutrition: calories 186, fat 3, fiber 1, carbs 4, protein 20

Cider Clams

Preparation time: 10 minutes | Cooking time: 2 hours | Servings: 4

Ingredients:
- 2 pounds clams, scrubbed
- 3 ounces pancetta
- 1 tablespoon olive oil
- 3 tablespoons butter, melted
- 2 garlic cloves, minced
- 1 bottle infused cider
- Salt and black pepper to the taste
- Juice of ½ lemon
- 1 small green apple, chopped
- 2 thyme springs, chopped

Directions:
Heat up a pan with the oil over medium-high heat, add pancetta, brown for 3 minutes and transfer to your Slow cooker. Add butter, garlic, salt, pepper, shallot, cider, clams, thyme, lemon juice and apple, cover and cook on High for 2 hours. Divide everything into bowls and serve.

Nutrition: calories 270, fat 2, fiber 1, carbs 11, protein 20

Mustard Salmon

Preparation time: 10 minutes | Cooking time: 2 hours | Servings: 1

Ingredients:
- 1 big salmon fillet
- Salt and black pepper to the taste
- 2 tablespoons mustard
- 1 tablespoon olive oil
- 1 tablespoon maple extract

Directions:
In a bowl, mix maple extract with mustard and whisk well. Season salmon with salt and pepper, brush with the mustard mix, put in your Slow cooker, cover and cook on High for 2 hours. Serve the salmon with a side salad.

Nutrition: calories 240, fat 7, fiber 1, carbs 15, protein 23

Salmon and Relish

Preparation time: 10 minutes | Cooking time: 2 hours | Servings: 2

Ingredients:
- 2 medium salmon fillets, boneless
- Salt and black pepper to the taste
- 1 shallot, chopped
- 1 tablespoon lemon juice
- 1 big lemon, peeled and cut into wedges
- ¼ cup olive oil+ 1 teaspoon
- 2 tablespoons parsley, finely chopped

Directions:
Brush salmon fillets with the olive oil, sprinkle with salt and pepper, put in your Slow cooker, add shallot and lemon juice, cover and cook on High for 2 hours. Shed salmon and divide into 2 bowls. Add lemon segments to your Slow cooker also add ¼-cup oil and parsley and whisk well. Divide this mix over salmon, toss and serve.

Nutrition: calories 200, fat 10, fiber 1, carbs 5, protein 20

Mussels Soup

Preparation time: 10 minutes | Cooking time: 2 hours | Servings: 6

Ingredients:
- 2 pounds mussels
- 28 ounces canned tomatoes, crushed
- 28 ounces canned tomatoes, chopped
- 2 cup chicken stock
- 1 teaspoon red pepper flakes, crushed
- 3 garlic cloves, minced
- 1 handful parsley, chopped
- 1 yellow onion, chopped
- Salt and black pepper to the taste
- 1 tablespoon olive oil

Directions:
In your Slow cooker, mix mussels with canned and crushed tomatoes, stock, pepper flakes, garlic, parsley, onion, salt, pepper and oil, stir, cover and cook on High for 2 hours. Divide into bowls and serve.

Nutrition: calories 250, fat 3, fiber 3, carbs 8, protein 12

Fish and Olives Mix

Preparation time: 10 minutes | Cooking time: 2 hours | Servings: 4

Ingredients:
- 4 white fish fillets, boneless
- 1 cup olives, pitted and chopped
- 1 pound cherry tomatoes, halved
- A pinch of thyme, dried
- 1 garlic clove, minced
- A drizzle of olive oil
- Salt and black pepper to the taste
- ¼ cup chicken stock

Directions:
Put the stock in your Slow cooker, add fish, olives, tomatoes, thyme, garlic, oil, salt and pepper, cover and cook on High for 2 hours. Divide everything between plates and serve.

Nutrition: calories 200, fat 3, fiber 3, carbs 12, protein 20

Indian Fish

Preparation time: 10 minutes | Cooking time: 2 hours | Servings: 6

Ingredients:
- 6 white fish fillets, cut into medium pieces
- 1 tomato, chopped
- 14 ounces coconut milk
- 2 yellow onions, sliced
- 2 red bell peppers, cut into strips
- 2 garlic cloves, minced
- 6 curry leaves
- 1 tablespoons coriander, ground
- 1 tablespoon ginger, finely grated
- ½ teaspoon turmeric, ground
- 2 teaspoons cumin, ground
- Salt and black pepper to the taste
- ½ teaspoon fenugreek, ground
- 1 teaspoon hot pepper flakes
- 2 tablespoons lemon juice

Directions:
In your Slow cooker, mix fish with tomato, milk, onions, bell peppers, garlic cloves, curry leaves, coriander, turmeric, cumin, salt, pepper, fenugreek, pepper flakes and lemon juice, cover and cook on High for 2 hours. Toss fish, divide the whole mix between plates and serve.

Nutrition: calories 231, fat 4, fiber 6, carbs 16, protein 22

Cod and Peas

Preparation time: 15 minutes | Cooking time: 2 hours | Servings: 4

Ingredients:

- 16 ounces cod fillets
- 1 tablespoon parsley, chopped
- 10 ounces peas
- 9 ounces wine
- ½ teaspoon oregano, dried
- ½ teaspoon paprika
- 2 garlic cloves, chopped
- Salt and pepper to the taste

Directions:

In your food processor mix garlic with parsley, oregano, paprika and wine, blend well and add to your Slow cooker. Add fish, peas, salt and pepper, cover and cook on High for 2 hours. Divide into bowls and serve.

Nutrition: calories 251, far 2, fiber 6, carbs 7, protein 22

Salmon and Rice

Preparation time: 5 minutes | Cooking time: 2 hours | Servings: 2

Ingredients:

- 2 wild salmon fillets, boneless
- Salt and black pepper to the taste
- ½ cup jasmine rice
- 1 cup chicken stock
- ¼ cup veggie stock
- 1 tablespoon butter
- A pinch of saffron

Directions

In your Slow cooker mix stock with rice, stock, butter and saffron and stir. Add salmon, salt and pepper, cover and cook on High for 2 hours. Divide salmon on plates, add rice mix on the side and serve.

Nutrition: calories 312, fat 4, fiber 6, carbs 20, protein 22

Milky Fish

Preparation time: 10 minutes | Cooking time: 2 hours | Servings: 6

Ingredients:

- 17 ounces white fish, skinless, boneless and cut into medium chunks
- 1 yellow onion, chopped
- 13 ounces potatoes, peeled and cut into chunks
- 13 ounces milk
- Salt and black pepper to the taste
- 14 ounces chicken stock
- 14 ounces water
- 14 ounces half and half

Directions:

In your Slow cooker, mix fish with onion, potatoes, water, milk and stock, cover and cook on High for 2 hours. Add salt, pepper, half-and-half, stir, divide into bowls and serve.

Nutrition: calories 203, fat 4, fiber 5, carbs 20, protein 15

Salmon and Raspberry Vinaigrette

Preparation time: 2 hours | Cooking time: 2 hours | Servings: 6

Ingredients:
- 6 salmon steaks
- 2 tablespoons olive oil
- 4 leeks, sliced
- 2 garlic cloves, minced
- 2 tablespoons parsley, chopped
- 1 cup clam juice
- 2 tablespoons lemon juice
- Salt and white pepper to the taste
- 1 teaspoon sherry
- 1/3 cup dill, chopped

For the raspberry vinegar:
- 2 pints red raspberries
- 1-pint cider vinegar

Directions:
In a bowl, mix red raspberries with vinegar and salmon, toss, cover and keep in the fridge for 2 hours. In your Slow cooker, mix oil with parsley, leeks, garlic, clam juice, lemon juice, salt, pepper, sherry, dill and salmon, cover and cook on High for 2 hours. Divide everything between plates and serve.

Nutrition: calories 251, fat 6, fiber 7, carbs 16, protein 26

Fish Pudding

Preparation time: 10 minutes | Cooking time: 2 hours | Servings: 4

Ingredients:
- 1 pound cod fillets, cut into medium pieces
- 2 tablespoons parsley, chopped
- 4 ounces breadcrumbs
- 2 teaspoons lemon juice
- 2 eggs, whisked
- 2 ounces butter, melted
- ½ pint milk
- ½ pint shrimp sauce
- Salt and black pepper to the taste

Directions:
In a bowl, mix fish with crumbs, lemon juice, parsley, salt and pepper and stir. Add butter to your Slow cooker, add milk and whisk well. Add egg and fish mix, stir, cover and cook on High for 2 hours. Divide between plates and serve with shrimp sauce on top.

Nutrition: calories 231, fat 3, fiber 5, carbs 10, protein 5

Jambalaya

Preparation time: 10 minutes | Cooking time: 4 hours 30 minutes | Servings: 8

Ingredients:
- 1 pound chicken breast, chopped
- 1 pound shrimp, peeled and deveined
- 2 tablespoons extra virgin olive oil
- 1 pound sausage, chopped
- 2 cups onions, chopped
- 1 and ½ cups rice
- 2 tablespoons garlic, chopped
- 2 cups green, yellow and red bell peppers, chopped
- 3 and ½ cups chicken stock
- 1 tablespoon Creole seasoning
- 1 tablespoon Worcestershire sauce
- 1 cup tomatoes, crushed

Directions:
Add the oil to your Slow cooker and spread. Add chicken, sausage, onion, rice, garlic, mixed bell peppers, stock, seasoning, tomatoes and Worcestershire sauce, cover and cook on High for 4 hours. Add shrimp, cover, cook on High for 30 minutes more, divide everything between plates and serve.

Nutrition: calories 251, fat 10, fiber 3, carbs 20, protein 25

Tasty Tuna Mix

Preparation time: 5 minutes | *Cooking time:* 2 hours | *Servings:* 4

Ingredients:
- 14 ounces canned tuna, drained
- 16 ounces egg noodles
- 28 ounces cream of mushroom
- 1 cup peas, frozen
- 3 cups water
- 4 ounces cheddar cheese, grated
- ¼ cup breadcrumbs

Directions:

Add pasta and water to your Slow cooker; also add tuna, peas and cream, stir, cover and cook on High for 1 hour. Add cheese, stir, spread breadcrumbs all over, cover, cook on High for 1 more hour, divide into bowls and serve.

Nutrition: calories 251, fat 6, fiber 1, carbs 20, protein 12

Delicious Mackerel

Preparation time: 10 minutes | *Cooking time:* 2 hours | *Servings:* 4

Ingredients:
- 18 ounces mackerel, cut into pieces
- 3 garlic cloves, minced
- 8 shallots, chopped
- 1 teaspoon dried shrimp powder
- 1 teaspoon turmeric powder
- 1 tablespoon chili paste
- 2 lemongrass sticks, cut into halves
- 1 small piece of ginger, chopped
- 6 stalks laska leaves
- 3 and ½ ounces water
- 5 tablespoons vegetable oil
- 1 tablespoon tamarind paste mixed with 3 ounces water
- Salt to the taste
- 1 tablespoon sugar

Directions:

In your blender, mix garlic with shallots, chili paste, turmeric powder and shrimp powder and blend well. Add the oil to your Slow cooker, also add fish, spices paste, ginger, lemongrass, laska leaves, tamarind mix, water, salt and sugar, stir, cover, cook on High for 2 hours, divide between plates and serve.

Nutrition: calories 200, fat 3, fiber 1, carbs 20, protein 22

Chinese Mackerel

Preparation time: 10 minutes | *Cooking time:* 2 hours | *Servings:* 4

Ingredients:
- 2 pounds mackerel, cut into medium pieces
- 1 cup water
- 1 garlic clove, crushed
- 1 shallot, sliced
- 1-inch ginger piece, chopped
- 1/3 cup sake
- 1/3 cup mirin
- ¼ cup miso
- 1 sweet onion, thinly sliced
- 2 celery stalks, sliced
- 1 tablespoon rice vinegar
- 1 teaspoon Japanese hot mustard
- Salt to the taste
- 1 teaspoon sugar

Directions:

In your Slow cooker, mix mirin, sake, ginger, garlic and shallot. Add miso, water and mackerel, stir, cover the slow cooker and cook on High for 2 hours. Put onion and celery in a bowl and cover with ice water. In another bowl, mix vinegar with salt, sugar and mustard and stir well. Divide mackerel on plates, drain onion and celery well, mix with mustard dressing, divide next to mackerel and serve.

Nutrition: calories 300, fat 12, fiber 1, carbs 14, protein 20

Mackerel and Lemon

Preparation time: 10 minutes | Cooking time: 2 hours | Servings: 4

Ingredients:
- 4 mackerels
- 3 ounces breadcrumbs
- Juice and rind of 1 lemon
- 1 tablespoon chives, finely chopped
- Salt and black pepper to the taste
- 1 egg, whisked
- 1 tablespoon butter
- 1 tablespoon vegetable oil
- 3 lemon wedges

Directions:
In a bowl, mix breadcrumbs with lemon juice, lemon rind, salt, pepper, egg and chives, stir very well and coat mackerel with this mix. Add the oil and the butter to your Slow cooker and arrange mackerel inside. Cover, cook on High for 2 hours, divide fish between plates and serve with lemon wedges on the side.

Nutrition: calories 200, fat 3, fiber 1, carbs 3, protein 12

Mussels and Sausage Mix

Preparation time: 5 minutes | Cooking time: 2 hours | Servings: 4

Ingredients:
- 2 pounds mussels, scrubbed and debearded
- 12 ounces amber beer
- 1 tablespoon olive oil
- 1 yellow onion, chopped
- 8 ounces spicy sausage
- 1 tablespoon paprika

Directions:
Grease your Slow cooker with the oil, add onion, paprika, sausage, mussels and beer, cover and cook on High for 2 hours. Discard unopened mussels, divide the rest between bowls and serve.

Nutrition: calories 124, fat 3, fiber 1, carbs 7, protein 12

Mussels, Clams and Chorizo Mix

Preparation time: 10 minutes | Cooking time: 2 hours | Servings: 4

Ingredients:
- 15 small clams
- 30 mussels, scrubbed
- 2 chorizo links, sliced
- 1 pound baby red potatoes, peeled
- 1 yellow onion, chopped
- 10 ounces beer
- 2 tablespoons parsley, chopped
- 1 teaspoon olive oil
- Lemon wedges for serving

Directions:
Grease your Slow cooker with the oil, add clams, mussels, chorizo, potatoes, onion, beer and parsley, cover and cook on High for 2 hours. Add parsley, stir, divide into bowls and serve with lemon wedges on the side.

Nutrition: calories 251, fat 4, fiber 7, carbs 10, protein 20

Crab Legs

Preparation time: 5 minutes | Cooking time: 1 hour 30 minutes | Servings: 4

Ingredients:
- 4 pounds king crab legs, broken in half
- 3 lemon wedges
- ¼ cup butter, melted
- ½ cup chicken stock

Directions:
In your Slow cooker, mix stock with crab legs and butter, cover and cook on High for 1 hour and 30 minutes. Divide crab legs between bowls, drizzle melted butter all over and serve with lemon wedges on the side.

Nutrition: calories 100, fat 1, fiber 5, carbs 12, protein 3

Shrimp and Sausage Boil

Preparation time: 10 minutes | Cooking time: 2 hours 30 minutes | Servings: 4

Ingredients:
- 1 and ½ pounds shrimp, head removed
- 12 ounces Andouille sausage, already cooked and chopped
- 4 ears of corn, each cut into 3 pieces
- 1 tablespoon old bay seasoning
- 16 ounces beer
- Salt and black pepper to the taste
- 1 teaspoon red pepper flakes, crushed
- 2 sweet onions, cut into wedges
- 1 pound potatoes, cut into medium chunks
- 8 garlic cloves, crushed
- French baguettes for serving

Directions:
In your Slow cooker, mix beer with old bay seasoning, red pepper flakes, salt, black pepper, onions, garlic, potatoes, corn and sausage, cover and cook on High for 2 hours. Add shrimp, cover, cook on High for 30 minutes more, divide into bowls and serve with French baguettes on the side.

Nutrition: calories 261, fat 5, fiber 6, carbs 20, protein 16

Mushroom and Shrimp Curry

Preparation time: 10 minutes | Cooking time: 2 hours 30 minutes | Servings: 4

Ingredients:
- 1 pound shrimp, peeled and deveined
- 1 cup bouillon
- 4 lemon slices
- Salt and black pepper to the taste
- ½ teaspoon curry powder
- ¼ cup mushrooms, sliced
- ¼ cup yellow onion, chopped
- 1 tablespoon olive oil
- ½ cup raisins
- 3 tablespoons flour
- 1 cup milk

Directions:
In your Slow cooker, mix bouillon with lemon, salt, pepper, curry powder, mushrooms, onion, flour and milk, whisk well, cover and cook on High for 2 hours. Add shrimp and raisins, cover and cook on High for 30 minutes more. Divide curry into bowls and serve.

Nutrition: calories 300, fat 4, fiber 2, carbs 30, protein 17

Dill Shrimp Mix

Preparation time: 10 minutes | Cooking time: 1 hours | Servings: 4

Ingredients:
- 1 pound shrimp, peeled and deveined
- 2 tablespoons olive oil
- 1 tablespoon yellow onion, chopped
- 1 cup white wine
- 2 tablespoons cornstarch
- ¾ cup milk
- 1 tablespoon dill, chopped

Directions:
In your Slow cooker, mix oil with onion, cornstarch, milk, wine, dill and shrimp, cover and cook on High for 1 hour. Divide everything into bowls and serve.

Nutrition: calories 300, fat 13, fiber 2, carbs 10, protein 10

Japanese Shrimp

Preparation time: 10 minutes | Cooking time: 1 hours | Servings: 4

Ingredients:
- 1 pounds shrimp, peeled and deveined
- 2 tablespoons soy sauce
- ½ pound pea pods
- 3 tablespoons vinegar
- ¾ cup pineapple juice
- 1 cup chicken stock
- 3 tablespoons sugar

Directions:
Put shrimp and pea pods in your Slow cooker, add soy sauce, vinegar, pineapple juice, stock and sugar, stir, cover and cook on High for 1 hour, Divide between plates and serve.

Nutrition: calories 251, fat 4, fiber 1, carbs 12, protein 30

Octopus and Veggies Mix

Preparation time: 1 hour | Cooking time: 3 hours | Servings: 4

Ingredients:
- 1 octopus, already prepared
- 1 cup red wine
- 1 cup white wine
- 1 cup water
- 1 cup olive oil
- 2 teaspoons pepper sauce
- 1 tablespoon hot sauce
- 1 tablespoon paprika
- 1 tablespoon tomato sauce
- Salt and black pepper to the taste
- ½ bunch parsley, chopped
- 2 garlic cloves, minced
- 1 yellow onion, chopped
- 4 potatoes cut into quarters.

Directions:
Put octopus in a bowl, add white wine, red one, water, half of the oil, pepper sauce, hot sauce, paprika, tomato paste, salt, pepper and parsley, toss to coat, cover and keep in a cold place for 1 day. Add the rest of the oil to your Slow cooker and arrange onions and potatoes on the bottom. Add the octopus and the marinade, stir, cover, cook on High for 3 hours, divide everything between plates and serve.

Nutrition: calories 230, fat 4, fiber 1, carbs 7, protein 23

Mediterranean Octopus

Preparation time: 1 hour 10 minutes | Cooking time: 3 hours | Servings: 6

Ingredients:
- 1 octopus, cleaned and prepared
- 2 rosemary springs
- 2 teaspoons oregano, dried
- ½ yellow onion, roughly chopped
- 4 thyme springs
- ½ lemon
- 1 teaspoon black peppercorns
- 3 tablespoons extra virgin olive oil

For the marinade:
- ¼ cup extra virgin olive oil
- Juice of ½ lemon
- 4 garlic cloves, minced
- 2 thyme springs
- 1 rosemary spring
- Salt and black pepper to the taste

Directions:
Put the octopus in your Slow cooker, add oregano, 2 rosemary springs, 4 thyme springs, onion, lemon, 3 tablespoons olive oil, peppercorns and salt, stir, cover and cook on High for 2 hours. Transfer octopus on a cutting board, cut tentacles, put them in a bowl, mix with ¼-cup olive oil, lemon juice, garlic, 1 rosemary springs, 2 thyme springs, salt and pepper, toss to coat and leave aside for 1 hour. Transfer octopus and the marinade to your Slow cooker again, cover and cook on High for 1 more hour. Divide octopus on plates, drizzle the marinade all over and serve.

Nutrition: calories 200, fat 4, fiber 3, carbs 10, protein 11

Stuffed Squid

Preparation time: 10 minutes | Cooking time: 3 hours | Servings: 4

Ingredients:
- 4 squid
- 1 cup sticky rice
- 14 ounces dashi stock
- 2 tablespoons sake
- 4 tablespoons soy sauce
- 1 tablespoon mirin
- 2 tablespoons sugar

Directions:
Chop tentacles from 1 squid, mix with the rice, stuff each squid with this mix and seal ends with toothpicks. Place squid in your Slow cooker, add stock, soy sauce, sake, sugar and mirin, stir, cover and cook on High for 3 hours. Divide between plates and serve.

Nutrition: calories 230, fat 4, fiber 4, carbs 7, protein 11

Flavored Squid

Preparation time: 10 minutes | Cooking time: 3 hours | Servings: 4

Ingredients:
- 17 ounces squids
- 1 and ½ tablespoons red chili powder
- Salt and black pepper to the taste
- ¼ teaspoon turmeric powder
- 2 cups water
- 5 pieces coconut, shredded
- 4 garlic cloves, minced
- ½ teaspoons cumin seeds
- 3 tablespoons olive oil
- ¼ teaspoon mustard seeds
- 1-inch ginger pieces, chopped

Directions:
Put squids in your Slow cooker, add chili powder, turmeric, salt, pepper and water, stir, cover and cook on High for 2 hours. In your blender, mix coconut with ginger, oil, garlic and cumin and blend well. Add this over the squids, cover and cook on High for 1 more hour. Divide everything into bowls and serve.

Nutrition: calories 261, fat 3, fiber 8, carbs 19, protein 11

Slow Cooker Dessert Recipes

Pudding Cake

Preparation time: 10 minutes | *Cooking time:* 2 hours 30 minutes | *Servings:* 8

Ingredients:
- 1 and ½ cup sugar
- 1 cup flour
- ¼ cup cocoa powder+ 2 tablespoons
- ½ cup chocolate almond milk
- 2 teaspoons baking powder
- 2 tablespoons vegetable oil
- 1 teaspoon vanilla extract
- 1 and ½ cups hot water
- Cooking spray

Directions:
In a bowl, mix flour with 2 tablespoons cocoa, baking powder, milk, oil and vanilla extract, whisk well and spread on the bottom of the Slow cooker, greased with cooking spray. In another bowl, mix sugar with the rest of the cocoa and the water, whisk well, spread over the batter in the Slow cooker, cover; cook your cake on High for 2 hours and 30 minutes. Leave the cake to cool down, slice and serve.

Nutrition: calories 250, fat 4, fiber 3, carbs 40, protein 4

Peanut Butter Cake

Preparation time: 10 minutes | *Cooking time:* 2 hours 30 minutes | *Servings:* 8

Ingredients:
- 1 cup sugar
- 1 cup flour
- 3 tablespoons cocoa powder+ ½ cup
- 1 and ½ teaspoons baking powder
- ½ cup milk
- 2 tablespoons vegetable oil
- 2 cups hot water
- 1 teaspoon vanilla extract
- ½ cup peanut butter
- Cooking spray

Directions:
In a bowl, mix half of the sugar with 3 tablespoons cocoa, flour, baking powder, oil, vanilla and milk, stir well and pour into your Slow cooker greased with cooking spray. In another bowl, mix the rest of the sugar with the rest of the cocoa, peanut butter and hot water, stir well and pour over the batter in the slow cooker. Cover slow cooker, cook on High for 2 hours and 30 minutes, slice cake and serve.

Nutrition: calories 242, fat 4, fiber 7, carbs 8, protein 4

Blueberry Cake

Preparation time: 10 minutes | *Cooking time:* 1 hours | *Servings:* 6

Ingredients:
- ½ cup flour
- ¼ teaspoon baking powder
- ¼ teaspoon sugar
- ¼ cup blueberries
- 1/3 cup milk
- 1 teaspoon olive oil
- 1 teaspoon flaxseed, ground
- ½ teaspoon lemon zest, grated
- ¼ teaspoon vanilla extract
- ¼ teaspoon lemon extract
- Cooking spray

Directions:
In a bowl, mix flour with baking powder, sugar, blueberries, milk, oil, flaxseeds, lemon zest, vanilla extract and lemon extract and whisk well. Spray your slow cooker with cooking spray, line it with parchment paper, pour cake batter, cover slow cooker, cook on High for 1 hour, and leave the cake to cool down, slice and serve.

Nutrition: calories 200, fat 4, fiber 4, carbs 10, protein 4

Peach Pie

*Preparation time: 10 minutes | **Cooking time:** 4 hours | Servings: 4*

Ingredients:
- 4 cups peaches, peeled and sliced
- 1 cup sugar
- ½ teaspoon cinnamon powder
- 1 and ½ cups crackers, crushed
- ¼ teaspoon nutmeg, ground
- ½ cup milk
- 1 teaspoon vanilla extract
- Cooking spray

Directions:
In a bowl, mix peaches with half of the sugar and cinnamon and stir. In another bowl, mix crackers with the rest of the sugar, nutmeg, milk and vanilla extract and stir. Spray your Slow cooker with cooking spray, spread peaches on the bottom, and add crackers mix, spread, cover and cook on Low for 4 hours. Divide cobbler between plates and serve.

Nutrition: calories 212, fat 4, fiber 4, carbs 7, protein 3

Sweet Strawberry Mix

*Preparation time: 10 minutes | **Cooking time:** 3 hours | Servings: 10*

Ingredients:
- 2 tablespoons lemon juice
- 2 pounds strawberries
- 4 cups sugar
- 1 teaspoon cinnamon powder
- 1 teaspoon vanilla extract

Directions:
In your Slow cooker, mix strawberries with sugar, lemon juice, cinnamon and vanilla, cover, cook on Low for 3 hours, divide into bowls and serve cold.

Nutrition: calories 100, fat 1, fiber 1, carbs 6, protein 2

Sweet Plums

*Preparation time: 10 minutes | **Cooking time:** 3 hours | Servings: 6*

Ingredients:
- 14 plums, halved
- 1 and ¼ cups sugar
- 1 teaspoon cinnamon powder
- ¼ cup water

Directions:
Put the plums in your Slow cooker, add sugar, cinnamon and water, stir, cover, cook on Low for 3 hours, divide into bowls and serve cold.

Nutrition: calories 150, fat 2, fiber 1, carbs 5, protein 3

Bananas and Sweet Sauce

Preparation time: 10 minutes | Cooking time: 2 hours | Servings: 4

Ingredients:
- Juice of ½ lemon
- 3 tablespoons agave nectar
- 1 tablespoon vegetable oil
- 4 bananas, peeled and sliced
- ½ teaspoon cardamom seeds

Directions:
Put the bananas in your Slow cooker, add agave nectar, lemon juice, oil and cardamom, cover, cook on Low for 2 hours, divide bananas between plates, drizzle agave sauce all over and serve.

Nutrition: calories 120, fat 1, fiber 2, carbs 8, protein 3

Orange Cake

Preparation time: 10 minutes | Cooking time: 5 hours | Servings: 4

Ingredients:
- Cooking spray
- 1 teaspoon baking powder
- 1 cup flour
- 1 cup sugar
- ½ teaspoon cinnamon powder
- 3 tablespoons vegetable oil
- ½ cup milk
- ½ cup pecans, chopped
- ¾ cup water
- ½ cup raisins
- ½ cup orange peel, grated
- ¾ cup orange juice

Directions:
In a bowl, mix flour with half of the sugar, baking powder, cinnamon, 2 tablespoons oil, milk, pecans and raisins, stir and pour this into your Slow cooker greased with cooking spray. Heat up a small pan over medium heat, add water, orange juice, orange peel, the rest of the oil and the rest of the sugar, stir, bring to a boil, pour over the mix in the Slow cooker, cover and cook on Low for 5 hours. Divide into dessert bowls and serve cold.

Nutrition: calories 182, fat 3, fiber 1, carbs 4, protein 3

Apples Stew

Preparation time: 10 minutes | Cooking time: 1 hour 30 minutes | Servings: 5

Ingredients:
- 5 apples, tops cut off and cored
- 1/3 cup sugar
- ¼ cup pecans, chopped
- 2 teaspoons lemon zest, grated
- ½ teaspoon cinnamon powder
- 1 tablespoon lemon juice
- 1 tablespoon vegetable oil
- ½ cup water

Directions:
Arrange apples in your Slow cooker, add sugar, pecans, lemon zest, cinnamon, lemon juice, coconut oil and water, toss, cover and cook on High for 1 hour and 30 minutes. Divide apple stew between plates and serve.

Nutrition: calories 200, fat 1, fiber 2, carbs 6, protein 3

Pears and Sauce

Preparation time: 10 minutes | Cooking time: 4 hours | Servings: 4

Ingredients:
- 4 pears, peeled and cored
- 2 cups orange juice
- ¼ cup maple syrup
- 2 teaspoons cinnamon powder
- 1 tablespoon ginger, grated

Directions:
In your Slow cooker, mix pears with orange juice, maple syrup, cinnamon and ginger, cover and cook on Low for 4 hours. Divide pears and sauce between plates and serve warm.

Nutrition: calories 210, fat 1, fiber 2, carbs 6, protein 4

Vanilla Cookies

Preparation time: 10 minutes | Cooking time: 2 hours 30 minutes | Servings: 12

Ingredients:
- 2 eggs
- ¼ cup vegetable oil
- 1 cup sugar
- ½ teaspoon vanilla extract
- 1 teaspoon baking powder
- 1 and ½ cups almond meal
- ½ cup almonds, chopped

Directions:
In a bowl, mix oil with sugar, vanilla extract and eggs and whisk. Add baking powder, almond meal and almonds and stir well. Line your slow cooker with parchment paper, spread cookie mix on the bottom of the slow cooker, cover and cook on Low for 2 hours and 30 minutes. Leave cookie sheet to cool down, cut into medium pieces and serve.

Nutrition: calories 220, fat 2, fiber 1, carbs 3, protein 6

Pumpkin Pie

Preparation time: 10 minutes | Cooking time: 2 hours 20 minutes | Servings: 10

Ingredients:
- 1 and ½ teaspoons baking powder
- Cooking spray
- 1 cup pumpkin puree
- 2 cups flour
- ½ teaspoon baking soda
- 1 and ½ teaspoons cinnamon powder
- ¼ teaspoon ginger, grated
- 1 tablespoon vegetable oil
- 2 eggs
- 1 tablespoon vanilla extract
- 1/3 cup maple syrup
- 1 teaspoon lemon juice

Directions:
In a bowl, flour with baking powder, baking soda, cinnamon, ginger, eggs, oil, vanilla, pumpkin puree, maple syrup and lemon juice, stir and pour in your slow cooker greased with cooking spray and lined. Cover slow cooker and cook on Low for 2 hours and 20 minutes. Leave the cake to cool down, slice and serve.

Nutrition: calories 182, fat 3, fiber 2, carbs 10, protein 3

Strawberries Marmalade

Preparation time: 10 minutes | Cooking time: 4 hours | Servings: 10

Ingredients:
- 32 ounces strawberries, chopped
- 2 pounds sugar
- Zest of 1 lemon, grated
- 4 ounces raisins
- 3 ounces water

Directions:
In your slow cooker, mix strawberries with coconut sugar, lemon zest, raisins and water, stir, cover and cook on High for 4 hours. Divide into small jars and serve cold.

Nutrition: calories 140, fat 3, fiber 2, carbs 2, protein 1

Rhubarb Marmalade

Preparation time: 10 minutes | Cooking time: 3 hours | Servings: 8

Ingredients:
- 1/3 cup water
- 2 pounds rhubarb, chopped
- 2 pounds strawberries, chopped
- 1 cup sugar
- 1 tablespoon mint, chopped

Directions:
In your Slow cooker, mix water with rhubarb, strawberries, sugar and mint, stir, cover and cook on High for 3 hours. Divide into cups and serve cold.

Nutrition: calories 100, fat 1, fiber 4, carbs 10, protein 2

Sweet Potato Pudding

Preparation time: 10 minutes | Cooking time: 5 hours | Servings: 8

Ingredients:
- 1 cup water
- 1 tablespoon lemon peel, grated
- ½ cup sugar
- 3 sweet potatoes peeled and sliced
- ¼ cup butter
- ¼ cup maple syrup
- 1 cup pecans, chopped

Directions:
In your Slow cooker, mix water with lemon peel, sugar, potatoes, butter, maple syrup and pecans, stir, cover and cook on High for 5 hours. Divide sweet potato pudding into bowls and serve cold.

Nutrition: calories 200, fat 4, fiber 3, carbs 10, protein 4

Cherry Jam

Preparation time: 10 minutes | Cooking time: 3 hours | Servings: 6

Ingredients:
- 2 tablespoons lemon juice
- 3 tablespoons gelatin
- 4 cups cherries, pitted
- 2 cups sugar

Directions:
In your Slow cooker, mix lemon juice with gelatin, cherries and coconut sugar, stir, cover and cook on High for 3 hours. Divide into cups and serve cold.

Nutrition: calories 211, fat 3, fiber 1, carbs 3, protein 3

Sweet Cookies

Preparation time: 10 minutes | Cooking time: 2 hours 30 minutes | Servings: 10

Ingredients:
- 1 egg white
- ¼ cup vegetable oil
- 1 cup sugar
- ½ teaspoon vanilla extract
- 1 teaspoon baking powder
- 1 and ½ cups almond meal
- ½ cup dark chocolate chips

Directions:
In a bowl, mix coconut oil with sugar, vanilla extract and egg white and beat well using your mixer. Add baking powder and almond meal and stir well. Fold in chocolate chips and stir gently. Line your slow cooker with parchment paper and grease it. Transfer cookie mix to your Slow cooker, press it on the bottom, cover and cook on low for 2 hours and 30 minutes. Take cookie sheet out of the Slow cooker, cut in 10 bars and serve.

Nutrition: calories 220, fat 2, fiber 1, carbs 3, protein 6

Maple Pears

Preparation time: 10 minutes | Cooking time: 4 hours | Servings: 4

Ingredients:
- 4 pears, peeled and tops cut off and cored
- 5 cardamom pods
- 2 cups orange juice
- ¼ cup maple syrup
- 1 cinnamon stick
- 1-inch ginger, grated

Directions:
Put the pears in your Slow cooker, add cardamom, orange juice, maple syrup, cinnamon and ginger, cover and cook on Low for 4 hours. Divide pears between plates and serve them with the sauce on top.

Nutrition: calories 200, fat 4, fiber 2, carbs 3, protein 4

Stuffed Apples

Preparation time: 10 minutes | Cooking time: 1 hour 30 minutes | Servings: 5

Ingredients:
- 5 apples, tops cut off and cored
- 5 figs
- 1/3 cup sugar
- 1 teaspoon dried ginger
- ¼ cup pecans, chopped
- 2 teaspoons lemon zest, grated
- ¼ teaspoon nutmeg, ground
- ½ teaspoon cinnamon powder
- 1 tablespoon lemon juice
- 1 tablespoon vegetable oil
- ½ cup water

Directions:

In a bowl, mix figs with sugar, ginger, pecans, lemon zest, nutmeg, cinnamon, oil and lemon juice, whisk really well, stuff your apples with this mix and put them in your Slow cooker. Add the water, cover, cook on High for 1 hour and 30 minutes, divide between dessert plates and serve.

Nutrition: calories 200, fat 1, fiber 2, carbs 4, protein 7

Chocolate Cake

Preparation time: 10 minutes | Cooking time: 3 hours | Servings: 10

Ingredients:
- 1 cup flour
- 3 egg whites, whisked
- ½ cup cocoa powder
- ½ cup sugar
- 1 and ½ teaspoons baking powder
- 3 eggs
- 4 tablespoons vegetable oil
- ¾ teaspoon vanilla extract
- 2/3 cup milk
- 1/3 cup dark chocolate chips

Directions:

In a bowl, mix sugar with flour, egg whites, cocoa powder, baking powder, milk, oil, eggs, chocolate chips and vanilla extract and whisk really well. Pour this into your lined and greased Slow cooker and cook on Low for 2 hours. Leave the cake aside to cool down, slice and serve.

Nutrition: calories 200, fat 12, fiber 4, carbs 8, protein 6

Berry Cobbler

Preparation time: 10 minutes | Cooking time: 2 hours | Servings: 6

Ingredients:
- 1 pound fresh blackberries
- 1 pound fresh blueberries
- ¾ cup water
- ¾ cup sugar+ 2 tablespoons
- ¾ cup flour
- ¼ cup tapioca flour
- ½ cup arrowroot powder
- 1 teaspoon baking powder
- 2 tablespoons palm sugar
- 1/3 cup milk
- 1 egg, whisked
- 1 teaspoon lemon zest, grated
- 3 tablespoons vegetable oil

Directions:

Put blueberries, blackberries, ¾-cup sugar, water and tapioca in your Slow cooker, cover and cook on High for 1 hour. In a bowl, mix flour with arrowroot, the rest of the sugar and baking powder and stir well. In a second bowl, mix the egg with milk, oil and lemon zest. Combine egg mixture with flour mixture, stir well, drop tablespoons of this mix over the berries, cover and cook on High for 1 more hour. Leave cobbler to cool down, divide into dessert bowls and serve.

Nutrition: calories 240, fat 4, fiber 3, carbs 10, protein 6

Apple Bread

Preparation time: 10 minutes | Cooking time: 2 hours 20 minutes | Servings: 6

Ingredients:

- 3 cups apples, cored and cubed
- 1 cup sugar
- 1 tablespoon vanilla extract
- 2 eggs
- 1 tablespoon apple pie spice
- 2 cups flour
- 1 tablespoon baking powder
- 1 tablespoon butter

Directions:

In a bowl, mix apples with sugar, vanilla, eggs, apple spice, flour, baking powder and butter, whisk well, pour into your Slow cooker, cover and cook on High for 2 hours and 20 minutes. Leave the bread to cool down, slice and serve.

Nutrition: calories 236, fat 2, fiber 4, carbs 12, protein 4

Banana Cake

Preparation time: 10 minutes | Cooking time: 2 hours | Servings: 6

Ingredients:

- ¾ cup sugar
- 1/3 cup butter, soft
- 1 teaspoon vanilla
- 1 egg
- 3 bananas, mashed
- 1 teaspoon baking powder
- 1 and ½ cups flour
- ½ teaspoons baking soda
- 1/3 cup milk
- Cooking spray

Directions:

In a bowl, mix butter with sugar, vanilla extract, eggs, bananas, baking powder, flour, baking soda and milk and whisk. Grease your Slow cooker with the cooking spray, add the batter, spread, cover and cook on High for 2 hours. Leave the cake to cool down, slice and serve.

Nutrition: calories 300, fat 4, fiber 4, carbs 27, protein 4

Chocolate Pudding

Preparation time: 10 minutes | Cooking time: 1 hours | Servings: 4

Ingredients:

- 4 ounces heavy cream
- 4 ounces dark chocolate, cut into chunks
- 1 teaspoon sugar

Directions:

In a bowl, mix the cream with chocolate and sugar, whisk well, pour into your slow cooker, cover and cook on High for 1 hour. Divide into bowls and serve cold.

Nutrition: calories 232, fat 12, fiber 6, carbs 9, protein 4

Cauliflower Pudding

Preparation time: 5 minutes | Cooking time: 2 hours | Servings: 6

Ingredients:
- 1 tablespoon butter, melted
- 7 ounces cauliflower rice
- 4 ounces water
- 16 ounces milk
- 3 ounces sugar
- 1 egg
- 1 teaspoon cinnamon powder
- 1 teaspoon vanilla extract

Directions:
In your Slow cooker, mix butter with cauliflower rice, water, milk, sugar, egg, cinnamon and vanilla extract, stir, cover and cook on High for 2 hours. Divide pudding into bowls and serve cold.

Nutrition: calories 202, fat 2, fiber 6, carbs 18, protein 4

Chia Pudding

Preparation time: 10 minutes | Cooking time: 1 hours | Servings: 4

Ingredients:
- 1 cup milk
- ½ cup pumpkin puree
- 2 tablespoons maple syrup
- ½ cup coconut milk
- ¼ cup chia seeds
- ½ teaspoon cinnamon powder
- ¼ teaspoon ginger, grated

Directions:
In your Slow cooker, mix milk with coconut milk, pumpkin puree, maple syrup, chia, cinnamon and ginger, stir, cover and cook on High for 1 hour. Divide pudding into bowls and serve.

Nutrition: calories 105, fat 2, fiber 7, carbs 11, protein 4

Stewed Grapefruit

Preparation time: 10 minutes | Cooking time: 2 hours | Servings: 6

Ingredients:
- 1 cup water
- 1 cup maple syrup
- ½ cup mint, chopped
- 64 ounces red grapefruit juice
- 2 grapefruits, peeled and chopped

Directions:
In your Slow cooker, mix grapefruit with water, maple syrup, mint and grapefruit juice, stir, cover and cook on High for 2 hours. Divide into bowls and serve cold.

Nutrition: calories 170, fat 1, fiber, 2, carbs 5, protein 1

Cocoa Cherry Compote

Preparation time: 10 minutes | Cooking time: 2 hours | Servings: 6

Ingredients:
- ½ cup dark cocoa powder
- ¾ cup red cherry juice
- ¼ cup maple syrup
- 1 pound cherries, pitted and halved
- 2 tablespoons sugar
- 2 cups water

Directions:
In your Slow cooker, mix cocoa powder with cherry juice, maple syrup, cherries, water and sugar, stir, cover and cook on High for 2 hours. Divide into bowls and serve cold.

Nutrition: calories 197, fat 1, fiber 4, carbs 5, protein 2

Cashew Cake

Preparation time: 10 minutes | Cooking time: 2 hours | Servings: 6

Ingredients:

For the crust:
- ½ cup dates, pitted
- 1 tablespoon water
- ½ teaspoon vanilla
- ½ cup almonds

For the cake:
- 2 and ½ cups cashews, soaked for 8 hours
- 1 cup blueberries
- ¾ cup maple syrup
- 1 tablespoon vegetable oil

Directions:
In your blender, mix dates with water, vanilla and almonds, pulse well, transfer dough to a working surface, flatten and arrange on the bottom of your Slow cooker. In your blender, mix maple syrup with the oil, cashews and blueberries, blend well, spread over crust, cover and cook on High for 2 hours. Leave the cake to cool down, slice and serve.

Nutrition: calories 200, fat 3, fiber 5, carbs 12, protein 3

Lemon Pudding

Preparation time: 10 minutes | Cooking time: 1 hours | Servings: 4

Ingredients:
- 1/3 cup butter, soft
- 1 and ½ tablespoons vegetable oil
- 5 tablespoons lemon juice
- ½ teaspoon lemon zest, grated
- 1 tablespoons maple syrup

Directions:
In a bowl, mix butter with oil, lemon juice, lemon zest and maple syrup and stir really well. Pour into your Slow cooker, cook on High for 1 hour, divide into bowls and serve.

Nutrition: calories 182, fat 4, fiber 0, carbs 6, protein 1

Lemon Jam

Preparation time: 10 minutes | Cooking time: 2 hours | Servings: 8

Ingredients:
- 2 pounds lemons, sliced
- 2 cups dates
- 1 cup water
- 1 tablespoon vinegar
- 2 tablespoons sugar

Directions:
Put dates in your blender, add water, pulse really well, transfer to your Slow cooker, add lemon slices, sugar and vinegar, stir, cover and cook on Low for 2 hours. Divide into small jars and serve cold.

Nutrition: calories 172, fat 2, fiber 1, carbs 2, protein 4

Chocolate Cream

Preparation time: 10 minutes | Cooking time: 2 hours | Servings: 4

Ingredients:
- 1 cup chocolate chips
- 2 tablespoons butter
- 2/3 cup heavy cream
- 2 teaspoons brandy
- 2 tablespoons sugar
- ¼ teaspoon vanilla extract

Directions:
In your Slow cooker, mix chocolate chips with butter, cream, brandy, sugar and vanilla extract, cover and cook on Low for 2 hours. Divide into bowls and serve warm.

Nutrition: calories 150, fat 5, fiber 4, carbs 6, protein 1

Coconut and Macadamia Cream

Preparation time: 10 minutes | Cooking time: 1 hours 30 minutes | Servings: 4

Ingredients:
- 4 tablespoons vegetable oil
- 3 tablespoons macadamia nuts, chopped
- 2 tablespoons sugar
- 1 cup heavy cream
- 5 tablespoons coconut powder

Directions:
Put the oil in your Slow cooker, add nuts, sugar, coconut powder and cream, stir, cover, and cook on Low for 1 hour and 30 minutes. Stir well, divide into bowls and serve.

Nutrition: calories 154, fat 1, fiber 0, carbs 7, protein 2

Strawberry Pie

Preparation time: 10 minutes | Cooking time: 2 hours | Servings: 12

Ingredients:
For the crust:
- 1 cup coconut, shredded
- 1 cup sunflower seeds
- ¼ cup butter
- Cooking spray

For the filling:
- 1 teaspoon gelatin
- 8 ounces cream cheese
- 4 ounces strawberries
- 2 tablespoons water
- ½ tablespoon lemon juice
- ¼ teaspoon stevia
- ½ cup heavy cream
- 8 ounces strawberries, chopped for serving
- 16 ounces heavy cream for serving

Directions:
In your food processor, mix sunflower seeds with coconut and butter and stir well. Put this into your Slow cooker greased with cooking spray. Heat up a pan with the water over medium heat, add gelatin, stir until it dissolves, and take off heat and leave aside to cool down. Add this to your food processor, mix with 4 ounces strawberries, cream cheese, lemon juice and stevia and blend well. Add ½-cup heavy cream, stir well and spread this over crust. Top with 8 ounces strawberries, cover and cook on High for 2 hours. Spread heavy cream all over, leave the cake to cool down and keep it in the fridge until you serve it.

Nutrition: calories 234, fat 23, fiber 2, carbs 6, protein 7

Sweet Raspberry Mix

Preparation time: 10 minutes | Cooking time: 1 hours | Servings: 12

Ingredients:
- ½ cup coconut butter
- ½ cup vegetable oil
- ½ cup raspberries, dried
- ¼ cup sugar
- ½ cup coconut, shredded

Directions:
In your food processor, blend dried berries very well. In a bowl, mix oil, coconut and sugar and spread half of this mix on the bottom of your Slow cooker. Add raspberry powder, spread, and top with the rest of the butter mix, spread, cover and cook on High for 1 hour. Cut into pieces and serve.

Nutrition: calories 234, fat 22, fiber 2, carbs 4, protein 2

Sweet Mascarpone Cream

Preparation time: 10 minutes | Cooking time: 1 hours | Servings: 12

Ingredients:
- 8 ounces mascarpone cheese
- ¾ teaspoon vanilla extract
- 1 tablespoon sugar
- 1 cup whipping cream
- ½ pint blueberries
- ½ pint strawberries

Directions:
In your Slow cooker, mix whipping cream with sugar, vanilla and mascarpone and blend well. Add blueberries and strawberries cover cook on High for 1 hour, stir your cream, divide it into glasses and serve cold.

Nutrition: calories 143, fat 12, fiber 1, carbs 6, protein 2

Lemon Cream

Preparation time: 10 minutes | Cooking time: 1 hours | Servings: 4

Ingredients:
- 1 cup heavy cream
- 1 teaspoon lemon zest, grated
- ¼ cup lemon juice
- 8 ounces mascarpone cheese

Directions:
In your Slow cooker, mix heavy cream with mascarpone, lemon zest and lemon juice, stir, cover and cook on Low for 1 hour. Divide into dessert glasses and keep in the fridge until you serve.

Nutrition: calories 165, fat 7, fiber 0, carbs 7, protein 4

Coconut Vanilla Cream

Preparation time: 10 minutes | Cooking time: 1 hours | Servings: 4

Ingredients:
- 14 ounces canned coconut milk
- 1 teaspoon vanilla extract
- 2 tablespoons sugar
- 4 ounces blueberries
- 2 tablespoons walnuts, chopped

Directions:
In a bowl, mix coconut milk with sugar and vanilla extract and whisk using your mixer. In another bowl, mix berries with walnuts and stir. Pour half of the vanilla cream in your Slow cooker, add a layer of berries and walnuts, add the rest of the vanilla cream, cover and cook on Low for 1 hour. Spoon this into dessert cups and serve cold.

Nutrition: calories 160, fat 23, fiber 4, carbs 6, protein 7

Avocado Pudding

Preparation time: 2 hours | Cooking time: 1 hours | Servings: 3

Ingredients:
- ½ cup vegetable oil
- ½ tablespoon sugar
- 1 tablespoon cocoa powder

For the pudding:
- 1 teaspoon peppermint oil
- 14 ounces coconut milk
- 1 avocado, pitted, peeled and chopped
- 1 tablespoon sugar

Directions:
In a bowl, mix vegetable oil with cocoa powder and ½-tablespoon sugar, stir well, transfer to a lined container, keep in the fridge for 1 hour and chop into small pieces. In your blender, mix coconut milk with avocado, 1-tablespoon sugar and peppermint oil, pulse well, transfer to your Slow cooker, cook on Low for 1 hour and mix with the chocolate chips you made at the beginning. Divide pudding into bowls and keep in the fridge for 1 more hour before serving.

Nutrition: calories 140, fat 3, fiber 2, carbs 3, protein 4

Coconut Pudding

Preparation time: 10 minutes | Cooking time: 1 hours | Servings: 4

Ingredients:
- 1 and 2/3 cups coconut milk
- 1 tablespoon gelatin
- 6 tablespoons sugar
- 3 egg yolks
- ½ teaspoon vanilla extract

Directions:

In a bowl, mix gelatin with 1-tablespoon coconut milk and stir. Put the rest of the milk in your Slow cooker, add whisked egg yolks, gelatin, vanilla and sugar, stir everything, cover, cook on High for 1 hour, divide into bowls and serve cold.

Nutrition: calories 170, fat 2, fiber 0, carbs 6, protein 2

Simple Cake

Preparation time: 2 hours | Cooking time: 2 hours | Servings: 3

Ingredients:
- 10 tablespoons flour
- 3 tablespoon butter, melted
- 4 teaspoons sugar
- 1 tablespoon cocoa powder
- 4 eggs
- ¼ teaspoon vanilla extract
- ½ teaspoon baking powder

Directions:

In a bowl, mix butter with sugar, cocoa powder, eggs, vanilla extract and baking powder and stir well. Add flour, stir the whole batter really well, pour into your Slow cooker, cover and cook on High for 2 hours. Slice cake, divide it between plates and serve.

Nutrition: calories 240, fat 34, fiber 7, carbs 10, protein 20

Dark Chocolate Cream

Preparation time: 1 hour | Cooking time: 1 hours | Servings: 6

Ingredients:
- ½ cup heavy cream
- 4 ounces dark chocolate, unsweetened and chopped

Directions:

In your Slow cooker, mix cream with chocolate, stir, cover, cook on High for 1 hour, divide into bowls and serve cold.

Nutrition: calories 78, fat 1, fiber 1, carbs 2, protein 1

Mango Cream

Preparation time: 10 minutes | Cooking time: 1 hours | Servings: 4

Ingredients:
- 1 mango, sliced
- 14 ounces coconut cream

Directions:
In your Slow cooker, mix mango with the cream, cover and cook on High for 1 hour. Divide into bowls and serve right away.

Nutrition: calories 150, fat 12, fiber 2, carbs 6, protein 1

Lime Cheesecake

Preparation time: 10 minutes | Cooking time: 1 hours | Servings: 10

Ingredients:
- 2 tablespoons butter, melted
- 2 teaspoons sugar
- 4 ounces almond meal
- ¼ cup coconut, shredded
- Cooking spray
- 1 pound cream cheese
- Zest of 1 lime
- Juice from 1 lime
- 2 sachets lime jelly
- 2 cup hot water

For the filling:

Directions:
In a bowl, mix coconut with almond meal, butter and sugar, stir well and press on the bottom of your Slow cooker greased with cooking spray. Put the water in a bowl, add jelly sachets and stir until they dissolve. Put cream cheese in a bowl, add jelly, lime juice and lime zest, blend well and spread over your crust. Cover the slow cooker, cook on High for 1 hour and then keep in the fridge until you serve it.

Nutrition: calories 300, fat 23, fiber 2, carbs 5, protein 7

Caramel Cream

Preparation time: 10 minutes | Cooking time: 2 hours | Servings: 2

Ingredients:
- 1 and ½ teaspoons caramel extract
- 1 cup water
- 2 ounces cream cheese
- 2 eggs
- 1 and ½ tablespoons sugar

For the caramel sauce:
- 2 tablespoons sugar
- 2 tablespoons butter, melted
- ¼ teaspoon caramel extract

Directions:
In your blender, mix cream cheese with water, 1 and ½ tablespoons sugar, 1 and ½ teaspoons caramel extract and eggs and blend well. Pour this into your Slow cooker, cover and cook on High for 2 hours. Put the butter in a slow cooker, heat up over medium heat add ¼-teaspoon caramel extract and 2 tablespoons sugar stir well and cook until everything melts. Pour this over caramel cream, leave everything to cool down and serve in dessert cups.

Nutrition: calories 254, fat 24, fiber 1, carbs 6, protein 8

Ricotta Cream

Preparation time: 2 hours 10 minutes | Cooking time: 1 hour | Servings: 10

Ingredients:
- ½ cup hot coffee
- 2 cups ricotta cheese
- 2 and ½ teaspoons gelatin
- 1 teaspoon vanilla extract
- 1 teaspoon espresso powder
- 1 teaspoon sugar
- 1 cup whipping cream

Directions:
In a bowl, mix coffee with gelatin, stir well and leave aside until coffee is cold. In your Slow cooker, mix espresso, sugar, vanilla extract and ricotta and stir. Add coffee mix and whipping cream, cover, cook on Low for 1 hour. Divide into dessert bowls and keep in the fridge for 2 hours before serving.

Nutrition: calories 200, fat 13, fiber 0, carbs 5, protein 7

Green Tea Pudding

Preparation time: 10 minutes | Cooking time: 1 hour | Servings: 2

Ingredients:
- ½ cup coconut milk
- 1 and ½ cup avocado, pitted and peeled
- 2 tablespoons green tea powder
- 2 teaspoons lime zest, grated
- 1 tablespoon sugar

Directions:
In your Slow cooker, mix coconut milk with avocado, tea powder, lime zest and sugar, stir, cover and cook on Low for 1 hour. Divide into cups and serve cold.

Nutrition: calories 107, fat 5, fiber 3, carbs 6, protein 8

Sweet Lemon Mix

Preparation time: 5 minutes | Cooking time: 1 hour | Servings: 4

Ingredients:
- 2 cups heavy cream
- Sugar to the taste
- 2 lemons, peeled and roughly chopped

Directions:
In your Slow cooker, mix cream with sugar and lemons, stir, cover and cook on Low for 1 hour. Divide into glasses and serve very cold.

Nutrition: calories 177, fat 0, fiber 0, carbs 6, protein 1

Banana Bread

Preparation time: 10 minutes | Cooking time: 3 hours | Servings: 6

Ingredients:
- ¾ cup sugar
- 1/3 cup butter, soft
- 1 teaspoon vanilla extract
- 1 egg
- 2 bananas, mashed
- 1 teaspoon baking powder
- 1 and ½ cups flour
- ½ teaspoons baking soda
- 1/3 cup milk
- 1 and ½ teaspoons cream of tartar
- Cooking spray

Directions:
In a bowl, combine milk with cream of tartar and stir well. Add sugar, butter, egg, vanilla and bananas and stir everything. In another bowl, mix flour with salt, baking powder and soda. Combine the 2 mixtures and stir them well. Grease your Slow cooker with cooking spray, add bread batter, cover, and cook on High for 3 hours. Leave the bread to cool down, slice and serve it.

Nutrition: calories 300, fat 3, fiber 4, carbs 28, protein 5

Candied Lemon

Preparation time: 20 minutes | Cooking time: 4 hours | Servings: 4

Ingredients:
- 5 lemons, peeled and cut into medium segments
- 3 cups white sugar
- 3 cups water

Directions:
In your Slow cooker, mix lemons with sugar and water, cover, cook on Low for 4 hours, transfer them to bowls and serve cold.

Nutrition: calories 62, fat 3, fiber 5, carbs 3, protein 4

Chocolate and Liquor Cream

Preparation time: 10 minutes | Cooking time: 2 hours | Servings: 4

Ingredients:
- 3.5 ounces crème fraiche
- 3.5 ounces dark chocolate, cut into chunks
- 1 teaspoon liquor
- 1 teaspoon sugar

Directions:
In your Slow cooker, mix crème fraiche with chocolate, liquor and sugar, stir, cover, cook on Low for 2 hours, divide into bowls and serve cold

Nutrition: calories 200, fat 12, fiber 4, carbs 6, protein 3

Butternut Squash Sweet Mix

Preparation time: 10 minutes | Cooking time: 3 hours | Servings: 8

Ingredients:
- 2 pounds butternut squash, steamed, peeled and mashed
- 2 eggs
- 1 cup milk
- ¾ cup maple syrup
- 1 teaspoon cinnamon powder
- ½ teaspoon ginger powder
- ¼ teaspoon cloves, ground
- 1 tablespoon cornstarch
- Whipped cream for serving

Directions:
In a bowl, mix squash with maple syrup, milk, eggs, cinnamon, cornstarch, ginger, cloves and cloves and stir very well. Pour this into your Slow cooker, cover, cook on Low for 2 hours, divide into cups and serve with whipped cream on top.

Nutrition: calories 152, fat 3, fiber 4, carbs 16, protein 4

Tapioca Pudding

Preparation time: 10 minutes | Cooking time: 1 hour | Servings: 6

Ingredients:
- 1 and ¼ cups milk
- 1/3 cup tapioca pearls, rinsed
- ½ cup water
- ½ cup sugar
- Zest of ½ lemon

Directions:
In your Slow cooker, mix tapioca with milk, sugar, water and lemon zest, stir, cover, cook on Low for 1 hour, divide into cups and serve warm.

Nutrition: calories 200, fat 4, fiber 2, carbs 37, protein 3

Orange Cream Mix

Preparation time: 1 hour | Cooking time: 1 hour | Servings: 6

Ingredients:
- 2 cups fresh cream
- 1 teaspoon cinnamon powder
- 6 egg yolks
- 5 tablespoons white sugar
- Zest of 1 orange, grated
- A pinch of nutmeg for serving
- 4 tablespoons sugar
- 2 cups water

Directions:
In a bowl, mix cream, cinnamon and orange zest and stir. In another bowl, mix the egg yolks with white sugar and whisk well. Add this over the cream, stir, strain and divide into ramekins. Put ramekins in your Slow cooker, add 2 cups water to the slow cooker, cover, cook on Low for 1 hour, leave cream aside to cool down and serve.

Nutrition: calories 200, fat 4, fiber 5, carbs 15, protein 5

Pears and Wine Sauce

Preparation time: 10 minutes | Cooking time: 1 hour 30 minutes | Servings: 6

Ingredients:
- 6 green pears
- 1 vanilla pod
- 1 cloves
- A pinch of cinnamon
- 7 oz. sugar
- 1 glass red wine

Directions:
In your Slow cooker, mix wine with sugar, vanilla and cinnamon. Add pears and clove cover slow cooker and cook on High for 1 hour and 30 minutes. Transfer pears to bowls and serve with the wine sauce all over.

Nutrition: calories 162, fat 4, fiber 3, carbs 6, protein 3

Pears and Grape Sauce

Preparation time: 10 minutes | Cooking time: 1 hour 30 minutes | Servings: 4

Ingredients:
- 4 pears
- Juice and Zest of 1 lemon
- 26 ounces grape juice
- 11 ounces currant jelly
- 4 garlic cloves
- ½ vanilla bean
- 4 peppercorns
- 2 rosemary springs

Directions:
Put the jelly, grape juice, lemon zest, lemon juice, vanilla, peppercorns, rosemary and pears in your Slow cooker, cover and cook on High for 1 hour and 30 minutes. Divide everything between plates and serve.

Nutrition: calories 152, fat 3, fiber 5, carbs 12, protein 4

Rice Pudding

Preparation time: 10 minutes | Cooking time: 2 hours | Servings: 6

Ingredients:
- 1 tablespoon butter
- 7 ounces long grain rice
- 4 ounces water
- 16 ounces milk
- 3 ounces sugar
- 1 egg
- 1 tablespoon cream
- 1 teaspoon vanilla extract

Directions:
In your Slow cooker, mix butter with rice, water, milk, sugar, egg, cream and vanilla, stir, cover and cook on High for 2 hours. Stir pudding one more time, divide into bowls and serve.

Nutrition: calories 152, fat 4, fiber 4, carbs 6, protein 4

Orange Marmalade

Preparation time: 10 minutes | Cooking time: 3 hours | Servings: 8

Ingredients:
- Juice of 2 lemons
- 3 pounds sugar
- 1 pound oranges, peeled and cut into segments
- 1-pint water

Directions:
In your Slow cooker, mix lemon juice with sugar, oranges and water, cover and cook on High for 3 hours. Stir one more time, divide into cups and serve cold.

Nutrition: calories 100, fat 4, fiber 4, carbs 12, protein 4

Berry Marmalade

Preparation time: 10 minutes | Cooking time: 3 hours | Servings: 12

Ingredients:
- 1 pound cranberries
- 1 pound strawberries
- ½ pound blueberries
- 3.5 ounces black currant
- 2 pounds sugar
- Zest of 1 lemon
- 2 tablespoon water

Directions:
In your Slow cooker, mix strawberries with cranberries, blueberries, currants, lemon zest, sugar and water, cover, cook on High for 3 hours, divide into jars and serve cold.

Nutrition: calories 100, fat 4, fiber 3, carbs 12, protein 3

Pears Jam

Preparation time: 10 minutes | Cooking time: 3 hour | Servings: 12

Ingredients:
- 8 pears, cored and cut into quarters
- 2 apples, peeled, cored and cut into quarters
- ½ cup apple juice
- 1 teaspoon cinnamon, ground

Directions:
In your Slow cooker, mix pears with apples, cinnamon and apple juice, stir, cover and cook on High for 3 hours. Blend using an immersion blender, divide jam into jars and keep in a cold place until you serve it.

Nutrition: calories 100, fat 1, fiber 2, carbs 20, protein 3

Conclusion

As we journey together through the final page of this cookbook, it's time for an epicurean reflection. Likely, you'd have never imagined the towering heights of culinary delight your Slow Cooker would usher into your life.

The Slow Cooker, more than being a mere kitchen appliance, is a remarkable companion that aids you in becoming your own kitchen star. With its support, you've discovered that creating sumptuous feasts isn't just a skill reserved for professional chefs.

Like many others around the globe, you've experienced first-hand the wonders of this efficient tool. From spontaneous weeknight dinners to lavish celebratory meals, you've delved deep into the alluring world of Slow Cooker cuisine, truly a culinary revelation.

So, once again, what's stopping you? With this impactful cookbook in your possession, you're fully equipped to concoct the most tantalizing masterpieces. The best dishes of your life are now not a far-off dream, but a tangible, near future reality.

Through the wealth of recipes shared in this cookbook, you truly have the world at your stovetop, from regional classics to innovative fusions, all ready to be savored.

Enjoy experimenting and exploring with your Slow Cooker, as the realm of culinary artistry it opens is immense and immensely pleasurable. Remember that the table is where love is shared and memories are made, your Slow Cooker meals now a cherished part of those golden moments.

So, as the last page turns, here begins an unending adventure of slow cooked love, flavor, and magic. Happy slow cooking, here's to creating boundless memories and the best dishes of your life! Enjoy the ride, and bon appétit!

Recipe Index

AGAVE
Bananas and Sweet Sauce, 171

ALFREDO SAUCE
Cauliflower and Broccoli Mix, 66

ALMOND MILK
Breakfast Zucchini Oatmeal, 14
Quinoa and Oats Mix, 17
Vanilla Oats, 20
Breakfast Rice Pudding, 24
Chia Seeds Mix, 27
Cauliflower Rice Pudding, 30
Veggies Casserole, 30
Veggie Spread, 98

ALMONDS
Vanilla Cookies, 172
Sweet Cookies, 174
Cranberry Quinoa, 15
Quinoa Breakfast Bars, 18
Butternut Squash Oatmeal, 21
Coconut Granola, 22
Tropical Granola, 22
Chia Seeds Mix, 27
Creamy Breakfast, 32
Sweet Potato Soup, 59
Cauliflower and Broccoli Mix, 66
Cashew Cake, 178

AMBER BEER
Mussels and Sausage Mix, 165

ANAHEIM CHILIES
Chili Cream, 53

ANDOUILLE SAUSAGE
Shrimp and Sausage Boil, 166

APPLE CIDER
White Bean Spread, 97

APPLE VINEGAR
Apple Pork Ribs, 129
Pork Chops and Pineapple Mix, 129
Mexican Pork Roast, 130
Lamb and Fennel Mix, 145

APPLES
Dates Quinoa, 25
Thai Chicken Soup, 48
Maple Sweet Potatoes, 70
Sweet Potato Mash, 71
Maple Brussels Sprouts, 73
Apple Jelly Sausage Snack, 101
Flavored Chicken Thighs, 112
Apple Crumble, 14
Apple Oatmeal, 17
Butternut Squash Oatmeal, 21
Apple Breakfast Rice, 24
Turkey Lunch, 34
Teriyaki Pork, 35
Apple and Onion Lunch Roast, 36
Apples and Potatoes, 74
Apple Dip, 91
Turkey Breast and Cranberries, 110
Pork Tenderloin and Apples, 130
Pork Belly and Applesauce, 139
Apples Stew, 171
Stuffed Apples, 175
Apple Bread, 176
Pears Jam, 188

APRICOT PRESERVES
Chicken and Sauce, 126

APRICOTS
Quinoa and Apricots, 25

ARROWROOT
Berry Cobbler, 175

ARUGULA
Arugula Frittata, 30
Carrot and Beet Side Salad, 79
Tuna and Chimichurri, 159

ASPARAGUS
Cod and Asparagus, 61
Asparagus Mix, 75
Worcestershire Asparagus Casserole, 31
Asparagus and Mushroom Mix, 75

AVOCADO
Chicken Frittata, 33
Pork and Chorizo Lunch Mix, 58
Beans, Carrots and Spinach Salad, 65
Mexican Rice, 84
Black Bean Salsa Salad, 99
Calamari and Shrimp, 158
Avocado Pudding, 181
Green Tea Pudding, 184
Tuna and Chimichurri, 159

AVOCADO OIL
    Lamb and Mint Pesto, 145
    Veal Stew, 146
    Veal and Tomatoes, 146
    Sausage Soup, 147
    Salmon and Green Onions Mix, 149

BACON
    Egg Bake, 21
    Brussels Sprouts Omelet, 32
    Peas and Ham Mix, 41
    Lamb and Bacon Stew, 59
    Creamy Chipotle Sweet Potatoes, 71
    Green Beans and Mushrooms, 85
    Chicken and Lentils, 125
    Italian Sausage Soup, 148
    Veggie Casserole, 16
    Bacon and Egg Casserole, 23
    Veggies Casserole, 30
    Chicken Frittata, 33
    Hearty Chicken, 42
    Corn and Bacon, 64
    Sweet Potatoes with Bacon, 66
    BBQ Chicken Dip, 87
    Cheesy Mix, 93
    Cheeseburger Meatballs, 94
    Cheeseburger Dip, 104
    Onion Dip, 104
    Chicken Chowder, 111
    Chicken and Mustard Sauce, 117
    Chicken and Creamy Mushroom Sauce, 118
    Slow Cooker Chicken Breasts, 119
    Pork Loin and Cauliflower Rice, 137
    Pork Chops, 140
    Clam Chowder, 158

BALSAMIC VINEGAR
    Orange Salmon, 159
    Easy and Veggies Mix, 76
    Herbed Beets, 80
    Eggplant Salsa, 97
    Eggplant Dip, 101
    Balsamic Chicken, 108
    Turkey Breast and Cranberries, 110
    Chicken Salad, 124
    Coca Cola Chicken, 124
    Tuna and Chimichurri, 159

BANANAS
    Banana and Coconut Oatmeal, 14
    Breakfast Banana Bread, 16
    Quinoa and Banana Mix, 24
    Quinoa Breakfast Bake, 28
    Bananas and Sweet Sauce, 171
    Banana Cake, 176
    Banana Bread, 185

BARLEY
    Wild Rice and Barley Pilaf, 74

BARRAMUNDI
    Italian Barramundi and Tomato Relish, 156

BASIL
    Summer Squash Mix, 80
    Easy Veggie Side Salad, 80
    Pecans Snack, 101

BASIL PESTO
    Italian Veggie Mix, 74

BBQ SAUCE
    BBQ Chicken Thighs, 45
    BBQ Chicken Dip, 87
    Glazed Sausages, 93
    Cheeseburger Meatballs, 94
    Flavored Chicken Thighs, 112

BEANS
    Stuffed Peppers, 37
    Beans and Pumpkin Chili, 37

BEEF
    Beef and Chipotle Dip, 92
    Cheeseburger Meatballs, 94
    Sauerkraut Dip, 95
    Beef Meatballs, 100
    Jalapeno Poppers, 100
    Cheeseburger Dip, 104
    Fennel Short Ribs, 128
    Seasoned Beef, 133
    Beef Soup, 133
    Beef Meatloaf, 137
    Beef Stuffed Squash, 142
    Beef and Tzatziki, 142
    German Beef Soup, 143
    Beef and Pancetta, 145
    Spicy Beef Mix, 148
    Lunch Roast, 34
    Fajitas, 35
    Beef Stew, 36
    Apple and Onion Lunch Roast, 36
    Orange Beef Dish, 39
    Pork Stew, 40
    Beef Chili, 42
    Lunch Meatloaf, 43

Beef Strips, 44
Slow Cooker Roast, 45
Taco Soup, 49
Beef and Onions, 131
Roast and Pepperoncinis, 132
Balsamic Beef Cheeks, 133
Herbed and Cinnamon Beef, 134
Beef Brisket and Turnips Mix, 134
Smoky Lamb, 135
Sausage and Onion Jam, 136
Jamaican Pork , 136
Pork Loin and Cauliflower Rice, 137
Lamb Stew, 138
Beef Meatballs Casserole, 142
Sausage Soup, 147
Beef Curry, 148
Beef Chuck Roast, 129
Roast and Pepperoncinis, 132
Beef and Veggie Stew, 41
Beef Roast, 128

BEEF SAUSAGE
Beef Meatballs Casserole, 142

BEER
Mexican Lunch Mix, 43
Tex Mex Dip, 88
Beer and Cheese Dip, 89
Fajita Dip, 105
Mussels, Clams and Chorizo Mix, 165
Shrimp and Sausage Boil, 166

BEETS
Beets and Carrots, 73
Roasted Beets, 78
Thyme Beets, 78
Beets Side Salad, 78
Lemony Beets, 79
Carrot and Beet Side Salad, 79
Herbed Beets, 80

BEEL PEPPERS
Veggie Casserole, 16
Breakfast Stuffed Peppers, 21

BLACK BEANS
Black Bean Soup, 49
Black Beans Mix, 86

BLACK CURRANT
Berry Marmalade, 188

BLACK OLIVES
Pizza Dip, 95

Cheesy Corn Dip, 96
Chicken and Tomatillos, 123
Paprika Lamb, 143
Italian Barramundi and Tomato Relish, 156

BLACK PEPPERS
Mexican Eggs, 17

BLACKBERRIEWS
Vanilla Oats, 20
Berry Cobbler, 175

BLACK-EYED PEAS
Peas and Ham Mix, 41
Peas Dip, 98

BLUE CHEESE
Scalloped Potatoes, 65
Mushrooms Stuffed With Chicken, 120

BLUEBERRIES
Quinoa and Banana Mix, 24
Blueberry Quinoa Oatmeal, 26
Chia Seeds Mix, 27
Turkey Lunch, 34
Nut and Berry Side Salad, 82
Blueberry and Spinach Salad, 82
Blueberry Cake, 169
Berry Cobbler, 175
Cashew Cake, 178
Sweet Mascarpone Cream, 180
Coconut Vanilla Cream, 181
Berry Marmalade, 188

BOCCONCINI
Veal and Tomatoes, 146

BOK CHOY STALKES
Creamy Sea Bass, 151

Bourbon
Bourbon Sausage Bites, 94

BOURSIN
Artichoke Dip, 88

BRAN FLAKRS
Apple Crumble, 14

BRANDY
Chocolate Cream, 179

BREAD
　Beef and Tzatziki, 142

BROCCOLI FLORETS
　Veggie Casserole, 16
　Asian Salmon Mix, 149
　Veggie Omelet, 19
　Broccoli Mix, 63
　Cauliflower and Broccoli Mix, 66
　Chicken and Broccoli Casserole, 117

BROWN LENTILS
　Lentils Curry, 51
　Lentils Rolls, 97

BROWN RISE
　Breakfast Rice Pudding, 24
　Apple Breakfast Rice, 24

BRUSSELS SPROUTS
　Brussels Sprouts Omelet, 32
　Maple Brussels Sprouts, 73
　Balsamic Chicken, 108

BUFFALO WINGS SAUCE
　Buffalo Meatballs, 93

BULGUR
　Bulgur Chili, 61
　Breakfast Butterscotch Pudding, 29
　Creamy Hash Brown Mix, 63
　Broccoli Mix, 63
　Green Beans Mix, 64
　Corn and Bacon, 64
　Peas and Carrots, 65
　Sweet Potatoes with Bacon, 66
　Wild Rice Mix, 66
　Mashed Potatoes, 67
　Orange Glazed Carrots, 67
　Mushrooms and Sausage Mix, 69
　Glazed Baby Carrots, 69
　Buttery Mushrooms, 70
　Cauliflower Rice and Spinach, 70
　Sweet Potato Mash, 71
　Dill Cauliflower Mash, 72
　Apples and Potatoes, 74
　Cauliflower and Carrot Gratin, 79
　Garlic Butter Green Beans, 81
　Zucchini Casserole, 82
　Caramel Corn, 94
　Caramel Dip, 105
　Alfredo Chicken, 108
　Turkey Wings and Sauce, 113
　Chicken Thighs and Mushrooms, 115
　Creamy Duck Breast, 115
　Red Chicken Soup, 118
　Chicken and Green Onion Sauce, 120
　Chicken Thighs and Romano Cheese Mix, 122
　Chicken and Chickpeas, 126
　Chicken Liver Stew, 127
　Roast and Pepperoncinis, 132
　Lamb Stew, 138
　Sausages and Celeriac Mash, 138
　Lamb Casserole, 144
　Beef and Pancetta, 145
　Wine Piccata, 146
　Fish Pie, 153
　Fish Pie, 153
　Buttery Trout, 153
　Salmon and Kimchi Sauce, 154
　Salmon and Caper Sauce, 154
　Tabasco Halibut, 155
　Italian Clams, 159
　Cider Clams, 160
　Salmon and Rice, 162
　Fish Pudding, 163
　Mackerel and Lemon, 165
　Crab Legs, 166
　Sweet Potato Pudding, 173
　Apple Bread, 176
　Banana Cake, 176
　Cauliflower Pudding, 177
　Lemon Pudding, 178
　Lemon Pudding, 178
　Chocolate Cream, 179
　Strawberry Pie, 180
　Simple Cake, 182
　Lime Cheesecake, 183
　Lime Cheesecake, 183
　Caramel Cream, 183
　Banana Bread, 185
　Rice Pudding, 187
　Lavender and Orange Lamb, 144
　Salmon Meatballs and Sauce, 154

BUTTERNUT SGUACH
　Butternut Squash Oatmeal, 21
　Butternut Squash Quinoa, 26
　Butternut Squash Sweet Mix, 186

CABBAGE
　Chicken and Cabbage Mix, 57
　Slow Cooked Turkey Delight, 116
　Beef Brisket and Turnips Mix, 134

CAJUN SEASONING
　Peas Dip, 98

195

CALAMARI
Calamari and Shrimp, 158

CANNED ARTICHOKE
Rice and Artichokes, 85
Creamy Spinach and Artichoke Chicken, 121
Artichoke Lamb Shoulder, 132
Artichoke Dip, 88
Artichoke Frittata, 19

CANNED BLACK BEANS
Quinoa Chili, 51
Black Beans Stew, 52
Quinoa Chili, 60
5 Bean Chili, 61
Bean Medley, 64
Black Bean Salsa Salad, 99

CANNED BLACK -EYED PEAS
Bean Medley, 64

CANNED CANNELLINI BEANS
Italian Veggie Mix, 74

CANNED CHISKPEAS
Winter Veggie Stew, 50
Chickpeas Stew, 50
Chicken and Chickpeas, 126

CANNED CHILI BEANS
4 Bean Chili, 61

CANNED CHILI CON CARNE
Tex Mex Dip, 88

CANNED CLAMS
Shrimp Stew, 62

CANNED COCONUT MILK
Shrimp and Baby Carrots Mix, 152
Coconut Vanilla Cream, 181

CANNED CORN
Bean Medley, 64
Tamale Dip, 87

CANNED CREAM
Broccoli Mix, 63
Scalloped Potatoes, 65

CANNED ENCHILADA SAUCE
Taco Dip, 88

CANNED FAVA BEANS
Italian Veggie Mix, 74

CANNED GARBANZO BEANS
Minestrone Soup, 53
Veggie and Garbanzo Mix, 68
Chicken and Tomatillos, 123

CANNED GREEN CHILIES
Taco Soup, 49
Bean Dip, 92
Chicken Chowder, 111
Chicken and Tomatillos, 123
Duck Chili, 125
Chorizo and Cauliflower Mix, 75
Mexican Dip, 87

CANNED KIDNEY BEANS
Pumpkin Chili, 60
3 Bean Chili, 61
Bulgur Chili, 61

CANNED LIMA BEANS
Bean Medley, 64

CANNED NORTHERN BEANS
Bean Medley, 64

CANNED PEACHES
Chicken with Peach and Orange Sauce, 111

CANNED PINTO BEANS
Bulgur Chili, 61

CANNED PLUM TOMATOES
Salsa Snack, 106

CANNED REFRIED BEANS
Bean Dip, 92

CANNED SAUERKRAUT
Sauerkraut Dip, 95

CANNED TOMATILLOS
Chicken and Tomatillos, 123

CANNED TOMATOES
French Veggie Stew, 52
Mexican Pork Roast, 130
Beef and Veggie Stew, 41
Beef Chili, 42
Lentils Curry, 51

Quinoa Chili, 60
Lentils and Quinoa Mix, 26
Butternut Squash Quinoa, 26
Pork Sandwiches, 41
BBQ Chicken Thighs, 45
Chicken Stew, 46
Taco Soup, 49
Winter Veggie Stew, 50
Quinoa Chili, 51
Sweet Potato Stew, 53
Minestrone Soup, 53
Chicken Chili, 55
Turkey Chili, 56
Chicken and Stew, 57
White Beans Stew, 59
Pumpkin Chili, 60
7 Bean Chili, 61
Seafood Stew, 62
Shrimp Stew, 62
Eggplant and Kale Mix, 72
Okra and Corn, 77
Beef Meatballs, 100
Italian Mussels Salad, 103
Cheeseburger Dip, 104
Turkey Curry, 116
Duck Chili, 125
Chicken and Chickpeas, 126
Fennel Short Ribs, 128
Lamb Shanks, 131
Flavored Pork Roast, 131
Smoky Lamb, 135
French Lamb, 136
Pork Rolls, 140
Beef Stuffed Squash, 142
German Beef Soup, 143
Veal and Tomatoes, 146
Sausage Soup, 147
Spicy Beef Mix, 148
Sriracha Shrimp, 157
Mussels Soup, 161
Oregano Pork Chops, 141
Spicy Dip, 96

CANNED TUNA
Tasty Tuna Mix, 164

CANOLA OIL
Slow Cooker Roast, 45
Nut and Berry Side Salad, 82
Cheesy Mix, 93

CAPERS
Eggplant Salsa, 97
Chicken Liver Stew, 127

Wine Piccata, 146
Salmon and Caper Sauce, 154

CARAMEL EXTRACT
Caramel Cream, 183

CARAMEL SAUCE
Apple Dip, 91

CARDAMOM
Balsamic Beef Cheeks, 133
Maple Pears, 174
Rice and Veggies, 84

CARROTS
Breakfast Zucchini Oatmeal, 14
Chicken Stew, 46
Quinoa Chili, 51
Veggie and Garbanzo Mix, 68
Turkey Wings and Veggies, 113
Mushrooms Stuffed With Chicken, 120
Fennel Short Ribs, 128
Beef Chuck Roast, 129
Balsamic Beef Cheeks, 133
Veal Stew, 146
Carrot Pudding, 33
Beef Stew, 36
Pork Stew, 40
Beef and Veggie Stew, 41
Hearty Chicken, 42
Slow Cooker Roast, 45
Chicken Noodle Soup, 47
Lentils Soup, 47
Creamy Chicken Soup, 49
Black Bean Soup, 49
Minestrone Soup, 53
Lamb Stew, 58
Lamb Curry, 58
Lamb and Bacon Stew, 59
White Beans Stew, 59
Peas and Carrots, 65
Beans, Carrots and Spinach Salad, 65
Wild Rice Mix, 66
Orange Glazed Carrots, 67
Squash Side Salad, 68
Glazed Baby Carrots, 69
Beets and Carrots, 73
Carrot and Beet Side Salad, 79
Cauliflower and Carrot Gratin, 79
Rice and Veggies, 84
Veggie Spread, 98
Chicken and Dumplings, 107
Slow Cooked Chicken, 109
Thyme Chicken, 110

Chicken Thighs Delight, 111
Chinese Duck, 112
Duck Chili, 125
Chicken and Lentils, 125
Beef Roast, 128
Lamb Shanks, 131
Seasoned Beef, 133
Beef Brisket and Turnips Mix, 134
Veggie Lamb Shanks, 135
Lamb Leg and Mushrooms Mix, 135
Pork Loin and Cauliflower Rice, 137
Lamb Stew, 138
Paprika Lamb, 143
Lamb Casserole, 144
Spicy Beef Mix, 148
Shrimp and Baby Carrots Mix, 152

CACHEWS
Thai Chicken, 55
White Bean Spread, 97
Veggie Spread, 98
Cashew Dip, 99
Cashew Cake, 178

CATFICH
Chili Catfish, 151

CAULIFLOWER FLORETS
Chorizo and Cauliflower Mix, 75
Cauliflower and Carrot Gratin, 79
Beef Chuck Roast, 129
Beef Soup, 133
Lamb Casserole, 144
Winter Veggie Stew, 50
Cauliflower Pudding, 177
Cauliflower and Broccoli Mix, 66
Veggie and Garbanzo Mix, 68
Mushrooms and Sausage Mix, 69
Veggie Spread, 98
Asian Salmon Mix, 149

CAULIFLOWER HEAD
Dill Cauliflower Mash, 72

CAULIFLOWER RISE
Cauliflower Pilaf, 68
Cauliflower Rice and Spinach, 70
Pork Loin and Cauliflower Rice, 137

CAYENNE PEPPER
Creamy Chicken, 46
Lentils Soup, 47
Taco Soup, 49
Chili Salmon, 54

Kale and Ham Mix, 71
Okra and Corn, 77
Queso Dip, 89
Flavored Chicken Thighs, 112
Classic Turkey Gumbo, 112
Beef Stuffed Squash, 142
Calamari and Sauce, 157
Stewed Okra, 77

CAYENNE SAUSE
Buffalo Chicken, 108

CELERIAC
Sausages and Celeriac Mash, 138
Lamb Casserole, 144

CELERY
Slow Cooker Roast, 45
Lamb and Bacon Stew, 59
Asparagus Mix, 75
Potato Salsa, 99
Red Chicken Soup, 118
Hot Chicken Wings, 124
Beef Roast, 128
Lamb Shanks, 131
Seasoned Beef, 133
Herbed and Cinnamon Beef, 134
Seafood Chowder, 149
Lentils and Quinoa Mix, 26
Beef Stew, 36
Pork Stew, 40
Seafood Stew, 40
Beef and Veggie Stew, 41
Hearty Chicken, 42
Creamy Chicken, 46
Chicken Stew, 46
Chicken Noodle Soup, 47
Creamy Chicken Soup, 49
Black Bean Soup, 49
Minestrone Soup, 53
Lamb Curry, 58
Sweet Potato Soup, 59
White Beans Stew, 59
Shrimp Stew, 62
Bean Medley, 64
Mushrooms and Sausage Mix , 69
Rice and Beans, 86
Eggplant Dip, 101
Chicken and Dumplings, 107
Thyme Chicken, 110
Chinese Duck, 112
Turkey Wings and Veggies, 113
Turkey Soup, 116
Chicken Stroganoff, 119

Beef Chuck Roast, 129
Lamb Casserole, 144
Clam Chowder, 158
Chinese Mackerel, 164

CHARD
White Beans Stew, 59

CHARDONNAY WINE
Chicken and Creamy Mushroom Sauce, 118

CHEDDAR CHEESE
Veggie Casserole, 16
Veggie Omelet, 19
Hash Browns and Sausage Casserole, 20
Egg Bake, 21
Breakfast Stuffed Peppers, 21
Breakfast Potatoes, 23
Hash Brown Mix, 23
Bacon and Egg Casserole, 23
Veggies Casserole, 30
Mixed Egg and Sausage Scramble, 31
Creamy Hash Brown Mix, 63
Broccoli Mix, 63
Cauliflower and Carrot Gratin, 79
Zucchini Casserole, 82
Tamale Dip, 87
BBQ Chicken Dip, 87
Artichoke Dip, 88
Beer and Cheese Dip, 89
Cheeseburger Meatballs, 94
Cheesy Corn Dip, 96
Cheeseburger Dip, 104
Onion Dip, 104
Chicken Cordon Bleu Dip, 105
Slow Cooked Turkey Delight, 116
Chicken and Broccoli Casserole, 117
Slow Cooker Chicken Breasts, 119
Chicken and Tomatillos, 123
Sausages and Celeriac Mash, 138
Fish Pie, 153
Tasty Tuna Mix, 164
Asparagus Mix, 75

CHEERIOS
Slow Cooked Dip, 90

CHEESE DRESSING
Buffalo Meatballs, 93

CHEESE TORTELLINI
Chicken Noodle Soup, 47
Spinach and Mushroom Soup, 48

CHERRIES
Wild Rice Mix, 66
Maple Sweet Potatoes, 70
Apples and Potatoes, 74
Rice and Farro Pilaf, 83
Easy Farro, 84
Cherry Jam, 174
Cocoa Cherry Compote, 178

CHERRY TOMSTOES
Easy and Veggies Mix, 76
Okra Side Dish, 76
Salsa Corn Dip, 96
Chicken Salad, 124
Beef and Tzatziki, 142
Italian Barramundi and Tomato Relish, 156
Fish and Olives Mix, 161

CHIA SEEDS
Chia Seeds Mix, 27
Chia Seeds and Chicken Breakfast, 27
Chia Pudding, 177

CHICKEN
Butternut Squash Quinoa, 26
Chia Seeds and Chicken Breakfast, 27
Chicken Frittata, 33
Lemon Chicken, 46
Lentils Soup, 47
Winter Veggie Stew, 50
Thai Chicken, 55
Wild Rice Mix, 66
Tamale Dip, 87
BBQ Chicken Dip, 87
Taco Dip, 88
Buffalo Meatballs, 93
Rotisserie Chicken, 107
Alfredo Chicken, 108
Slow Cooked Chicken, 109
Thyme Chicken, 110
Chicken and Sauce, 113
Lemony Chicken, 114
Chicken Meatloaf, 121
Thai Peanut Chicken, 122
Cuban Chicken, 125
Chicken and Sauce, 126
Veggie Lamb Shanks, 135
Beef Stuffed Squash, 142
German Beef Soup, 143
Mussels Soup, 161
Salmon and Rice, 162
Beans and Pumpkin Chili, 37

Chicken and Peppers Mix, 38
Chicken Tacos, 38
Chicken with Couscous, 39
Hearty Chicken, 42
Flavored Turkey, 44
BBQ Chicken Thighs, 45
Creamy Chicken, 46
Chicken Stew, 46
Chicken Noodle Soup, 47
Thai Chicken Soup, 48
Creamy Chicken Soup, 49
Chickpeas Stew, 50
Black Beans Stew, 52
Sweet Potato Stew, 53
Pulled Chicken, 54
Chicken Chili, 55
Salsa Chicken, 55
Chicken Thighs Mix, 57
Chicken and Stew, 57
Chicken and Cabbage Mix, 57
Lamb Curry, 58
Creamy Hash Brown Mix, 63
Beans, Carrots and Spinach Salad, 65
Scalloped Potatoes, 65
Mashed Potatoes, 67
Kale and Ham Mix, 71
Rice and Farro Pilaf, 83
Pink Rice, 83
Rice and Artichokes, 85
Green Beans and Mushrooms, 85
Mexican Dip, 87
Chicken Bites, 91
Chicken Wings, 92
Spicy Mussels, 104
Chicken Cordon Bleu Dip, 105
Fajita Dip, 105
Chicken and Dumplings, 107
Balsamic Chicken, 108
Buffalo Chicken, 108
Chicken Breasts, 109
Mediterranean Chicken, 110
Chicken Chowder, 111
Chicken Thighs Delight, 111
Chicken with Peach and Orange Sauce, 111
Flavored Chicken Thighs, 112
Chinese Duck, 112
Turkey Wings and Veggies, 113
Chicken Wings and Mint Sauce, 114
Chicken and Paprika Sauce, 114
Chicken Thighs and Mushrooms, 115
Chicken and Mustard Sauce, 117
Chicken Casserole, 117
Chicken and Broccoli Casserole, 117
Red Chicken Soup, 118
Citrus Chicken, 118
Chicken and Creamy Mushroom Sauce, 118
Slow Cooker Chicken Breasts, 119
Chicken and Sour Cream, 119
Chicken Stroganoff, 119
Pepperoni Chicken, 120
Chicken and Green Onion Sauce, 120
Mushrooms Stuffed With Chicken, 120
Creamy Spinach and Artichoke Chicken, 121
Chicken Thighs and Romano Cheese Mix, 122
Slow Cooker Chicken Thighs, 123
Chicken and Tomatillos, 123
Chicken Salad, 124
Hot Chicken Wings, 124
Coca Cola Chicken, 124
Chicken and Lentils, 125
Chicken and Chickpeas, 126
Lamb Leg and Sweet Potatoes, 130
Chinese Pork Shoulder, 132
Pork Rolls, 140
Pork Chops, 140
Rosemary Pork, 141
Wine Piccata, 146
Italian Sausage Soup, 148
Shrimp Mix, 150
Dill Trout, 152
Shrimp and Peas Soup, 157
Clam Chowder, 158
Fish and Olives Mix, 161
Milky Fish, 162
Jambalaya, 163
Crab Legs, 166
Japanese Shrimp, 167

CHICKEN LIVERS
Chicken Liver Stew, 127

CHICKEN STOCK
Moist Pork Loin, 42
Zucchini Casserole, 82

CHICKPEARS
Hummus, 98

CHILI
Chicken Chili, 55

CHILI OIL
Shrimp and Peas Soup, 157

CHILI PEPPER
Quinoa Chili, 51
Coca Cola Chicken, 124
Beef Chili, 42

CHILI POWDER
Tostadas, 103
Spicy Pork, 141

CHILI SAUCE
Lunch Meatloaf, 43
Bourbon Sausage Bites, 94
Goose and Sauce, 127
Chinese Pork Shoulder, 132

CHILIES
Orange Beef Dish, 39
Cheeseburger Dip, 104

CHINESE 5 SPICE
Apple Pork Ribs, 129
Chinese Pork Shoulder, 132

CHINESE SPICE
Chicken Thighs and Romano Cheese Mix, 122

CHIPOTLE CHILIES
Chili Salmon, 54
Beef and Chipotle Dip, 92

CHIPOTLE PEPPER
Creamy Chipotle Sweet Potatoes, 71

CHIPS
Bean Dip, 92

CHOCOLATE
Chocolate Pudding, 176
Dark Chocolate Cream, 182
Chocolate and Liquor Cream, 185
Chocolate Quinoa, 27
Mocha Latte Quinoa Mix, 28
Sweet Cookies, 174
Chocolate Cake, 175
Chocolate Cream, 179

CHOCOLATE ALMOND MILK
Pudding Cake, 169

CHOCOLATE CHIPS
Peanut Snack, 91

CHORIZO
Pork and Chorizo Lunch Mix, 58
Chorizo and Cauliflower Mix, 75
Jalapeno Poppers, 100
Mussels, Clams and Chorizo Mix, 165

CIDER
Cider Clams, 160

CILANTRO
Salmon and Cilantro Sauce, 54
Salsa Chicken, 55
Mexican Rice, 84
Chicken and Sauce, 113
Duck Chili, 125
Stuffed Pork, 139
Tuna and Chimichurri, 159

CLAMS
Salmon and Raspberry Vinaigrette, 163
Seafood Stew, 40
Clam Chowder, 158
Italian Clams, 159
Cider Clams, 160
Mussels, Clams and Chorizo Mix, 165

CLOVES
Duck Chili, 125
Balsamic Beef Cheeks, 133
Fish Pie, 153
Pears and Wine Sauce, 187

COCA COLA
Tostadas, 103
Coca Cola Chicken, 124

COCOA POWDER
Simple Cake, 182
Cocoa Cherry Compote, 178
Avocado Pudding, 181
Thai Cocoa Pork, 134
Chocolate Cake, 175

COCONUT
Quinoa Breakfast Bake, 28
Flavored Squid, 168
Coconut and Macadamia Cream, 179
Strawberry Pie, 180
Sweet Raspberry Mix, 180
Lime Cheesecake, 183
Mocha Latte Quinoa Mix, 28

COCONUT BUTTER
Sweet Raspberry Mix, 180

COCONUT CREAM
   Cauliflower Rice and Spinach, 70
   Creamy Chipotle Sweet Potatoes, 71
   Apples and Potatoes, 74
   Chicken Chowder, 111
   Turkey Curry, 116
   Turkey Curry, 116
   Creamy Sea Bass, 151
   Salmon Meatballs and Sauce, 154
   Mustard Fish Mix, 156
   Mango Cream, 183

COCONUT FLAKES
   Cranberry Quinoa, 15

COCONUT MILK
   Banana and Coconut Oatmeal, 14
   Breakfast Zucchini Oatmeal, 14
   Breakfast Rice Pudding, 24
   Chocolate Quinoa, 27
   Worcestershire Asparagus Casserole, 31
   Thai Chicken Soup, 48
   Taco Soup, 49
   Winter Veggie Stew, 50
   Lentils Curry, 51
   Lamb Curry, 58
   Veggie and Garbanzo Mix, 68
   Squash Side Salad, 68
   Thai Side Salad, 72
   Asparagus and Mushroom Mix, 75
   Chicken and Paprika Sauce, 114
   Chicken Stroganoff, 119
   Chicken Thighs and Romano Cheese Mix, 122
   Sausages and Celeriac Mash, 138
   Beef Curry, 148
   Seafood Chowder, 149
   Sriracha Shrimp, 157
   Indian Fish, 161
   Chia Pudding, 177
   Avocado Pudding, 181
   Coconut Pudding, 182
   Green Tea Pudding, 184

COCONUT OIL
   Chicken and Paprika Sauce, 114
   Turkey Curry, 116
   Beef Chuck Roast, 129
   Mexican Pork Roast, 130
   Pork Rolls, 140

COD
   Poached Cod and Pineapple Mix, 150
   Chinese Cod, 155
   Cod and Asparagus, 61
   Flavored Cod Fillets, 152
   Cod and Peas, 162
   Fish Pudding, 163

COFFEE
   Mocha Latte Quinoa Mix, 28
   Bulgur Chili, 61
   Ricotta Cream, 184

CONDENSET MILK
   Caramel Dip, 105

CORN
   Beef Stew, 36
   Stuffed Peppers, 37
   Quinoa Chili, 51
   Chili Cream, 53
   Corn and Bacon, 64
   Okra and Corn, 77
   Salsa Corn Dip, 96
   Cheesy Corn Dip, 96
   Shrimp and Sausage Boil, 166
   Rice and Veggies, 84

CORN CEREAL
   Cheesy Mix, 93

CORN SYRUP
   Caramel Corn, 94
   Caramel Dip, 105

CORN TORTILLAS
   Tostadas, 103

CORNFLAKES
   Creamy Hash Brown Mix, 63

CORNSTARCH
   Dill Shrimp Mix, 167
   Butternut Squash Sweet Mix, 186

COTIJA
   Queso Dip, 89

COUSCOUS
   Chicken with Couscous, 39

CRAB
   Crab Legs, 166

CRABMEAT
   Seafood Stew, 40
   Crab Dip, 90

CRASCKERS
  Broccoli Mix, 63
  Zucchini Casserole, 82

CRANBERRIES
  Cranberry Quinoa, 15
  Turkey and Potatoes, 56
  Mushrooms and Sausage Mix, 69
  Turkey Breast and Cranberries, 110
  Turkey Wings and Sauce, 113
  Berry Marmalade, 188

CREAM
  Creamy Breakfast, 32
  Pink Rice, 83
  Chicken and Creamy Mushroom Sauce, 118
  Chicken and Chickpeas, 126
  Veal Stew, 146
  Italian Sausage Soup, 148
  Clam Chowder, 158
  Chocolate Pudding, 176
  Chocolate Cream, 179
  Coconut and Macadamia Cream, 179
  Strawberry Pie, 180
  Sweet Mascarpone Cream, 180
  Lemon Cream, 181
  Dark Chocolate Cream, 182
  Ricotta Cream, 184
  Sweet Lemon Mix, 184
  Orange Cream Mix, 186
  Rice Pudding, 187

CREAM CHEESE
  Lime Cheesecake, 183
  Creamy Chicken Soup, 49
  Corn and Bacon, 64
  Rice and Artichokes, 85
  Tamale Dip, 87
  BBQ Chicken Dip, 87
  Mexican Dip, 87
  Tex Mex Dip, 88
  Taco Dip, 88
  Lasagna Dip, 89
  Beer and Cheese Dip, 89
  Crab Dip, 90
  Beef and Chipotle Dip, 92
  Pizza Dip, 95
  Sauerkraut Dip, 95
  Spicy Dip, 96
  Salsa Corn Dip, 96
  Cheesy Corn Dip, 96
  Cheeseburger Dip, 104
  Onion Dip, 104
  Chicken Cordon Bleu Dip, 105
  Fajita Dip, 105
  Slow Cooked Turkey Delight, 116
  Red Chicken Soup, 118
  Slow Cooker Chicken Breasts, 119
  Mushrooms Stuffed With Chicken, 120
  Creamy Spinach and Artichoke Chicken, 121
  Strawberry Pie, 180
  Caramel Cream, 183

CREAM FRAICHE
  Chocolate and Liquor Cream, 185

CREOLE SEASONING
  Spicy Creole Shrimp, 156

CUCUMBER
  Mediterranean Chicken, 110
  Beef and Tzatziki, 142

CUMIN SEEDS
  Black Beans Mix, 86

CURRANT JELLI
  Pears and Grape Sauce, 187

CURRY LEAVE
  Indian Fish, 161

CURRY PASTE
  Thai Chicken Soup, 48

DACHI
  Stuffed Squid, 168

DATES
  Lemon Jam, 179

DIJON MUSTARD
  Curried Meatballs, 95
  Apple Jelly Sausage Snack, 101
  Balsamic Chicken, 108
  Chicken Thighs and Mushrooms, 115
  Chicken and Mustard Sauce, 117
  Worcestershire Pork Chops, 140
  Salmon Meatballs and Sauce, 154

DILL
  Potato Salsa, 99
  Cheeseburger Meatballs, 94

DOUBLE CREAM
  French Breakfast Pudding, 29

DRIED APPLES
    Quinoa Breakfast Bars, 18

DRIED CHERRIES
    Slow Cooker Turkey Breast, 109

DRIED CRANBERRIES
    Slow Cooker Turkey Breast, 109

DUCK
    Chinese Duck, 112
    Duck and Potatoes, 123
    Duck Chili, 125
    Creamy Duck Breast, 115
    Duck Breast and Veggies, 115

EGGPLANT
    French Veggie Stew, 52
    Eggplant and Kale Mix, 72
    Easy Veggie Side Salad, 80
    Eggplant Salsa, 97
    Eggplant Dip, 101

EGGS
    Chocolate French Toast, 15
    Breakfast Banana Bread, 16
    Greek Breakfast Casserole, 16
    Veggie Casserole, 16
    Mexican Eggs, 17
    Quinoa Breakfast Bars, 18
    Artichoke Frittata, 18
    Spinach Frittata, 19
    Veggie Omelet, 19
    Hash Browns and Sausage Casserole, 20
    Ham Quiche, 20
    Egg Bake, 21
    Breakfast Stuffed Peppers, 21
    Bacon and Egg Casserole, 23
    Chia Seeds and Chicken Breakfast, 27
    Chai Breakfast Quinoa, 28
    Breakfast Butterscotch Pudding, 29
    French Breakfast Pudding, 29
    Eggs and Sausage Casserole, 29
    Veggies Casserole, 30
    Arugula Frittata, 30
    Mixed Egg and Sausage Scramble, 31
    Worcestershire Asparagus Casserole, 31
    Peppers, Kale and Cheese Omelet, 31
    Salmon Frittata, 32
    Brussels Sprouts Omelet, 32
    Chicken Frittata, 33
    Lunch Meatloaf, 43
    Asparagus and Mushroom Mix, 75
    Asparagus Mix, 75
    Buffalo Meatballs, 93
    Cheeseburger Meatballs, 94
    Beef Meatballs, 100
    Slow Cooked Turkey Delight, 116
    Chicken Casserole, 117
    Thai Cocoa Pork, 134
    Beef Meatloaf, 137
    Beef Meatballs Casserole, 142
    Fish Pie, 153
    Salmon Meatballs and Sauce, 154
    Fish Pudding, 163
    Mackerel and Lemon, 165
    Vanilla Cookies, 172
    Berry Cobbler, 175
    Apple Bread, 176
    Banana Cake, 176
    Cauliflower Pudding, 177
    Simple Cake, 182
    Caramel Cream, 183
    Banana Bread, 185
    Butternut Squash Sweet Mix, 186
    Rice Pudding, 187
    Candied Pecans, 90
    Veal Stew, 146
    Tasty Tuna Mix, 164
    Sweet Cookies, 174
    Chocolate Cake, 175
    Coconut Pudding, 182
    Orange Cream Mix, 186

ENCHILADA SAUCE
    Pork and Chorizo Lunch Mix, 58
    Tamale Dip, 87
    Tostadas, 103

ENDIVES
    Shrimp Salad, 158

FAJITA
    Fajita Dip, 105

FAVA BEAN
    Fava Bean Dip, 102

FANNEL
    Seafood Chowder, 149

FETA CHEESE
    Greek Breakfast Casserole, 16
    Artichoke Frittata, 19
    Peppers, Kale and Cheese Omelet, 31
    Beans, Carrots and Spinach Salad, 65
    Lamb and Spinach Salad, 138

FIGS
  Slow Cooker Turkey Breast, 109
  Lamb and Fennel Mix, 145
  Stuffed Apples, 175

FICH SAUCE
  Citrus Chicken, 118
  Chicken Thighs and Romano Cheese Mix, 122
  Shrimp and Peas Soup, 157

FLAXSEED
  Breakfast Rice Pudding, 24
  Blueberry Quinoa Oatmeal, 26

GALLON MILK
  Creamy Yogurt, 15

GARLIC
  Duck Chili, 125

GELATIN
  Cherry Jam, 174
  Coconut Pudding, 182
  Ricotta Cream, 184

GERMAN MUSTARD
  Beef Roast, 128

GINGER
  Tropical Granola, 22
  Beets and Carrots, 73
  Chicken Bites, 91
  Chicken Thighs Delight, 111
  Chinese Duck, 112
  Chicken Wings and Mint Sauce, 114
  Citrus Chicken, 118
  Thai Peanut Chicken, 122
  Chicken and Chickpeas, 126
  Chicken and Sauce, 126
  Chinese Pork Shoulder, 132
  Thai Cocoa Pork, 134
  Asian Steamed Fish, 150
  Flavored Cod Fillets, 152
  Chinese Cod, 155
  Mustard Fish Mix, 156
  Indian Fish , 161
  Delicious Mackerel, 164
  Flavored Squid, 168
  Pears and Sauce, 172
  Pumpkin Pie, 172
  Maple Pears, 174
  Chia Pudding, 177

  Chicken Thighs and Romano Cheese Mix, 122
  Duck and Potatoes, 123
  Poached Cod and Pineapple Mix, 150
  Chili Catfish, 151
  Creamy Sea Bass, 151
  Shrimp and Peas Soup, 157
  Chinese Mackerel, 164

GOAT CHEESE
  Arugula Frittata, 30
  Mushrooms Casserole, 33
  Nut and Berry Side Salad, 82
  Goat Cheese Rice, 85
  Mushroom Dip, 100

GOOSE
  Goose and Sauce, 127
  Goose Mix, 126

GOUDA CHEESE
  Scalloped Potatoes, 65
  Cheesy Sausage Casserole, 147

GRAHAM CRACKERS
  Rice and Artichokes, 85

GRAIN FARO
  Rice and Farro Pilaf, 83
  Easy Farro, 84

GRANOLA
  Apple Crumble, 14

GRAPE
  Pears and Grape Sauce, 187

GRAPEFRUIDS
  Stewed Grapefruit, 177

GREEN APPLE
  Cider Clams, 160

GREEN BEANS
  Veggie and Garbanzo Mix, 68
  Hearty Chicken, 42
  Minestrone Soup, 53
  Green Beans Mix, 64
  Green Beans and Red Peppers, 81
  Garlic Butter Green Beans, 81
  Rice and Veggies, 84
  Green Beans and Mushrooms, 85

GREEN CABBAGE
　　Lentils Rolls, 97

GREEN CHILI TOMATILLO SALSA
　　Pork Sirloin Salsa Mix, 137

GREEN CHILIES
　　Mexican Eggs, 17
　　Spicy Dip, 96
　　Mustard Fish Mix, 156

GREEN HOT SAUCE
　　Mexican Rice, 84

GREEN OLIVES
　　Chicken Bites, 91
　　Eggplant Salsa, 97
　　Chicken Thighs Delight, 111
　　Italian Barramundi and Tomato Relish, 156

GREEN ONIONS
　　Artichoke Frittata, 19
　　Easy Farro, 84

GREEN PEPPER
　　Creamy Chicken, 46
　　Winter Veggie Stew, 50
　　Quinoa Chili, 51
　　Turkey Chili, 56
　　Quinoa Chili, 60
　　Bean Medley, 64
　　Okra and Corn, 77
　　Easy Veggie Side Salad, 80
　　Rice and Beans, 86
　　Tomato Salsa, 106
　　Jalapeno Dip, 106
　　Shrimp and Baby Carrots Mix, 152
　　Pork Sandwiches, 41
　　French Veggie Stew, 52
　　6 Bean Chili, 61
　　Italian Squash and Peppers Mix, 81
　　Mushroom Dip, 100
　　Duck Breast and Veggies, 115

GUACAMOLE
　　Tostadas, 103

HADDOCK
　　Slow Cooked Haddock, 153
　　Seafood Stew, 40
　　Fish Pie, 153

HALIBUT
　　Tabasco Halibut, 155

HAM
　　Ham Quiche, 20
　　Breakfast Stuffed Peppers, 21
　　Peas and Ham Mix, 41
　　Chicken Cordon Bleu Dip, 105
　　Kale and Ham Mix, 71
　　Stuffed Pork, 139

HARISSA
　　Paprika Lamb, 143

HAZELNUTS
　　Quinoa and Apricots, 25
　　Rice and Farro Pilaf, 83

HEAVY CREAM
　　Alfredo Chicken, 108
　　Creamy Duck Breast, 115

HERBS DE PROVENCE
　　French Lamb, 136

HONEY
　　Cranberry Quinoa, 15
　　Coconut Granola, 22
　　Quinoa and Apricots, 25
　　Peas and Carrots, 65
　　Beets Side Salad, 78
　　Lemony Beets, 79
　　Nut and Berry Side Salad, 82
　　Cheeseburger Meatballs, 94
　　Balsamic Chicken, 108
　　Chicken Salad, 124
　　Hot Chicken Wings, 124
　　Chicken and Sauce, 126

HONEY MUSTARD
　　Green Beans and Red Peppers, 81

HOT PEPPER SAUCE
　　Spicy Pork, 141

HOT SAUCE
　　Beans and Rice, 52
　　Mushrooms Stuffed With Chicken, 120
　　Hot Chicken Wings, 124
　　Octopus and Veggies Mix, 167

HUMMUS
　　Cashew Dip, 99

JACK CHEESE
    Stuffed Peppers, 37

JALAPENO PEPPER
    Black Beans Stew, 52
    Tamale Dip, 87
    Taco Dip, 88
    Peas Dip, 98
    Italian Mussels Salad, 103
    Spicy Beef Mix, 148
    Poached Cod and Pineapple Mix, 150
    Tuna Loin Mix, 151
    Creamy Sea Bass, 151
    Tuna and Chimichurri, 159
    Chili Cream, 53
    Peas and Ham Mix, 41
    Mexican Lunch Mix, 43
    Pumpkin Chili, 60
    Sweet Potato Stew, 53
    Queso Dip, 89
    Jalapeno Poppers, 100
    Tomato Salsa, 106
    Salsa Snack, 106
    Jalapeno Dip, 106
    Slow Cooker Chicken Breasts, 119
    Sausage Soup, 147

JASMINE RICE
    Salmon and Rice, 162

KALAMATA OLIVES
    Mediterranean Chicken, 110
    Flavored Pork Roast, 131
    Beef and Onions, 131

KALE
    Peppers, Kale and Cheese Omelet, 31
    Kale and Ham Mix, 71
    Eggplant and Kale Mix, 72
    Onion Sausage Mix, 147

KETCHUP
    Bean Medley, 64
    Cheeseburger Dip, 104
    Pork Chops and Pineapple Mix, 129
    Beef Meatloaf, 137

KETO JAMAICAN SPICE MIX
    Jamaican Pork, 136

KIDNEY BEANS
    Bean Medley, 64

KIMCHI
    Salmon and Kimchi Sauce, 154

LAMB
    Lamb and Spinach Salad, 138
    Paprika Lamb, 143
    Lamb Stew, 58
    Lamb Curry, 58
    Lamb and Bacon Stew, 59
    Lamb Leg and Sweet Potatoes, 130
    Lamb Shanks, 131
    Artichoke Lamb Shoulder, 132
    Veggie Lamb Shanks, 135
    Lamb Leg and Mushrooms Mix, 135
    Smoky Lamb, 135
    French Lamb, 136
    Lamb Stew, 138
    Lamb Casserole, 144
    Lavender and Orange Lam, 144
    Lamb and Orange Sauce, 144
    Lamb and Mint Pesto, 145
    Lamb and Fennel Mix, 145

LASKA LEAVES
    Delicious Mackerel, 164

LEEK
    French Lamb, 136
    Salmon and Raspberry Vinaigrette, 163

LEMON
    Crab Dip, 90
    Slow Cooked Chicken, 109
    Thyme Chicken, 110
    Chicken and Broccoli Casserole, 117
    Chicken and Chickpeas, 126
    Mexican Pork Roast, 130
    Flavored Pork Roast, 131
    Artichoke Lamb Shoulder, 132
    Lamb and Spinach Salad, 138
    Beef and Pancetta, 145
    Shrimp Mix, 150
    Salmon Meatballs and Sauce, 154
    Tabasco Halibut, 155
    Spicy Creole Shrimp, 156
    Mackerel and Lemon, 165
    Mediterranean Octopus, 168
    Sweet Strawberry Mix, 170
    Bananas and Sweet Sauce, 171
    Strawberries Marmalade, 173
    Tapioca Pudding, 186
    Pears and Grape Sauce, 187
    Berry Marmalade, 188
    Mushrooms Casserole, 33

Lunch Roast, 34
Fajitas, 35
Flavored Turkey, 44
Lemon Chicken, 46
Lentils Soup, 47
Turkey and Potatoes, 56
Cod and Asparagus, 61
Beans, Carrots and Spinach Salad, 65
Lemony Beets, 79
Carrot and Beet Side Salad, 79
Easy Farro, 84
Goat Cheese Rice, 85
Chicken Bites, 91
Hummus, 98
Fava Bean Dip, 102
Chicken with Peach and Orange Sauce, 111
Chicken and Sauce, 113
Pork Belly and Applesauce, 139
Beef and Tzatziki, 142
Lamb and Mint Pesto, 145
Salmon and Green Onions Mix, 149
Asian Salmon Mix, 149
Dill Trout, 152
Slow Cooked Haddock, 153
Buttery Trout, 153
Salmon and Caper Sauce, 154
Italian Barramundi and Tomato Relish, 156
Calamari and Sauce, 157
Calamari and Shrimp, 158
Shrimp Salad, 158
Cider Clams, 160
Salmon and Relish, 160
Indian Fish, 161
Salmon and Raspberry Vinaigrette, 163
Fish Pudding, 163
Crab Legs, 166
Mushroom and Shrimp Curry, 166
Blueberry Cake, 169
Apples Stew, 171
Pumpkin Pie, 172
Sweet Potato Pudding, 173
Sweet Potato Pudding, 173
Cherry Jam, 174
Stuffed Apples, 175
Berry Cobbler, 175
Strawberry Pie, 180
Lemon Cream, 181
Lemon Peel Snack, 102
Mediterranean Chicken, 110
Lemony Chicken, 114
Orange Salmon, 159
Lemon Jam, 179

Sweet Lemon Mix, 184
Candied Lemon, 185
Orange Marmalade, 188

LEMON PEPPER
Worcestershire Pork Chops, 140

LEMONGRASS
Flavored Chicken Drumsticks, 122

LENTILS
Lentils and Quinoa Mix, 26
Chicken Stew, 46
Minestrone Soup, 53
Chicken and Lentils, 125

LETTUCE LEAVES
Tostadas, 103

LIMA BEANS
Wild Rice and Barley Pilaf, 74

LIME
Sweet Potato Stew, 53
Chicken Wings and Mint Sauce, 114
Chicken Thighs and Romano Cheese Mix, 122
Chinese Pork Shoulder, 132
Lime Cheesecake, 183
Flavored Turkey, 44
Salmon and Cilantro Sauce, 54
Chicken and Paprika Sauce, 114
Spicy Pork, 141
Sriracha Shrimp, 157
Shrimp Salad, 158
Green Tea Pudding, 184
Stuffed Pork, 139

LIGUOR
Chocolate and Liquor Cream, 185

MACADAMIA NUTS
Coconut and Macadamia Cream, 179

MACARONI
Tex Mex Dip, 88

MACKEREL
Delicious Mackerel, 164
Chinese Mackerel, 164
Fish Pie, 153
Mackerel and Lemon, 165

MANGO
  Mango Cream, 183
  Spicy Pork, 141
  Black Beans Stew, 52
  Chicken Tacos, 38

MAPLE SYYRUP
  Turkey Breast and Cranberries, 110
  Apple Crumble, 14
  Creamy Yogurt, 15
  Quinoa and Oats Mix, 17
  Quinoa Breakfast Bars, 18
  Vanilla Oats, 20
  Quinoa and Banana Mix, 24
  Blueberry Quinoa Oatmeal, 26
  Chocolate Quinoa, 27
  Breakfast Butterscotch Pudding, 29
  Cauliflower Rice Pudding, 30
  Carrot Pudding, 33
  Pulled Chicken, 54
  Maple Sweet Potatoes, 70
  Maple Brussels Sprouts, 73
  Blueberry and Spinach Salad, 82
  Jalapeno Poppers, 100
  Pork Tenderloin and Apples, 130
  Asian Salmon Mix, 149
  Pears and Sauce, 172
  Pumpkin Pie, 172
  Sweet Potato Pudding, 173
  Maple Pears, 174
  Chia Pudding, 177
  Stewed Grapefruit, 177
  Cocoa Cherry Compote, 178
  Cashew Cake, 178
  Lemon Pudding, 178
  Butternut Squash Sweet Mix, 186

MARINARA SAUSE
  Lasagna Dip, 89
  Lentils Rolls, 97
  Chicken Casserole, 117
  Chicken Meatloaf, 121
  Beef Meatballs Casserole, 142

MARJORAM
  Chicken and Sauce, 126

MARSALA WINE
  Veal Stew, 146

MASA HARINA
  Tamales, 102

MASCARPONE CHEESE
  Sweet Mascarpone Cream, 180
  Lemon Cream, 181

MEATBALLS
  Curried Meatballs, 95

MEDJOL DATES
  Dates Quinoa, 25

MEXICAN CHEESE
  Tex Mex Dip, 88
  Bean Dip, 92
  Tostadas, 103

MILK
  Veggie Omelet, 19
  Chocolate French Toast, 15
  Greek Breakfast Casserole, 16
  Veggie Casserole, 16
  Spiced Pumpkin Oatmeal, 18
  Raspberry Oatmeal, 18
  Spinach Frittata, 19
  Hash Browns and Sausage Casserole, 20
  Egg Bake, 21
  Butternut Squash Oatmeal, 21
  Breakfast Stuffed Peppers, 21
  Creamy Strawberries Oatmeal, 22
  Hash Brown Mix, 23
  Bacon and Egg Casserole, 23
  Apple Breakfast Rice, 24
  Dates Quinoa, 25
  Cinnamon Quinoa, 25
  Chai Breakfast Quinoa, 28
  Breakfast Butterscotch Pudding, 29
  Arugula Frittata, 30
  Mixed Egg and Sausage Scramble, 31
  Carrot Pudding, 33
  Sweet Potato Soup, 59
  Creamy Hash Brown Mix, 63
  Corn and Bacon, 64
  Mashed Potatoes, 67
  Cauliflower and Carrot Gratin, 79
  Cheeseburger Meatballs, 94
  Beef and Tzatziki, 142
  Milky Fish, 162
  Mushroom and Shrimp Curry, 166
  Dill Shrimp Mix, 167
  Peanut Butter Cake, 169
  Peanut Butter Cake, 169
  Blueberry Cake, 169
  Peach Pie, 170
  Orange Cake, 171
  Chocolate Cake, 175

Berry Cobbler, 175
Banana Cake, 176
Cauliflower Pudding, 177
Banana Bread, 185
Butternut Squash Sweet Mix, 186
Tapioca Pudding, 186
Rice Pudding, 187
Chia Pudding, 177

MINT SAUCE
Lamb Casserole, 144

MIRIN
Chinese Mackerel, 164
Stuffed Squid, 168

MIXED BEANS
Spicy Beef Mix, 148

MIXED SALAD
Chicken Salad, 124

MONTEREY
Mexican Eggs, 17

MONTEREY JACK CHEESE
Mexican Dip, 87
Beef and Chipotle Dip, 92
Salsa Corn Dip, 96
Tamale Dip, 87

MAZZARELLA CHEESE
Lasagna Dip, 89
Cheeseburger Dip, 104
Chicken Casserole, 117
Pepperoni Chicken, 120
Creamy Spinach and Artichoke Chicken, 121
Chicken Meatloaf, 121
Beef Meatballs Casserole, 142
Spinach Frittata, 19
Hash Browns and Sausage Casserole, 20
Pizza Dip, 95

MUSHROOM CREAM
Goose Mix, 126

MUSHROOMS
Tasty Tuna Mix, 164
Mushrooms Stuffed With Chicken, 120
Hash Brown Mix, 23
Worcestershire Asparagus Casserole, 31
Mushrooms Casserole, 33
Orange Beef Dish, 39
Beef Strips, 44
Spinach and Mushroom Soup, 48
Bulgur Chili, 61
Wild Rice Mix, 66
Creamy Risotto, 67
Mushrooms and Sausage Mix, 69
Buttery Mushrooms, 70
Thai Side Salad, 72
Asparagus and Mushroom Mix, 75
Easy and Veggies Mix, 76
Okra Side Dish, 76
Green Beans and Mushrooms, 85
Lentils Rolls, 97
Mushroom Dip, 100
Chicken Thighs and Mushrooms, 115
Chicken and Creamy Mushroom Sauce, 118
Chicken Stroganoff, 119
Chinese Pork Shoulder, 132
Lamb Leg and Mushrooms Mix, 135
Veal Stew, 146
Mushroom and Shrimp Curry, 166

MUSSEIS
Mussels Salad, 103
Italian Mussels Salad, 103
Spicy Mussels, 104
Mussels Soup, 161
Mussels and Sausage Mix, 165
Mussels, Clams and Chorizo Mix, 165

MUSTARD SEEDS
Mustard Fish Mix, 156

NOTHERN BEANS
Beans, Carrots and Spinach Salad, 65
Duck Chili, 125

NUTMEG
Ham Quiche, 20
Butternut Squash Oatmeal, 21
Apple Breakfast Rice, 24
Dates Quinoa, 25
Chai Breakfast Quinoa, 28
Creamy Breakfast, 32
Carrot Pudding, 33
Chili Salmon, 54
Turkey and Potatoes, 56
Glazed Baby Carrots, 69
Sweet Potato Mash, 71
Pink Rice, 83
Apple Dip, 91
Chicken Breasts, 109
Mexican Pork Roast, 130

Pork Tenderloin and Apples, 130
Flavored Cod Fillets, 152
Fish Pie, 153
Peach Pie, 170
Stuffed Apples, 175
Orange Cream Mix, 186

OATS
Apple Oatmeal, 17
Coconut Granola, 22
Tropical Granola, 22
Creamy Strawberries Oatmeal, 22
Quinoa and Apricots, 25
Blueberry Quinoa Oatmeal, 26
Chia Seeds Mix, 27

OCTOPUS
Octopus and Veggies Mix, 167
Mediterranean Octopus, 168

OKRA
Okra Side Dish, 76
Okra Side Dish, 76
Okra Mix, 77
Stewed Okra, 77
Okra and Corn, 77

OLIVES
Fish and Olives Mix, 161

OMAINE LETTUCE
Black Bean Salsa Salad, 99

ORANGE
BBQ Chicken Thighs, 45
Stuffed Pork, 139
Lamb and Mint Pesto, 145
Orange Cream Mix, 186
Orange Beef Dish, 39
Slow Cooker Roast, 45
Sweet Potatoes with Bacon, 66
Orange Glazed Carrots, 67
Herbed Beets, 80
Blueberry and Spinach Salad, 82
Chicken with Peach and Orange Sauce, 111
Turkey Wings and Sauce, 113
Citrus Chicken, 118
Citrus Chicken, 118
Orange Cake, 171
Pears and Sauce, 172
Maple Pears, 174
Herbed and Cinnamon Beef, 134
Orange Marmalade, 188

ORANGE PEPPERS
Cheesy Sausage Casserole, 147

OY SAUCE
Shrimp and Peas Soup, 157

PAIE ALE
Spicy Beef Mix, 148

PALM SUGAR
Berry Cobbler, 175

PANCETTA
Beef and Pancetta, 145
Cider Clams, 160

PARMESAN CHEESE
Egg Bake, 21
Chia Seeds and Chicken Breakfast, 27
Chicken and Peppers Mix, 38
Spinach and Mushroom Soup, 48
Garlic Butter Green Beans, 81
Rice and Artichokes, 85
Artichoke Dip, 88
Lasagna Dip, 89
Crab Dip, 90
Cheesy Mix, 93
Chicken and Dumplings, 107
Alfredo Chicken, 108
Chicken Casserole, 117
Slow Cooker Chicken Breasts, 119
Chicken Meatloaf, 121
Beef Meatloaf, 137
Pork Rolls, 140
Beef Meatballs Casserole, 142
Tabasco Halibut, 155
Creamy Salmon, 155
Slow Cooked Turkey Delight, 116
Scalloped Potatoes, 65

PEA PODS
Japanese Shrimp, 167

PEACHES
Glazed Baby Carrots, 69
Peach Pie, 170

PEANUT BUTTER
Thai Peanut Chicken, 122

PEANUTS
Sweet Potato Stew, 53
Slow Cooked Dip, 90
Peanut Snack, 91

PEARS
- Pears and Sauce, 172
- Maple Pears, 174
- Pears and Wine Sauce, 187
- Pears and Grape Sauce, 187
- Pears Jam, 188

PEAS
- Beef Stew, 36
- Beef and Veggie Stew, 41
- Creamy Chicken Soup, 49
- Peas and Carrots, 65
- Rice and Veggies, 84
- Chicken and Dumplings, 107
- Shrimp and Peas Soup, 157
- Cod and Peas, 162
- Tasty Tuna Mix, 164

PECANS
- Tropical Granola, 22
- Blueberry and Spinach Salad, 82
- Goat Cheese Rice, 85
- Candied Pecans, 90
- Beef and Chipotle Dip, 92
- Peas Dip, 98
- Pecans Snack, 101
- Lamb and Spinach Salad, 138
- Orange Cake, 171
- Apples Stew, 171
- Sweet Potato Pudding, 173
- Stuffed Apples, 175

PEPPER
- Beans and Pumpkin Chili, 37
- Chicken and Peppers Mix, 38
- Pork Stew, 40
- Taco Dip, 88
- Peppers, Kale and Cheese Omelet, 31
- Chicken Tacos, 38
- Chicken with Couscous, 39

PEPPER JACK CHEESE
- Fajita Dip, 105

PEPPER SAUCE
- Octopus and Veggies Mix, 167

PEPPERONCINIS
- Roast and Pepperoncinis, 132

PEPPERONI
- Pepperoni Chicken, 120

PICKLES
- Stuffed Pork, 139

PINE NUTS
- Chicken Thighs Mix, 57
- Lentils Rolls, 97

PINEAPPLE
- Tropical Granola, 22
- Pork Chops and Pineapple Mix, 129
- Poached Cod and Pineapple Mix, 150
- Curried Meatballs, 95
- Chicken Tacos, 38
- Chicken Wings, 92
- Glazed Sausages, 93
- Japanese Shrimp, 167

PINT MILK
- Fish Pudding, 163

PINTO BEANS
- Lentils and Quinoa Mix, 26
- Beans and Rice, 52

PISTACHIOS
- Beans, Carrots and Spinach Salad, 65
- Lamb and Mint Pesto, 145

PIZZA SAUCE
- Pizza Dip, 95
- Pepperoni Chicken, 120

PLUMS
- Pork Stew, 40
- Sweet Plums, 170

POBLANO CHILIES
- Chili Cream, 53

POLENTA
- Italian Veggie Mix, 74

POMEGRANATE
- Beets and Carrots, 73
- Chia Seeds Mix, 27

POPCORN
- Caramel Corn, 94

PORCINI MUSHROOMS
- Creamy Risotto, 67

PORK
- Pork and Chorizo Lunch Mix, 58
- Apple Pork Ribs, 129

Teriyaki Pork, 35
Pork Stew, 40
Pork Sandwiches, 41
Moist Pork Loin, 42
Tamales, 102
Tostadas, 103
Pork Chops and Pineapple Mix, 129
Mexican Pork Roast, 130
Pork Tenderloin and Apples, 130
Flavored Pork Roast, 131
Chinese Pork Shoulder, 132
Jamaican Pork, 136
Pork Sirloin Salsa Mix, 137
Pork Loin and Cauliflower Rice, 137
Pork Belly and Applesauce, 139
Pork Rolls, 140
Pork Chops, 140
Rosemary Pork, 141
Oregano Pork Chops, 141
Spicy Pork, 141
Italian Sausage Soup, 148
Worcestershire Pork Chops, 140

PORK BUTT
Thai Cocoa Pork, 134

PORK SAUSAGE
Mushrooms and Sausage Mix, 69
Onion Sausage Mix, 147
Cheesy Sausage Casserole, 147
Sausage Soup, 147
Sausage and Onion Jam, 136
Sausages and Celeriac Mash, 138

PORTOBELLO MUSHROOMS
Beef Stuffed Squash, 142
Cauliflower Pilaf, 68

POTATOES
Thai Chicken Soup, 48
Chicken Chowder, 111
Duck and Potatoes, 123
Breakfast Potatoes, 23
Beef Stew, 36
Chicken with Couscous, 39
Beef and Veggie Stew, 41
Hearty Chicken, 42
Slow Cooker Roast, 45
Creamy Chicken Soup, 49
Winter Veggie Stew, 50
Turkey and Potatoes, 56
Lamb Stew, 58
Lamb and Bacon Stew, 59
Sweet Potato Soup, 59

Quinoa Chili, 60
Seafood Stew, 62
Scalloped Potatoes, 65
Sweet Potatoes with Bacon, 66
Mashed Potatoes, 67
Maple Sweet Potatoes, 70
Creamy Chipotle Sweet Potatoes, 71
Sweet Potato Mash, 71
Thai Side Salad, 72
Rosemary Potatoes, 73
Apples and Potatoes, 74
Potato Salsa, 99
Balsamic Chicken, 108
Slow Cooker Turkey Breast, 109
Cuban Chicken, 125
Lamb Leg and Sweet Potatoes, 130
Flavored Pork Roast, 131
Seasoned Beef, 133
Beef Curry, 148
Seafood Chowder, 149
Milky Fish, 162
Mussels, Clams and Chorizo Mix, 165
Shrimp and Sausage Boil, 166
Octopus and Veggies Mix, 167

PRETZELS
Slow Cooked Dip, 90
Cheesy Mix, 93

POSCIUTTO
Pork Rolls, 140

PRUNES
Chicken Thighs Delight, 111

PUMPKIN
Beans and Pumpkin Chili, 37
Apples and Potatoes, 74
Pink Rice, 83
Pumpkin Pie, 172
Chia Pudding, 177

PUMPKIN PUREE
Spiced Pumpkin Oatmeal, 18
Pumpkin Chili, 60

QUINOA
Cranberry Quinoa, 15
Quinoa and Oats Mix, 17
Quinoa Breakfast Bars, 18
Quinoa and Banana Mix, 24
Dates Quinoa, 25
Cinnamon Quinoa, 25
Quinoa and Apricots, 25

Blueberry Quinoa Oatmeal, 26
Lentils and Quinoa Mix, 26
Butternut Squash Quinoa, 26
Chocolate Quinoa, 27
Chai Breakfast Quinoa, 28
Quinoa Breakfast Bake, 28
Mocha Latte Quinoa Mix, 28
Quinoa Chili, 51
Quinoa Chili, 60

RADICCHIO
Italian Veggie Mix, 74
Mussels Salad, 103

RADICHES
Duck Breast and Veggies, 115
Paprika Lamb, 143
Italian Sausage Soup, 148

RAISINS
Quinoa Breakfast Bars, 18
Lentils Rolls, 97
Mushroom and Shrimp Curry, 166
Orange Cake, 171
Strawberries Marmalade, 173

RANCH SEASONING
Buffalo Chicken, 108

RSPBERRIS
Raspberry Oatmeal, 18
Turkey Lunch, 34
Sweet Raspberry Mix, 180
Salmon and Raspberry Vinaigrette, 163

RED BEANS
Sweet Potato Stew, 53

RED CHILI PEPPERS
Chili Catfish, 151

RED CURRY PASTE
Lentils Curry, 51

RED GRAPEFRUIT
Stewed Grapefruit, 177

RED KIDNEY BEANS
Rice and Beans, 86

RED LENTILS
Lentils Soup, 47
Pumpkin Chili, 60

RED ONION
BBQ Chicken Dip, 87
Jalapeno Dip, 106
Mushrooms Stuffed With Chicken, 120
Lamb Casserole, 144
Mustard Fish Mix, 156
Tuna and Chimichurri, 159
Mediterranean Chicken, 110

RED ORANGE
Lavender and Orange Lam, 144
Orange Salmon, 159

RED PEPPER
Fajitas, 35
Peas and Ham Mix, 41
Winter Veggie Stew, 50
Quinoa Chili, 51
Black Beans Stew, 52
Chicken Chili, 55
Turkey Chili, 56
Bulgur Chili, 61
Wild Rice and Barley Pilaf, 74
Easy Veggie Side Salad, 80
Green Beans and Red Peppers, 81
Glazed Sausages, 93
Pizza Dip, 95
Spicy Mussels, 104
Tomato Salsa, 106
Jalapeno Dip, 106
Chicken and Paprika Sauce, 114
Onion Sausage Mix, 147
Sriracha Shrimp, 157
Artichoke Frittata, 19
Stuffed Peppers, 37
Taco Soup, 49
Sweet Potato Stew, 53
Italian Squash and Peppers Mix, 81
Fajita Dip, 105
Chicken Breasts, 109
Beef Soup, 133
Tuna Loin Mix, 151
Indian Fish, 161

RED PEPPER FLEKES
Italian Mussels Salad, 103

RED THAI CHILIES
Chickpeas Stew, 50

RED WINE
Beef Roast, 128
Fennel Short Ribs, 128
Octopus and Veggies Mix, 167

Pears and Wine Sauce, 187

RHUBARB
Pork Loin and Cauliflower Rice, 137
Rhubarb Marmalade, 173

RICE
Cauliflower Rice Pudding, 30
Stuffed Peppers, 37
Thai Chicken Soup, 48
Beans and Rice , 52
Black Beans Stew, 52
Wild Rice Mix, 66
Creamy Risotto, 67
Wild Rice and Barley Pilaf, 74
Rice and Farro Pilaf, 83
Pink Rice, 83
Rice and Veggies, 84
Mexican Rice, 84
Goat Cheese Rice, 85
Rice and Artichokes, 85
Rice and Beans, 86
Lentils Rolls, 97
Chicken and Tomatillos, 123
Jambalaya, 163
Rice Pudding, 187
Slow Cooked Dip, 90
Cheesy Mix, 93

RICOTTA CHEESE
Lasagna Dip, 89
Chicken Meatloaf, 121
Pork Rolls, 140
Beef Meatballs Casserole, 142
Ricotta Cream, 184

RIGATONI
Alfredo Chicken, 108

ROSEMARY
Beets Side Salad, 78
Rosemary Pork, 141
Lamb Casserole, 144
Lavender and Orange Lam, 144
Lamb Leg and Sweet Potatoes, 130
Mediterranean Octopus, 168
Mediterranean Octopus, 168
Pears and Grape Sauce, 187

SALMON
Salmon Frittata, 32
Salmon and Cilantro Sauce, 54
Chili Salmon, 54
Salmon and Kimchi Sauce, 154
Salmon Meatballs and Sauce, 154
Salmon and Caper Sauce, 154
Orange Salmon, 159
Salmon and Green Onions Mix, 149
Seafood Chowder, 149
Asian Salmon Mix, 149
Asian Steamed Fish, 150
Fish Pie, 153
Creamy Salmon, 155
Mustard Salmon, 160
Salmon and Relish, 160
Salmon and Rice, 162
Salmon and Raspberry Vinaigrette, 163
Peppers, Kale and Cheese Omelet, 31

SALSA
Black Bean Soup, 49
Chicken Chili, 55
Salsa Chicken, 55
Black Bean Salsa Salad, 99
Tostadas, 103

SALSA VERDE
Mexican Dip, 87
Salsa Corn Dip, 96
Cheesy Corn Dip, 96

SAUERKRAUT
German Beef Soup, 143

SAUSAGE
Hash Browns and Sausage Casserole, 20
Breakfast Potatoes, 23
Eggs and Sausage Casserole, 29
Rice and Beans, 86
Bourbon Sausage Bites, 94
Spicy Dip, 96
Jambalaya, 163
Mussels and Sausage Mix, 165
Mixed Egg and Sausage Scramble, 31
Glazed Sausages, 93
Apple Jelly Sausage Snack, 101

SEA BASS
Creamy Sea Bass, 151

SEA SCALLOPAS
Seafood Chowder, 149

SEAFOOD MIXED
Seafood Stew, 62

SERRANO PEPPER
    Chicken Wings and Mint Sauce, 114

SESSAME OIL
    Shrimp and Peas Soup, 157

SHALLOT
    Carrot and Beet Side Salad, 79
    Rice and Farro Pilaf, 83
    Chili Catfish, 151
    Salmon and Relish, 160
    Chinese Mackerel, 164
    Creamy Chipotle Sweet Potatoes, 71
    Delicious Mackerel, 164

SHERRY VINEGAR
    Chicken and Lentils, 125

SHERRY WINE
    Salmon and Raspberry Vinaigrette, 163
    Duck and Potatoes, 123

SHRIMP
    Seafood Stew, 40
    Shrimp Stew, 62
    Seafood Chowder, 149
    Shrimp Mix, 150
    Shrimp and Baby Carrots Mix, 152
    Spicy Creole Shrimp, 156
    Sriracha Shrimp, 157
    Shrimp and Peas Soup, 157
    Calamari and Shrimp, 158
    Shrimp Salad, 158
    Jambalaya, 163
    Shrimp and Sausage Boil, 166
    Mushroom and Shrimp Curry, 166
    Dill Shrimp Mix, 167
    Japanese Shrimp, 167

SHRIMP SAUCE
    Fish Pudding, 163

SNOW PEAS
    Orange Beef Dish, 39

SOUR CREAM
    Sauerkraut Dip, 95
    Spicy Dip, 96
    Cheeseburger Dip, 104
    Onion Dip, 104
    Fajita Dip, 105
    Red Chicken Soup, 118
    Chicken and Sour Cream, 119
    Chicken and Green Onion Sauce, 120
    Creamy Salmon, 155
    Shrimp Salad, 158

SOY SAUCE
    Teriyaki Pork, 35
    Apple and Onion Lunch Roast, 36
    Thai Chicken, 55
    Green Beans Mix, 64
    Chicken Wings, 92
    Black Bean Salsa Salad, 99
    Chicken with Peach and Orange Sauce, 111
    Thai Peanut Chicken, 122
    Chicken Thighs and Romano Cheese Mix, 122
    Slow Cooker Chicken Thighs, 123
    Duck and Potatoes, 123
    Apple Pork Ribs, 129
    Pork Chops and Pineapple Mix, 129
    Chinese Pork Shoulder, 132
    Roast and Pepperoncinis, 132
    Asian Salmon Mix, 149
    Asian Steamed Fish, 150
    Chili Catfish, 151
    Creamy Sea Bass, 151
    Chinese Cod, 155
    Japanese Shrimp, 167
    Stuffed Squid, 168
    Chicken and Cabbage Mix, 57
    Citrus Chicken, 118

SPAGHETTI SGUASH
    Beef Stuffed Squash, 142

SPINACH
    Greek Breakfast Casserole, 16
    Spinach Frittata, 19
    Breakfast Stuffed Peppers, 21
    Mushrooms Casserole, 33
    Spinach and Mushroom Soup, 48
    Winter Veggie Stew, 50
    Sweet Potato Soup, 59
    Beans, Carrots and Spinach Salad, 65
    Spinach and Squash Side Salad, 69
    Cauliflower Rice and Spinach, 70
    Italian Veggie Mix, 74
    Nut and Berry Side Salad, 82
    Blueberry and Spinach Salad, 82
    Goat Cheese Rice, 85
    Artichoke Dip, 88
    Mussels Salad, 103
    Creamy Duck Breast, 115
    Turkey Curry, 116

Creamy Spinach and Artichoke Chicken, 121
Creamy Spinach and Artichoke Chicken, 121
Chicken and Chickpeas, 126
Lamb and Spinach Salad, 138
Beef and Tzatziki, 142
Italian Sausage Soup, 148
Dill Trout, 152

SGUASH
Squash Side Salad, 68
Spinach and Squash Side Salad, 69
Thai Side Salad, 72
Summer Squash Mix, 80
Easy Veggie Side Salad, 80
Italian Squash and Peppers Mix, 81
Turkey Soup, 116
Chicken Casserole, 117

SGUID
Calamari and Sauce, 157
Stuffed Squid, 168
Stuffed Squid, 168

SRIRACHA SAUCE
Sriracha Shrimp, 157
Calamari and Sauce, 157

STEEL OATS
Banana and Coconut Oatmeal, 14
Quinoa and Oats Mix, 17
Spiced Pumpkin Oatmeal, 18
Raspberry Oatmeal, 18
Vanilla Oats, 20

STEVIA
Cinnamon Quinoa, 25
Beets and Carrots, 73
Strawberry Pie, 180

STRAWBERRIES
Creamy Strawberries Oatmeal, 22
Nut and Berry Side Salad, 82
Sweet Strawberry Mix, 170
Strawberries Marmalade, 173
Rhubarb Marmalade, 173
Strawberry Pie, 180
Sweet Mascarpone Cream, 180
Berry Marmalade, 188

SUN-DRIED TOMATOES
Greek Breakfast Casserole, 16
Cheesy Sausage Casserole, 147

SUNFLIWER
Strawberry Pie, 180

SWEET PEPPER
Bean Medley, 64

SWISS CHEESE
Ham Quiche, 20
Cauliflower and Broccoli Mix, 66
Sauerkraut Dip, 95
Chicken Cordon Bleu Dip, 105
Stuffed Pork, 139

TABASCO SAUCE
Peas Dip, 98
Tabasco Halibut, 155

TACO SAUCE
Mexican Eggs, 17

TACO SHELLS
Chicken Tacos, 38

TALIAN SAUSAGES
Chicken and Stew, 57

TAMARING PASTE
Delicious Mackerel, 164

TAPIOCA
Orange Glazed Carrots, 67
Fennel Short Ribs, 128
Berry Cobbler, 175
Seafood Chowder, 149
Shrimp and Baby Carrots Mix, 152
Tapioca Pudding, 186

TARRAGON
Herbed Beets, 80
Chicken Thighs and Mushrooms, 115
Shrimp Salad, 158

THAI RED CURRY PASTE
Thai Side Salad, 72

THYME
Thyme Beets, 78
Pink Rice, 83
Rice and Artichokes, 85
Rice and Beans, 86
Pecans Snack, 101

TOMATO PASTE
Veal Stew, 146

Pork Stew, 40
Mexican Lunch Mix, 43
Chickpeas Stew, 50
Turkey Chili, 56
Eggplant Dip, 101
Tostadas, 103
Fennel Short Ribs, 128
Lamb Shanks, 131
Artichoke Lamb Shoulder, 132
Veggie Lamb Shanks, 135
Lamb Leg and Mushrooms Mix, 135
Oregano Pork Chops, 141
Beef and Pancetta, 145
Shrimp and Baby Carrots Mix, 152
Calamari and Shrimp, 158

TOMATO SAUSE
Chicken and Peppers Mix, 38
BBQ Chicken Thighs, 45
Slow Cooker Roast, 45
Chicken and Stew, 57
Okra Side Dish, 76
Okra Mix, 77
Stewed Okra, 77
Mushroom Dip, 100
Chicken Liver Stew, 127
Beef Soup, 133
Beef Curry, 148
Octopus and Veggies Mix, 167

TOMATOES
Spinach Frittata, 19
Chicken Frittata, 33
Pork and Chorizo Lunch Mix, 58
Italian Veggie Mix, 74
Okra Side Dish, 76
BBQ Chicken Dip, 87
Eggplant Dip, 101
Veggie Lamb Shanks, 135
Lamb Stew, 138
Oregano Pork Chops, 141
Indian Fish, 161
Lunch Roast, 34
Beef Stew, 36
Seafood Stew, 40
Hot Chicken Wings, 124
Chicken Tacos, 38
Chicken with Couscous, 39
French Veggie Stew, 52
Pulled Chicken, 54
Pumpkin Chili, 60
Eggplant Salsa, 97
Spicy Mussels, 104
Tomato Salsa, 106

Salsa Snack, 106
Jalapeno Dip, 106
Chicken and Tomatillos, 123
Cuban Chicken, 125
Beef Soup, 133
Lamb Leg and Mushrooms Mix, 135
Jambalaya, 163

TOMATOES UN-DRIED
Beef and Onions, 131

TROUT
Dill Trout, 152
Buttery Trout, 153

TUNA
Tuna and Chimichurri, 159

TURKEY
Turkey Chili, 56
Turkey and Potatoes, 56
Slow Cooker Turkey Breast, 109
Beans and Pumpkin Chili, 37
Flavored Turkey, 44
Pizza Dip, 95
Turkey Breast and Cranberries, 110
Classic Turkey Gumbo, 112
Turkey Wings and Veggies, 113
Turkey Wings and Sauce, 113
Turkey Soup, 116
Slow Cooked Turkey Delight, 116
Turkey Curry, 116

TURRMERIC
Chicken Wings and Mint Sauce, 114

TURNIPS
Veggie Spread, 98
Beef Brisket and Turnips Mix, 134

TZATZIKI
Beef and Tzatziki, 142

VEAL
Veal Stew, 146
Veal and Tomatoes, 146
Wine Piccata, 146

VEGGIE STOCK
Mexican Rice, 84
Goat Cheese Rice, 85

VELVEETA
Queso Dip, 89

VIDALIA ONION
    Easy Veggie Side Salad, 80

WALNUTS
    Raspberry Oatmeal, 18
    Quinoa Breakfast Bake, 28
    Carrot Pudding, 33
    Turkey and Potatoes, 56
    Maple Sweet Potatoes , 70
    Carrot and Beet Side Salad, 79
    Nut and Berry Side Salad, 82
    Turkey Wings and Sauce, 113
    Coconut Vanilla Cream, 181

WHEAT CEREAL
    Slow Cooked Dip, 90
    Cheesy Mix, 93

WHIPPING CREAM
    Fish Pie, 153

WHITE BEANS
    White Beans Stew, 59
    White Bean Spread, 97

WHITE CHOCOLATE
    Peanut Snack, 91

WHITE FISH
    Mustard Fish Mix, 156
    Fish and Olives Mix, 161
    Indian Fish , 161
    Milky Fish , 162

WHITE VINEGAR
    Chinese Pork Shoulder, 132
    Poached Cod and Pineapple Mix, 150

WHITE WINE
    Chicken and Sauce, 126
    Wine Piccata, 146
    Italian Clams , 159
    Dill Shrimp Mix, 167
    Octopus and Veggies Mix, 167

WHOLE MILK
    Queso Dip, 89

WILD BERRIES
    Wild Rice and Barley Pilaf, 74

WORCESTERSHIRE SAUCE
    Beef Strips, 44
    Slow Cooked Dip, 90
    Cheeseburger Dip, 104
    Worcestershire Pork Chops, 140
    German Beef Soup, 143
    Asian Steamed Fish, 150
    Spicy Creole Shrimp, 156
    Calamari and Shrimp, 158
    Jambalaya, 163

YELLOW CORN
    Creamy Chicken Soup, 49

YELLOW PEPPERS
    Lentils Soup, 47
    Eggplant and Kale Mix, 72
    Classic Turkey Gumbo, 112
    Okra Side Dish, 76
    Cheesy Sausage Casserole, 147

YOGURT
    Creamy Yogurt, 15
    Creamy Strawberries Oatmeal, 22
    Hot Chicken Wings, 124

ZUCCHINI
    Breakfast Zucchini Oatmeal, 14
    Thai Chicken Soup, 48
    Thai Side Salad, 72
    Easy and Veggies Mix, 76
    Okra Side Dish, 76
    Easy Veggie Side Salad, 80
    Zucchini Casserole, 82
    Eggplant Dip, 101
    Chinese Pork Shoulder, 132
    French Veggie Stew, 52
    Minestrone Soup, 53
    Summer Squash Mix, 80
    Duck Breast and Veggies, 115
    Slow Cooked Turkey Delight, 116

Copyright © 2023 by William Jones

All rights reserved. No part of this cookbook may be reproduced in any form or by any electronic or mechanical means, including information storage and retrieval systems, without permission in writing from the publisher, except by a reviewer who may quote brief passages in a review.

This cookbook is intended to provide information and guidance to those interested in the culinary arts. The ideas, procedures, and suggestions contained in this book are not intended as a substitute for professional medical advice. All matters regarding health require medical supervision. Neither the author nor the publisher shall be liable or responsible for any loss or damage allegedly arising from any information or suggestion in this book.

Made in United States
Cleveland, OH
29 December 2024